Handbook of Human Rights
and
Criminal Justice in India

Third Edition

The Oxford India Handbooks are an important initiative in academic publishing.
Each volume offers a comprehensive survey of research in a critical subject area
and provides facts, figures, and analyses for a well-grounded perspective. The series
provides scholars, students, and policy planners with a balanced understanding
of a wide range of issues in the social sciences.

Handbook of Human Rights
and
Criminal Justice in India

The System and Procedure

Third Edition

SAHRDC
South Asia Human Rights Documentation Centre

OXFORD
UNIVERSITY PRESS

OXFORD
UNIVERSITY PRESS

Oxford University Press is a department of the University of Oxford.
It furthers the University's objective of excellence in research, scholarship,
and education by publishing worldwide. Oxford is a registered trademark of
Oxford University Press in the UK and in certain other countries

Published in India by
Oxford University Press
22 Workspace, 2nd Floor, 1/22 Asaf Ali Road, New Delhi 110002, India

First Edition published in 2006
Second edition 2007
Oxford India Paperbacks 2010
Digitally Printed in 2024

ISBN 13: 978-0-19-806951-5
ISBN 10: 0-19-806951-0

Typeset in AGaramond 11.5/13.5
by Le Studio Graphique, Gurgaon 122 001
Printed at Manipal Technologies Limited, Manipal

Contents

Boxes

Foreword

'The history of liberty has largely been the history of observance of procedural safeguards', Justice Felix Frankfurter remarked in 1943 in the famous case of *McNabb* v. *United States.*[*] The aphorism 'knowledge is power' is particularly true of knowledge of the law relating to procedural safeguards which ensure respect for individual liberty.

In the fifties, S.G. Vaze of Pune published a monthly *Civil Liberties Bulletin*. Its annual subscription was Rs 3. Vaze's erudition remained unmatched by all who came after him, till Ravi Nair entered the field. His scholarship and thoroughness in research live up to the highest standards set by civil libertarians the world over. The South Asia Human Rights Documentation Centre (SAHRDC), which he set up and runs as its Executive Director, deservedly enjoys special consultative status with the Economic and Social Council of the United Nations.

In the public mind, the Criminal Procedure Code, 1973 does not enjoy a flattering image. Few know that before the Constitution of India went into force on 26 January 1950, it was under section 491 of its predecessor, the Code of Criminal Procedure, 1898, that writs of *habeas corpus* were issued. The Code's provisions for bail, search-warrants, arrest, and for a special Bench of three judges of the High Court to decide on the validity of a ban on books (S.96), bear directly on the citizen's liberty. So, indeed, does the Code entire, particularly its notorious Section 144. It was invoked once in Mumbai to ban a meeting to criticize the policy of the Government of India on Afghanistan.

The *Handbook of Human Rights and Criminal Justice in India: The System and Procedure*, which Ravi Nair and his colleagues have painstakingly compiled is, in truth, a 'Primer to Civil Liberties'. It is written in so lucid a style as to serve as a text book for students, a guide for journalists, and even for the lay citizen. Its excellent documentation and citation of cases makes it a superb work of reference for trial lawyers, judges, and activists in the field. It is all too appropriate that it is published under the auspices of the SAHRDC.

While every work on British constitutional law discusses at length the status and powers of the police, books of the Constitution of India ignore the profound importance of the

---

[*] 318 U.S. 332 at 347.

police in a polity governed by the rule of law. This work discusses criminal procedure and criminal justice in the context of human rights. Particularly useful are its discussion of the essentials of a fair trial and safeguards against custodial torture. It fills a gaping void in Indian legal literature. Nothing like it has appeared before. All who are interested in the rule of law owe a deep gratitude to Ravi Nair and to his team at the South Asia Human Rights Documentation Centre.

Mumbai   A.G. NOORANI
26 September 2005

Preface to the Third Edition

The third edition of the *Handbook of Human Rights and Criminal Justice in India: The System and Procedure* includes a new chapter detailing recent developments in the criminal justice system in India. The new chapter lists, among other things, the amendments to the Criminal Procedure Code in 2008, various judgments by High Courts and the Supreme Court and reports by committees and commissions on reform of the criminal justice system.

The Code of Criminal Procedure (Amendment) Bill, 2010—seeks to bring in some of the provisions envisaged in those sections of the 2008 Amendment Act with some modifications. The proposed changes apply to, among others, the definition of 'victim', the law relating to arrest, and a significant revision of the provision for medical examination of an arrested person whereby the person having the custody of an accused is duty-bound to take reasonable care of the health and safety of the accused.

Some of the landmark cases discussed in the chapter include, among others, the Naz Foundation case, decided in July 2009, in which the Delhi High Court ruled that Section 377 (prohibiting same-sex intercourse) of the Indian Penal Code violated the constitutional right to privacy (read into the right to life and liberty contained in Article 21). This has the practical effect of decriminalizing same-sex intercourse in India. Also included are *Manish Jalan* v. *State of Karnataka* on payment of compensation, *Som Mittal* v. *Govt. of Karnataka* on the power of the courts under Section 482 CrPC, and the case of *Santosh Bariyar* v. *State of Maharashtra* in which the Supreme Court held that the 'rarest of rare' doctrine meant that for awarding the death penalty, the court would have to provide clear evidence as to why the convict is not fit for any kind of reformatory and rehabilitation scheme.

I am thankful to all those—interns, former interns, lawyers and others—who assisted in updating this Handbook and provided useful comments and suggestions. As with the first and second editions, I hope that the updated Handbook will serve as a useful resource and guide for academics, practitioners, students, and laypersons alike.

New Delhi
June 2010

RAVI NAIR
Executive Director
SAHRDC, New Delhi

Preface to the Second Edition

The first edition of the *Handbook of Human Rights and Criminal Justice in India: The System and Procedure* met with a good response and was sold out a little over a year and a half after it was published. I am very happy to be able to present an updated second edition. Many of the substantive changes in the second edition are related to the passage of the Code of Criminal Procedure (Amendment) Act, 2005 (CrPC Amendment Act). With a looming publication date scheduled only months after the passage of the CrPC Amendment Act, the first edition of the *Handbook* included only a brief discussion of the major changes wrought by the new law as a separate chapter at the end of the book.

With the passage of time and the opportunity to publish a second edition, we have more fully developed explanations of the various provisions affected by the CrPC Amendment Act and have integrated those explanations into their logical location in the discussions of various substantive topics. Thus, rather than grouping all of the CrPC Amendment Act provisions together, we discuss the newly created Directorate of Prosecution in the context of the system of Prosecution in Chapter 1, Section 1.5; the new requirement for police to inform friends or relatives of the arrestee of the arrest is discussed in the context of one's rights when under arrest in Chapter 4, Section 4.3; the new maximum permitted length of detention for under trial prisoners is now situated in its rightful place in the length of detention section in Chapter 6; and so on.

Even though we were able to include a discussion of the CrPC Amendment Act in the first edition, we were too close to our publishing deadline to be able to include an analysis of the Criminal Law (Amendment) Act, 2005 which was passed in January 2006. This Act is potentially a very important piece of legislation because it establishes procedures and guidelines for plea-bargaining—that is, negotiation between the accused and the prosecution whereby the accused agrees to plead guilty in exchange for a relatively less onerous sentence. Legislators and commentators hope that this new provision will assist in reducing the massive backlog of criminal cases in Indian courts. However, the amendment legislation allows for the same judge who assesses a potential plea agreement for the accused, to later preside over a trial, if the plea bargaining application is not successful, thus raising concerns about the fairness of the trial.

Lastly, we have also included in the second edition a discussion of a few recent Indian Supreme Court cases with the potential for a significant impact on the criminal justice system. The first, *Prakash Singh* v. *Union of India,* deals with long overdue police administration reforms. In this case the Court ordered a number of key changes in police organisation intended to reduce political interference in policing, to more clearly separate the police's peacekeeping and investigative functions, and to provide a complaint mechanism for the public against alleged police abuses. The second, *Sube Singh* v. *State of Haryana,* places important limits on the right to be compensated when one's rights are violated by the police while under arrest or custody. Only very clear and severe human rights violations resulting in death and disability are assured of compensation after *Sube Singh.*

In conclusion, I would like to express my thanks yet again to everyone at SAHRDC as well as many others who have contributed to putting together the first and second editions of the *Handbook.* The success of the *Handbook* is in great measure the result of all their efforts.

New Delhi
June 2007

RAVI NAIR
Executive Director
SAHRDC
New Delhi

Acknowledgements

This book would not have been possible without the untiring efforts of Jane Wysocki and Swagata Raha who coordinated the work on successive editions, attended to every detail, and insisted on excellence.

The South Asia Human Rights Documentation Centre (SAHRDC) also extends its thanks to all interns at the Centre who contributed to the drafting, editing, and proofreading of the chapters.

The following individuals provided invaluable suggestions on earlier drafts of this text: Dr S Krishnamurthy, former Additional Director General of Police (Crime and Technical Services), Office of the Director General of Police, Karnataka State; Mr Ashok Aggarwal, Advocate; Mr Rajesh Talwar, Advocate; and Ms Nitya Ramakrishnan, Advocate.

Abbreviations

AIR	All India Reports
Cri LJ	Criminal Law Journal
CrPC	Code of Criminal Procedure, 1973
FIR	First Information Report
ICCPR	International Covenant on Civil and Political Rights
IPC	Indian Penal Code, 1860
IEA	Indian Evidence Act, 1872
NHRC	National Human Rights Commission
NSA	National Security Act, 1980
POTA	Prevention of Terrorism Act, 2002
SCC	Supreme Court Cases
SCR	Supreme Court Reports
UDHR	Universal Declaration on Human Rights
SAHRDC	South Asia Human Rights Documentation Centre

Introduction

Handbook of Human Rights and Criminal Justice in India—The System and Procedure is designed to assist in the protection of the civil and political rights of those people who are confronted with the criminal justice system. Civil and political rights are fundamental rights that provide for fair and equal treatment under the law, and protection against harm by the state. Civil and political rights are recognized by international law and Indian domestic law, where they are found primarily in the Constitution of India, 1950, but are also safeguarded by other legislation such as the Code of Criminal Procedure, 1973, and the Indian Evidence Act, 1872. Importantly, these rights are also protected by the common law, (rules and principles of law that are based on the outcome of cases decided by the superior courts) and to some extent influenced by guidelines and recommendations issued by statutory bodies such as the National Human Rights Commission.

This handbook seeks to familiarize non-governmental organizations, lawyers, human rights activists, and concerned citizens with the law in relation to criminal procedure. Each section sets out the relevant statute and case law, and specifies the nature of a person's rights, and how they can seek redress should their rights be violated.

A. What are Human Rights?

Human rights are rights to which all human beings are entitled, simply because we are human. Our human rights are inalienable and they belong to all of us, whatever our caste, class, race, age, gender, religion or belief, and should not be taken away from us under any circumstances. The term 'human rights' covers a broad range of rights, from the right to freedom of religion to the right to food and shelter. All are as important as each other and are owed to us in equal measure.

Human rights are universal. This means that human rights are so important that the international community has deemed that everyone has them, regardless of where they live, or their economic, social or political situation. Regardless of whether you live in China, the United States, India, or any other country, you have certain rights that are guaranteed by international law, and sometimes also by domestic law. Human Rights are not a 'western concept.' For example, no culture in the world has ever condoned torture or extra-judicial executions.

There are two main kinds of rights:

1. economic, social and cultural rights; and
2. civil and political rights.

This guide is concerned exclusively with civil and political rights, because these are the rights that are often subject to abuse in the criminal justice process.

B. International Law

In the past 50 years a considerable body of international law has evolved which has resulted in internationally accepted standards and guarantees for human rights. The Universal Declaration of Human Rights, adopted by the United Nations in 1948, contains the basic rights of all people, regardless of race, religion, place of residence or gender. While the Universal Declaration of Human Rights is not a legally binding document, it represents the will of the international community that human rights should be respected. Further, the Indian Supreme Court has ruled that 'the rules of customary international law which are not contrary to the municipal law shall be deemed to be incorporated in the domestic law.'[1] The basic rights found in the Universal Declaration of Human Rights have since been expanded, developed, and made legally binding on countries through other international conventions.

The main convention that is discussed in this guide is the International Covenant on Civil and Political Rights (ICCPR). However, there are many other international declarations, rules, and conventions that affect the criminal justice system. These include—the United Nations Standard Minimum Rules for the Treatment of Prisoners; the Body of Principles for the Protection of All Persons under Any Form of Detention or Imprisonment; the United Nations Rules for the Protection of Juveniles Deprived of their Liberty; the Declaration on the Protection of All Persons from Being Subjected to Torture and Other Cruel, Inhuman or Degrading Treatment or Punishment; the Convention against Torture and Other Cruel, Inhuman or Degrading Treatment or Punishment; Principles of Medical Ethics relevant to the Role of Health Personnel, particularly Physicians, in the Protection of Prisoners and Detainees against Torture and other Cruel, Inhuman or Degrading Treatment or Punishment; the Code of Conduct for Law Enforcement Officials; Basic Principles on the Role of Lawyers; Guidelines on the Role of Prosecutors; the United Nations Standard Minimum Rules for Non-custodial Measures (the Tokyo Rules); the United Nations Standard Minimum Rules for the Administration of Juvenile Justice (the Beijing Rules); the Declaration of Basic Principles of Justice for Victims of Crime and Abuse of Power; the Basic Principles on the Independence of the Judiciary; the Declaration on the Protection of All Persons from Enforced Disappearance; and the Principles on the Effective Prevention and Investigation of Extra-legal, Arbitrary and Summary Executions.

---

[1] *PUCL v. Union of India* (1997) 1 SCC 301.

As a member of the international community, India should abide by these international instruments. Additionally, many of the rights espoused in these documents are protected in India by the Indian Constitution, the Indian Penal Code, Criminal Procedure Code, and the Indian Evidence Act.

C. Civil and Political Rights

This guide is concerned with the rights protected under the ICCPR. India ratified the ICCPR in 1979, meaning that India must uphold the rights it enshrines. At their very core, civil and political rights provide for fair and equal treatment under the law and protection from illegal or arbitrary harm by the authorities. As a result, many of the rights in the ICCPR relate to the criminal justice system—whether in relation to arrest procedures, trial processes or conditions of detention. Throughout this guide you will see reference to the ICCPR since many of the safeguards provided in Indian law are also demanded by international law.

Two of the very basic rights protected by the ICCPR are the right to be recognised before the law (Article 16) and the right to equality before the law (Article 26).

Box 1.1   International Covenant on Civil and Political Rights

Article 16: Everyone shall have the right to recognition everywhere as a person before the law.

Article 26: All persons are equal before the law and are entitled without any discrimination to the equal protection of the law. In this respect, the law shall prohibit any discrimination and guarantee to all persons equal and effective protection against discrimination on any ground such as race, colour, sex, language, religion, political or other opinion, national or social origin, property, birth or other status.

D. Using this Handbook

While Indian law guarantees certain rights, there is no 'human rights police.' A person must recognize and lay claim to their human rights in order to ensure that these rights be respected.

It should be noted that standing up for your rights in relation to the criminal process can be a long and frustrating ordeal. However, asserting your rights is the only way to realize justice and to highlight human rights violations.

The purpose of this handbook is two-fold:

1. to familiarize the reader with the criminal process so that the system is less daunting, and
2. to assist in recognizing and asserting rights in respect of the process.

It should be kept in mind that understanding the system better enables the accused to cope with the police and the judiciary in a more effective manner. This guide aims to make the process more accessible to ordinary people and empower them to stand up for their rights.

You should use the handbook in two ways. First, you should read it from cover to cover in an effort to gain a general knowledge and appreciation of criminal justice processes. Second, you should use the handbook as a reference point when a question of criminal procedure arises.

The structure of the handbook takes you through the basic steps of the criminal justice system, from reporting or being accused of a crime to the trial process. It also deals with other considerations such as rights in detention and the right to compensation. Each principle of law is accompanied by its source, usually statutes and/or judgements of courts. Statutes are laws passed by the Parliament. Court judgements interpret these statutes. These judicial interpretations provide an additional source of law, known as common law. In this handbook, references to legislation state the section of the statute, and where appropriate, the subsection, followed by the name of the law. For example, 'S. 32 (2) Indian Evidence Act' means section 32, clause 2 of the Indian Evidence Act. In reference to court judgements, the name of the case and its full citation are provided. The facts and findings of major cases, as well as the text of important statutory provisions, are also provided.

This handbook does use a number of legal terms and concepts. They have been included to familiarize you with terms that you can expect to hear as you progress through the criminal justice process. The meaning of these terms should be clarified as you read, by reference to the glossary at the back of the handbook.

Disclaimers: Please note that the law is not stagnant. Its substance and interpretation change with amendments to legislation and new decisions by the courts. Therefore, you should check the currency of this text before relying on it. You should also keep in mind that it is to be used as a guide only, and is not an adequate substitute for targeted and comprehensive legal advice.

Please also note that this handbook deals mainly with aspects of criminal law mentioned in the Indian Penal Code, Evidence Act, and Code of Criminal Procedure. This handbook does not mention substantive procedure arising from other criminal law, for example, the Dowry Prohibition Act or the Narcotic, Drugs, and Psychotropic Substances Act. Where relevant, however, it touches upon issues raised by security and anti-terrorism legislation such as the National Security Act (1980) (NSA) and the Unlawful Activities Prevention (Amendment) Ordinance 2004.

Finally, it should be noted that the handbook does not address in detail issues concerning gender and juvenile justice, or the treatment of other vulnerable groups such as the mentally ill, members of tribal groups, or scheduled castes. This is not because the human rights of such groups are not deserving of discussion in relation to the criminal justice system. On the contrary, vulnerable members of society often have specific needs in relation to the Criminal Justice System, and are particularly susceptible to abuse. Unfortunately, it is beyond the scope of this handbook to provide the detailed analysis required to ensure that the needs of all groups and individuals in Indian society are addressed in relation to the Criminal Justice System.

1 Criminal Procedure and Human Rights in India

1.1 CIVIL AND POLITICAL RIGHTS IN INDIA

The rights of individuals in the criminal justice system have long been an issue in South Asia. In 250 BC, in response to the Kalinga War between Ashoka's empire and the Kalinga Empire, the great Buddhist Emperor Ashoka banned torture. In the 12th and 13th centuries, the Kandyan Kings of what is now Sri Lanka abolished capital punishment in their realm, something that the Government of India has yet to do. And in the medieval period in India, the poet saint Vemana asked his kings to give suspects the right to produce evidence in their defence before a death sentence was passed. He called for what is now known as a 'fair trial.'

The principles of justice and fairness in the criminal justice system found in this guide are not new to India. However, in the past one hundred and fifty years, in particular, these rights have become enshrined in a variety of statutes in India, as well as in the common law. Chief among these laws is the Constitution of India.

1.2 CONSTITUTION OF INDIA

The Constitution of India, 1950, (the Constitution) is the supreme law of the land in India. It establishes the basic framework of the government, delineating the division of power between the central and state governments, and establishes the functions of various governmental organs, including the judicial system.

Part III of the Constitution guarantees an array of fundamental rights. Individuals can enforce these rights in courts when they are violated by the action or inaction of a government authority or official, but not when they are violated by other private individuals or companies.[1] However, certain fundamental rights are enforceable against private individuals as well.[2]

---

[1] This principle is embodied in the doctrine of 'state action' in Article 12 of the Constitution; *M.C. Mehta* v. *Union of India*, AIR 1987 SC 1086. When an individual's rights are violated by another private individual, recourse can be sought under the ordinary law.

[2] Rights contained in Articles 17, 18, 23 and 24 are enforceable against the State and private individuals.

Some important general clauses of the Constitution relating to criminal justice and human rights include:

Article 14: Right to Equality.[3]

'Equality before the law' in Article 14 means that every person in India, regardless of his or her social, political, or economic position, is equally subject to the jurisdiction of the courts. Thus, the fact that a person is a politician, a police officer, or is rich should not allow him or her to escape the legal system when he or she commits a crime.

'Equal protection of the laws' means that every person should enjoy the protection of the law without adverse discrimination or special treatment. However, this does not mean that the laws of India will affect all persons in the same way; it only ensures that the law will provide like treatment for people in similar circumstances.[4]

Article 19(1): Right to Freedom.[5]

Article 19(1) provides all citizens with the fundamental right to freedom of speech, expression, assembly, association, movement, residence, and profession. The freedoms enumerated in this Article do not encompass all the rights of a free person[6] but are basic rights that have been recognized as natural rights inherent in citizenship.[7]

However, none of these freedoms is absolute; each may be curtailed by laws made pursuant to sub-clauses (2) to (6) of Article 19. These clauses allow 'reasonable restrictions' in the interests of the general public, security of the State, and public order. While the Constitution does not define 'reasonable restriction,' the Supreme Court has held that the reasonableness of a restriction should be determined by the courts, not the legislature,[8] on a case by case basis,[9] and that the restrictions should not be arbitrary or of an excessive nature beyond what is required in the interests of the public.[10]

For example, the freedom to form associations guaranteed in Article 19(1)(c) may be restricted 'in the interests of the sovereignty and integrity of India or public order.'[11] Under

---

[3] Article 14: The State shall not deny to any person equality before the law or the equal protection of the laws within the territory of India.

[4] *Satish Chandra* v. *Union of India*, AIR 1953 SC 250, 252.

[5] Article 19(1): All citizens have the right (a) to freedom of speech and expression; (b) to assemble peaceably and without arms; (c) to form associations and unions; (d) to move freely throughout the territory of India; (e) to reside and settle in any part of the territory of India; (g) to practise any profession, or to carry on any occupation, trade or business.

[6] *A.K. Gopalan* v. *State of Madras*, AIR 1950 SC 27, 107.

[7] *State of W.B.* v. *Subodh Gopal Bose*, (1954) SCR 587, 592.

[8] *Chintaman Rao* v. *State of M.P.* (1950) SCR 759, 765.

[9] *State of Madras* v. *V.G. Row* (1952) SCR 597, 607.

[10] *Chintaman Rao* v. *State of M.P.* (1950) SCR 759 at 763.

[11] Article 19(3), Constitution of India.

the reasonable restrictions doctrine, section 129 CrPC empowers police officers to disband any assembly that is unlawful or is 'likely to cause a disturbance to public peace.'

Article 20: Protection in Respect of Conviction for Offences.[12]

Article 20 guarantees certain protections against conviction for offences. Article 20(1) provides that a person can only be convicted of an offence if the act charged against him or her was an offence under the law on the date of the commission of the act. This is called the protection against *ex post facto* laws. Article 20(2) dictates that no person shall be prosecuted and punished for the same offence more than once. This is termed the protection against double jeopardy. Finally, Article 20(3) embodies the principle of protection against self-incrimination, protecting an accused person from being compelled to be a witness against himself or herself.[13]

Article 21: Protection of Life and Personal Liberty.[14]

Article 21 is one of the most important constitutional provisions. It confers on every person the right to life and personal liberty,[15] and the Supreme Court has interpreted Article 21 to be very broad in scope. Article 21 has been interpreted to guarantee rights including: rights of prisoners,[16] the right to legal aid,[17] the right to a speedy trial,[18] and the right to claim compensation for the violation of the rights in Article 21.[19] Furthermore, the expression 'procedure established by law' in the article requires that there must be a valid law justifying an interference with a person's life or personal liberty, and the procedure provided by law must be strictly followed.[20]

Article 22: Protection Against Arrest and Detention in Certain Cases.[21]

Article 22 deals with protections against arrest and detention, and is important for its direct and immediate bearing on the rights of the accused and detainees in Indian law. It requires

---

[12] Article 20(1): No person shall be convicted of any offence except for violation of a law in force at the time of the commission of the act charged as an offence, nor be subjected to a penalty greater than that which might have been inflicted under the law in force at the time of the commission of the offence. 20(2) No person shall be prosecuted and punished for the same offence more than once. 20(3) No person accused of any offence shall be compelled to be a witness against himself.

[13] See Chapter 3: 'Investigation' for details.

[14] Article 21: No person shall be deprived of his life or personal liberty except according to procedure established by law.

[15] Bhagwati, J. in *Maneka Gandhi* v. *Union of India*, (1978) 1 SCC 248: AIR 1978 SC 597, 620 (interpreting the provision as conferring rights notwithstanding the negative language).

[16] *State of A.P.* v. *Challa Ramkrishna Reddy*, (2000) 5 SCC 712 (holding that a prisoner is entitled to all his fundamental rights unless his liberty has been constitutionally curtailed).

[17] *M.H. Hoskot* v. *State of Maharashtra*, (1978) 3 SCC 544.

[18] *Hussainara Khatoon* v. *Home Secretary, Bihar*, (1979) 1 SCR (3) 1276, 1277.

[19] *Rudul Sah* v. *State of Bihar*, (1983) 4 SCC 141.

[20] *A.K. Gopalan* v. *State of Madras*, AIR 1950 SC 27 at 111.

[21] Article 22(1): No person who is arrested shall be detained in custody without being informed, as soon as may be, of the grounds for such arrest nor shall he be denied the right to consult, and to be

that a person who is arrested be informed, as soon as may be, of the charges against him or her and provided with the right to obtain counsel. Furthermore, it provides every person who has been arrested with the right to be produced before the nearest magistrate within 24 hours of arrest, and the right not to be detained in custody beyond that period without the authority of the Court.

Article 23: Prohibition of Traffic in Human Beings and Forced Labour.[22]

Article 23 is designed to protect individuals not only against the State but also against other private citizens. Article 23 prohibits forced labour, begar (involuntary work without pay) and trafficking (selling or disposing of men, women or children as if they were goods).[23] Article 23(2) makes an exception in favour of the State and enables it to impose compulsory service for public purposes (e.g. conscription for the defence of the country) so long as the State does not discriminate on grounds of religion, race, caste or class.[24]

Article 51A: Fundamental Duties.[25]

Article 51A lists the fundamental duties of the citizens of India. There is no punishment for breach of the fundamental duties, unless a specific penal statute exists on the subject. However, the presence of these duties reinforces a notion that the Constitution is an integrated scheme

---

defended by, a legal practitioner of his choice. 22(2) Every person who is arrested and detained in custody shall be produced before the nearest magistrate within a period of twenty-four hours of such arrest excluding the time necessary for the journey from the place of arrest to court of the magistrate and no such person shall be detained in custody beyond the said period without the authority of a magistrate.

[22] Article 23(1): Traffic in human beings and *begar* and other similar forms of forced labour are prohibited and any contravention of this provision shall be an offence punishable in accordance with law. 23(2) Nothing in this article shall prevent the State from imposing compulsory service for public purposes, and in imposing such service the State shall not make any discrimination on grounds only of religion, race, caste or class or any of them.

[23] The Immoral Traffic (Prevention) Act, 1956 punishes trafficking of human beings; the Bonded Labour System (Abolition) Act, 1976 abolished the bonded labour system.

[24] See per Das, J. in *State of Bihar* v. *Kameshwar Singh*, AIR 1952 SC 252.

[25] Article 51A: It shall be the duty of every citizen of India—(a) to abide by the Constitution and respect its ideals and institutions, the National Flag and the National Anthem; (b) to cherish and follow the noble ideals which inspired our national struggle for freedom; (c) to uphold and protect the sovereignty, unity and integrity of India; (d) to defend the country and render national service when called upon to do so; (e) to promote harmony and the spirit of common brotherhood amongst all the people of India transcending religious, linguistic and regional or sectional diversities; to renounce practices derogatory to the dignity of women; (f) to value and preserve the rich heritage of our composite culture; (g) to protect and improve the natural environment including forests, lakes, rivers and wild life, and to have compassion for living creatures; (h) to develop the scientific temper, humanism and the spirit of inquiry and reform; (i) to safeguard public property and to abjure violence; (j) to strive towards excellence in all spheres of individual and collective activity so that the nation constantly rises to higher levels of endeavour and achievement.

of rights as well as duties and that constitutional rights must be in harmony with the fundamental duties in order to be legally valid.[26]

Article 32: Right to Constitutional Remedies.[27]

Article 32 confers the right to take proceedings in the Supreme Court for the enforcement of fundamental rights. Article 32(1) empowers the Supreme Court to issue directions, orders or writs, including the writ of *habeas corpus*.[28] Article 226 also empowers the High Courts to make such orders for the enforcement of fundamental rights.

1.3 AN OVERVIEW OF THE INDIAN CRIMINAL JUSTICE SYSTEM

The criminal law in India is contained in a number of sources. The Indian Penal Code of 1860, together with other Local and Special Laws such as the Dowry Prohibition Act 1961, the Protection of Civil Rights Act 1955, the Prevention of Food Adulteration Act 1954 and the Scheduled Castes and the Scheduled Tribes (Prevention of Atrocities) Act 1989, the Pre-Conception and Pre-Natal Diagnostic Techniques Act 1994, Protection of Women from Domestic Violence Act 2005, and others outline what constitute criminal offences under Indian law. The Indian Evidence Act sets forth the rules under which evidence is admissible in Indian courts. And the Code of Criminal Procedure of 1973 (CrPC), outlines the procedural mechanisms for prosecuting criminal acts, providing for the constitution of criminal courts, the procedure for conducting police investigations and arrests, and the procedure for holding criminal trials and inquiries.

The application of the CrPC generally extends to all criminal offences, and to the entire territory of India, excluding the State of Jammu and Kashmir, and some tribal areas.[29] Since Jammu and Kashmir is given special exemptive status from Parliamentary rule under Article 370 of the Constitution, it is not subject to the CrPC and has a separate criminal procedure code of its own.

---

[26] Shukla, V.N., *Constitution of India*, 1950, p. 124 (10th ed., by Mahendra P. Singh, Lucknow, 2001).

[27] Article 32(1): The right to move the Supreme Court by appropriate proceedings for the enforcement of the rights conferred by this Part is guaranteed. (2) The Supreme Court shall have power to issue directions or orders or writs, including writs in the nature of *habeas corpus, mandamus, prohibition, quo warranto* and *certiorari*, whichever may be appropriate, for the enforcement of any of the rights conferred by this Part. (3) Without prejudice to the powers conferred on the Supreme Court by clauses (1) and (2), Parliament may by law empower any other court to exercise within the local limits of its jurisdiction all or any of the powers exercisable by the Supreme Court under clause (2). (4) The right guaranteed by this article shall not be suspended except as otherwise provided for by this Constitution.

[28] A writ of habeas corpus is an order from the Court demanding that the detaining officer present the detained person before the court and inform the court of the grounds of his or her confinement. If it is revealed that there are no lawful grounds for the detainment, he or she will be released. Otherwise, the detention is sustained and the regular bail procedure is followed.

[29] S. 1 CrPC.

Generally speaking, the CrPC and other statutes are exhaustive enough to cover most situations. However, the criminal justice system in India operates based on a complex web of legislation and common law. The common law system allows judges the freedom to interpret legislation applicable to a particular case in a way that will bring about the most just and legal outcome. The common law is shaped through successive judicial interpretations of legislation and the legal principle of *stare decisis* (judicial adherence to prior case law). Thus, when a particular piece of legislation fails to adequately protect or outline a certain topic, judges are free to rely on common law to ascertain the most just and applicable rules. Yet, it should be noted that the common law applies only in areas where the legislature has not spoken, and it can therefore never be employed in direct contradiction of a particular piece of legislation.

1.4 POLICE ORGANIZATION

The Police Act of 1861 largely governs Indian police forces, aiming to make them a more 'efficient instrument for the prevention and detection of crime.'[30] The Police Act gives each State Government the power to establish its own police force.[31] In addition to the Police Act, other legislation such as the CrPC also regulates police operations.

In each State, the Inspector General of Police, presently designated as the Director General of Police, is responsible for the overall administration of the police in that State. Below the State level, the administration of the police and policing activity in each district is carried out by the District Superintendent of Police, under the supervision of the District Magistrate.[32] In cities with a Police Commissioner, the Police District is headed by a Deputy Commissioner of Police.

Each police station is managed by a senior police officer called the Station House Officer (SHO). The SHO is in charge of the administration of the police station, the operation of their staff, and other duties relating to detection, investigation, and prevention of offences. Under the Police Act of 1861, other officers of a higher rank than the SHO may exercise the same powers as an SHO within their local area of appointment.[33]

Finally, although police officers have fewer powers than the SHO, they still have a number of powers under the CrPC such as the ability to make arrests and to conduct searches.[34]

It must be remembered that each State has its own hierarchy and nomenclature. Some States employ the Police Commissioner System, while others use the traditional Directorate System described above.

It is also important to note that the police are not above the law. Police officers are not allowed to behave as they like or to violate the law just because they wear a badge. A person should fiercely defend his or her rights in relation to the police. Under the Police Act of

---

[30] Preamble, Police Act 1861.

[31] S. 2 Police Act 1861.

[32] S. 4 Police Act 1861.

[33] S. 36 CrPC.

[34] Ss. 41–51 CrPC.

1861, a police officer in violation of his duties may be subject to a fine of up to three months of pay, or imprisonment of up to three months or both.[35]

Commissions have been constituted to review the functioning of the police, identify the flaws within the existing system of administration, and make recommendations. In order to curb the threat of transfer, the National Police Commission recommended minimization of political interference in the daily working of the police and security of tenure. It also recommended setting up of a State Security Commission, which must lay down 'broad policy guidelines and directions for the performance of preventive tasks and service-oriented functions by the police'. The National Police Commission prepared a draft of a new Police Act to replace the archaic 1861 Act and incorporated its recommendations therein. Later Committees, the latest being the Soli Sorabjee Committee constituted in September 2005, have largely reiterated the above recommendations.

In 1996, Mr Prakash Singh, a retired police officer along with others petitioned the Supreme Court under Article 32,[36] urging for the 'issue of directions to Government of India to frame a new Police Act on the lines of the model Act drafted by the Commission in order to ensure that the police is made accountable essentially and primarily to the law of the land and the people.'[37] The Supreme Court referred to the recommendations made by several Committees on police reforms and culled four requisite points of reform:

(a) State Security Commission at State level;
(b) transparent procedure for the appointment of Police Chief and the desirability of giving him a minimum fixed tenure;
(c) separation of investigation work from law and order; and
(d) a new Police Act which should reflect the democratic aspirations of the people.

The Supreme Court chose not to wait for the Executive to act on the recommendations and proceeded to direct State Governments to establish a State Security Commission and a Police Establishment Board (to determine transfers, postings, promotions, etc.). The court outlined the procedure for selection of the Director General of Police, prescribed minimum two-year tenure for police officers, and directed police departments to separate the law and order function from the investigation function.[38] The Supreme Court also ordered the creation of a district and State level 'Police Complaints Authority' to deal with complaints against the police.[39]

---

[35] S. 29 Police Act 1861.

[36] Article 32(1) of the Indian Constitution provides that '[t]he right to move the Supreme Court by appropriate proceedings for the enforcement of the rights conferred by this Part [i.e., fundamental rights] is guaranteed.'

[37] *Prakash Singh* v. *Union of India* W.P (Civil) 310 of 1996, Judgment dated 22.09.06 at *http://judis.nic.in/ supremecourt/qrydisp.asp?tfnm=28072.*

[38] *Prakash Singh* v. *Union of India* W.P (Civil) 310 of 1996, Judgment dated 22.09.06 at *http://judis.nic.in/ supremecourt/qrydisp.asp?tfnm=28072.*

[39] *Prakash Singh* v. *Union of India* W.P (Civil) 310 of 1996, Judgment dated 22.09.06 at *http://judis.nic.in/ supremecourt/qrydisp.asp?tfnm=28072.*

1.5 THE PROSECUTION

In a criminal trial, the Public Prosecutor or Assistant Public Prosecutor conducts the prosecution of the accused on behalf of the State. Prosecutors play a crucial role in the administration of justice. The role of the prosecutor was described by the Law Commission of India, in its 14th Report in the following terms:

The purpose of a criminal trial being to determine the guilt or innocence of the accused person, the duty of the Public Prosecutor is not to represent any particular party, but the State. The prosecution of accused persons has to be conducted with the utmost fairness ... A Public Prosecutor should be personally indifferent to the result of the case. His duty should consist only in placing all the available evidence irrespective of the fact whether it goes against the accused or helps him, before the court, in order to aid the court in discovering the truth. It would thus be seen, that in the machinery of justice, a public prosecutor has to play a very responsible role: the impartiality of his conduct is as vital as the impartiality of the court itself.[40]

Thus, it is the duty of the prosecutor not to merely seek convictions, but to act impartially and place before the court the evidence to enable the court to decide on the accused person's innocence. Pursuant to the Code of Criminal Procedure (Amendment) Act, 2005, the CrPC now provides for the establishment of a Directorate of Prosecution comprising of a Director of Prosecution and required number of Deputy Directors of Prosecution, appointed by the State Government.[41] State Governments, through a notification, must lay down the mandate, powers and functions of the Directorate. The Director of Prosecution will operate under the administrative control of the Head of the Home Department in the State.[42]

An advocate with at least ten years of practice is eligible for appointment as Director or Deputy Director of Prosecution.[43] The State Government must make the appointments in concurrence with the Chief Justice of the High Court.[44]

1.6 THE COURTS

The court system in India is based on the British model. Enforcement of the criminal law is a state function, meaning that each state has its own facilities, in the form of state courts, for dealing with criminal offenders. Within each state there are lower courts at a district level called Magistrates Courts, middle courts at a session level called Courts of Sessions, and High Courts at a state level. The highest national court in India is the Supreme Court of India.

Most people only ever have dealings with the lower and middle courts. A person will go to the higher courts only if he or she appeals a case, or a case against him or her is appealed.

---

[40] Law Commission of India, *14th Report on Reform of Judicial Administration* 1958, p. 765 at para 2.

[41] S. 25A(1) CrPC.

[42] S. 25A(3) CrPC.

[43] S. 25A(2) CrPC.

[44] *Id.*

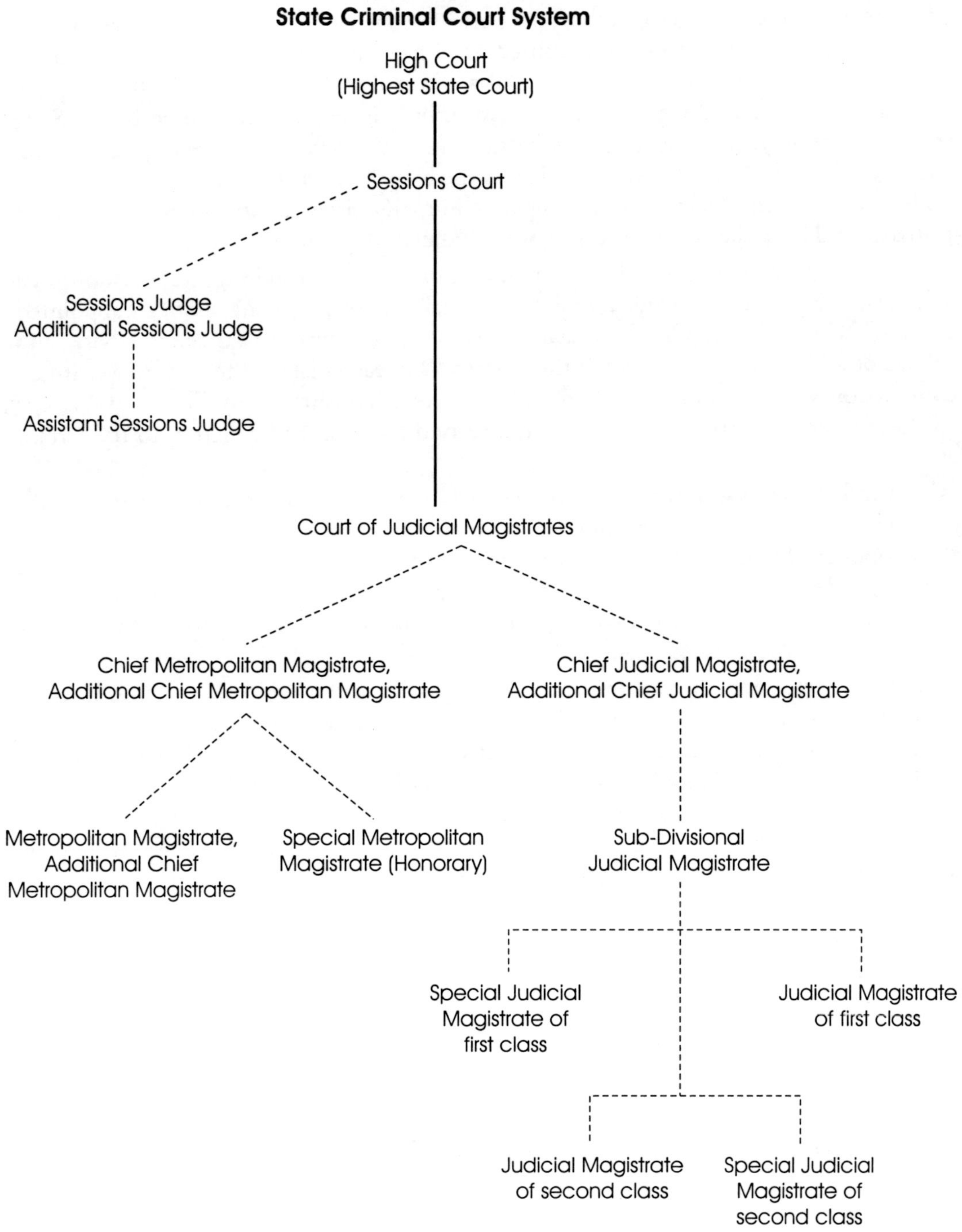

State Criminal Court System

High Court
(Highest State Court)

Sessions Court

Sessions Judge
Additional Sessions Judge

Assistant Sessions Judge

Court of Judicial Magistrates

Chief Metropolitan Magistrate,
Additional Chief Metropolitan Magistrate

Chief Judicial Magistrate,
Additional Chief Judicial Magistrate

Metropolitan Magistrate,
Additional Chief
Metropolitan Magistrate

Special Metropolitan
Magistrate (Honorary)

Sub-Divisional
Judicial Magistrate

Special Judicial
Magistrate of
first class

Judicial Magistrate
of first class

Judicial Magistrate
of second class

Special Judicial
Magistrate of
second class

FIGURE 1.1

If a person is accused of a crime, the first court he or she will have contact with will be the Magistrates Court. Magistrates are classified as either Judicial Magistrates or Executive Magistrates. However, if a person is accused of a criminal offence he or she will only come into contact with Judicial Magistrates, since Executive Magistrates, appointed by the State Government, are only empowered to issue certain orders to prevent breaches of public peace, and deal mainly with the civil law. In rural areas the Executive Magistrates may be known as Munsifs. Those Judicial Magistrates who operate in major cities are known as Metropolitan Magistrates, and have the same powers as other Judicial Magistrates.

Judicial Magistrates are divided into a hierarchy of Chief Judicial Magistrates, Additional Chief Judicial Magistrates, and Sub-Divisional Judicial Magistrates, all of whom are appointed by the High Court.[45] The Chief Judicial Magistrate has powers to guide, supervise, and control all other Judicial Magistrates in the District.[46] In each district the State Government in conjunction with the High Court decides on the establishment of Courts of Judicial Magistrates where magistrates of the first and second class have jurisdiction to try certain cases.[47]

Chief Judicial Magistrates and Chief Metropolitan Magistrates can pass sentences for imprisonment for terms not exceeding seven years.[48] Judicial Magistrates of the first class and Metropolitan Magistrates can pass sentences of imprisonment for terms not exceeding three years, and/or of fines not exceeding five thousand rupees.[49] Judicial Magistrates of the second class can only pass sentences of imprisonment not exceeding one year, and/or of fines not exceeding one thousand rupees.[50]

Depending upon the crime a person is accused of, he or she could alternatively be tried in a Court of Sessions. Each state of India is divided into at least one sessions division, for which the State must establish a Court of Sessions, to be presided over by a judge appointed by the High Court.[51] The High Court also appoints Additional Sessions Judges, and Assistant Sessions Judges.[52] Courts of Sessions can convict and sentence people for most crimes. However, any sentence of death passed by a Sessions Judge or Additional Sessions Judge is subject to confirmation by the High Court, and an Assistant Sessions Judge cannot pass a sentence of death, life imprisonment, or imprisonment for a term exceeding ten years.[53]

The highest state courts in India are the High Courts. Most states of India have a High Court, which hears cases on appeal from the lower courts and on rare occasions also deals

---

[45] S. 12 CrPC.
[46] Ss. 15 & 19 CrPC.
[47] S. 11 CrPC.
[48] S. 29(1)(4) CrPC.
[49] S. 29(2)(4) CrPC.
[50] S. 29(3)(4) CrPC.
[51] Ss. 7, 9(1)(2) CrPC.
[52] S. 9(3) CrPC.
[53] S. 28(2)(3) CrPC.

directly with cases under its original jurisdiction.[54] The Supreme Court is the highest court in India and is the final arbiter of all legal matters. Most people never have any contact with the Supreme Court of India, although it affects our lives by the decisions it makes.

Decisions of the Supreme Court of India are binding on state High Courts, which must follow the Supreme Court's interpretations of the law.[55] Subordinate courts will look first to the judgements of the High Court in their state and be bound by this. However, if there is no decision on the issue in question, subordinate courts will also follow the decision of the Supreme Court on the issue. Decisions of the High Courts are binding on lower courts within their jurisdiction, but are not binding on the Supreme Court, or on courts in other states. For example, a Sessions Court in Bombay is bound by the legal principles decided by the High Court of Bombay. However, a Sessions Court in Guwahati is not bound by the High Court of Bombay, but by the High Court of Guwahati. However, all courts in India are ultimately bound by the decisions of the Supreme Court of India.

[54] Article 214, Constitution of India.
[55] Article 141, Constitution of India.

2 Reporting a Crime: First Information Report

2.1 INTRODUCTION

Most people will have to report a crime at some stage—whether it is a theft, assault, or other crime. This chapter deals with the rules and procedures governing the reporting of crime, which is generally conducted through the filing of a First Information Report (FIR). This chapter also outlines what to do if a false FIR is lodged, or if the police refuse to register an FIR.

The procedure for reporting a crime varies depending upon the type of crime that has been committed. The filing of an FIR only occurs in the case of a 'cognizable offence', so it is necessary to know the difference between cognizable and non-cognizable offences.

A cognizable offence is a serious criminal offence that poses an immediate danger to society, such as murder, rape, or robbery. A police officer can investigate a cognizable offence without the order of a magistrate[1] and can make an arrest for a cognizable offence without a warrant.[2]

A non-cognizable offence is generally considered to be a less serious and less immediately dangerous offence, such as contempt of court or neglect of public duty. A police officer cannot make an arrest for a non-cognizable offence without a warrant,[3] nor can a police officer investigate a non-cognizable offence without an order from a magistrate.[4]

It is usually easy to tell the difference between cognizable and non-cognizable offences. Generally, serious offences with a minimum sentence of three years imprisonment are classified as cognizable. However, there are some exceptions to this general rule. The First Schedule of the CrPC contains a table in which offences are categorised as cognizable or non-cognizable.

[1] S. 156(1) CrPC.
[2] S. 2(c) CrPC.
[3] S. 2(l) CrPC.
[4] S. 155(2) CrPC.

Therefore, this Schedule should be consulted if there is any doubt as to the categorization of a crime. The First Schedule is reproduced in the Appendix of this handbook.

Examples of cognizable offences include the following:

- Murder[5] and attempted murder;[6]
- Doing an act that endangers the life or personal safety of others;[7]
- Rape;[8]
- Kidnapping;[9]
- Robbery,[10] theft,[11] and dishonestly receiving stolen property;[12]
- Criminal breach of trust by a public servant;[13]
- Trespassing;[14]
- Counterfeiting Indian coins,[15] currency-notes or bank-notes;[16] and
- Rioting.[17]

Where the information relates to two connected offences, one cognizable and one non-cognizable, the case will be treated as cognizable, and an FIR must be registered.[18]

Reporting a Non-Cognizable Offence

A person with information regarding the commission of a non-cognizable offence may still report it to the police, who will then record the information in the station diary.[19] However, this report does not have the status of being an FIR since an FIR must relate to the commission of a cognizable offence.

[5] S. 302 IPC.
[6] S. 307 IPC.
[7] S. 336 IPC.
[8] S. 376 IPC.
[9] S. 363 IPC.
[10] S. 392 IPC.
[11] S. 379 IPC.
[12] S. 411 IPC.
[13] S. 409 IPC.
[14] S. 447 IPC.
[15] S. 232 IPC.
[16] S. 489A IPC.
[17] S. 147 IPC.
[18] S. 155(4) CrPC.
[19] S. 155(1) CrPC.

2.2 WHAT IS A FIRST INFORMATION REPORT?

A First Information Report (FIR) is a formal statement given to and recorded by the police regarding a cognizable offence.[20] It is the earliest report made to the police and is intended to prompt the police into taking action. Whether particular information would constitute an FIR depends on the circumstances of each case.[21]

An FIR serves several purposes. First, it initiates a police investigation, and can lead to the arrest and prosecution of a criminal offender. Second, an FIR provides an early report of the commission of a criminal offence—before memories fail or stories are changed. For this reason, an FIR is an extremely important piece of evidence.

2.3 HOW TO LODGE AN FIR

As soon as a person is the victim of or witness to a crime, they should write and sign a statement noting exactly what happened. This information should be given to the officer-in-charge of investigations at the police station, or if the officer-in-charge is not available, to the next ranking officer in the station. If an oral statement is given to the police officer, then the police officer should write down the information on behalf of the informant (the person who lodged the FIR) and should read it back to him or her so that he or she may verify the contents. The informant should then sign the statement.[22]

An informant should not put anything that he or she knows to be untrue in the statement and should not embellish or exaggerate what happened. Giving false information to the police is an offence punishable with imprisonment under S. 203 IPC. He or she should simply state the facts of the offence to the best of his or her ability, trying to be as precise and clear as possible, as an FIR must not be vague and must be definite enough to enable the police to start an investigation.[23]

An FIR can be given over the telephone if the informant clearly identifies himself or herself, the officer-in-charge writes down the statement faithfully, and if the information clearly and completely discloses the commission of a cognizable offence.[24] An anonymous telephone call stating that a crime has been committed, which does not disclose the name of the accused or the commission of a cognizable offence, will not constitute an FIR.[25]

However, giving information over the telephone is a less reliable method of reporting a crime, and is more open to police abuse or inefficiency. It is much better that the informant

---

[20] The term 'FIR' is not defined in the CrPC, but is the name given to the information recorded by the police under S. 154 CrPC.

[21] *Tapinder Singh* v. *State of Punjab*, (1970) 2 SCC (Cri) 113; 1970 AIR 1566; 1971 SCR (1) 599.

[22] S. 154(1) CrPC.

[23] See *State of Assam* v. *U.N. Rajkhowa*, 1975 Cri LJ 354, 377 (Gau HC).

[24] See *Tohal Singh* v. *Rajasthan*, 1989 Cri LJ 1350 (Raj HC).

[25] See for example *Tapinder Singh* v. *State of Punjab*, (1970) 2 SCC (Cri) 113; 1970 AIR 1566; 1971 SCR (1) 599.

is present at the police station in person. Similarly, if a complaint is sent by post, it will be registered in a complaint register and will be inquired into by the police in a more leisurely fashion.

Even if an informant has spoken to the police at the scene of the crime, he or she should still go to the nearest police station to formally lodge an FIR for the offence. Information given to the police at the scene of the crime may not satisfy all the requirements for a valid FIR, for example, the officer at the scene of the crime may not be the officer-in-charge of the nearest police station.

It is possible that when a complaint is made, the police may record an FIR in a language that the informant does not understand. Usually, the FIR will be recorded in the local language of the police station where it is lodged. The police have no legal obligation to record the FIR in a language which the informant understands, nor are they under an obligation to translate it into any languages other than the one in which it was recorded. Therefore, in this situation the best course of action is for the informant to get the FIR translated himself or herself, and then get a certification as to the authenticity of the contents of this translation. The authenticity of such a translation should preferably be carried out by a notified translator, or by a government officer who has the appropriate authority in such matters, such as a notary public.

If the informant cannot read English or the language in which the FIR is recorded, then he or she must take with him or her a trustworthy person who can read the FIR and confirm that its contents correspond with the information that has been given to the police. If the informant cannot read the FIR, he or she will be left in an extremely vulnerable position whereby the police may read back the version of events given to them, but then record the FIR with false or wrong information. Therefore, it is essential that someone whom the informant trusts reads the FIR before it is signed to ensure that what is written is exactly what the informant told the police.

2.4 THE BASICS OF AN FIR

The FIR should meet the following criteria:[26]

1. The FIR should contain information related to the commission of a cognizable offence. The FIR should include:
   - The name and address of the informant/victim;
   - The name and address of the accused (if known);
   - The date, place, and time of the offence;
   - The details of the offence;
   - The identity of any witnesses;
   - An accurate description of what happened; and
   - The reasons for any delay in reporting the offence.

---

[26] S. 154(1) CrPC.

If the informant does not know all of this information, he or she should provide as much information as they can. However, it is neither customary nor necessary to mention every minute detail in the FIR.[27]

2. The information should be given to the officer-in-charge at the police station.

3. The FIR must be written down, either by the person making the complaint, or if the complaint is made orally, by the police officer.

4. The person making the complaint must sign the FIR. Refusal to sign an FIR is a criminal offence under S. 180 IPC. If that person is incapable of signing because of illiteracy or disability, the FIR should instead bear his/her fingerprint.

   Before an FIR is signed or submitted, the person making the complaint should carefully read it over, or have it read aloud by a trustworthy person. If the police officer, while writing down the statement, has left out something that the informant considers important, or has included something that the informant did not say, he or she should demand that it be corrected before signing the FIR.

5. The police are legally required to give the informant a copy of the FIR free of cost.[28] However, they do not always give the copy unless specifically requested. The informant should take care to keep the copy, because if the offence is investigated, it will be important to have a copy of his or her original statement. If the police refuse to give the informant a free copy of the FIR, he or she may make a complaint to the Superintendent of Police, or to a magistrate.

6. The FIR must be entered into the official diary of the police station at which it is registered.

   The following do not amount to an FIR:
   - Statements given to the police after the investigation has commenced;[29]
   - Vague or indefinite information;[30]
   - Cryptic messages;[31] or
   - An undated, unsigned, and anonymous letter.

2.5 QUESTIONS AND ANSWERS

A. Who can File an FIR?

Anyone can file an FIR. It is not necessary to be a victim of crime, or even a witness to a crime. You can register an FIR even if you hear of an offence second hand.[32] However,

---

[27] *Pedda Narayana and Ors* v. *State of Andhra Pradesh* 1975 AIR 1252; 1975 SCR 84; 1975 SCC (4) 153.

[28] S. 154(2) CrPC.

[29] *S.V. Madar* v. *State of Mysore*, 1979 SCC (Cri) 910; (1980) 1 SCC 479; 1979 Cri LJ 1358.

[30] *Emperor* v. *Khwaja*, AIR 1945 PC 18; 46 Cr LJ 413.

[31] *Binay Kumar Singh* v. *State of Bihar*, (1996) 4 CCR 253 (SC).

[32] See for example *Apren Joseph* v. *State of Kerala*, (1973) 3 SCC 114; AIR 1973 SC 1.

restraint and good judgement should be exercised before going to the police station whenever you hear about a crime.

B. Do you have to Register an FIR if a Crime has been Committed?

Under S. 39 of the CrPC, every person aware of the commission of, or of the intention of any other person, to commit certain offences punishable under the IPC, must give information regarding such offences to the nearest magistrate or police officer. The offences under the IPC to which this rule applies are listed in S. 39 and include murder, offences of robbery and dacoity, kidnapping, and house-trespass. The only exception to this would be, if it can be shown that the person had a reasonable excuse for not giving such information. The burden of proving the existence of such a reasonable excuse is placed on that person.

The intentional failure to provide the police with information regarding the commission of a crime which a person is legally bound to give information about is punishable with a term of imprisonment of up to six months and/or a fine.[33] Giving false information about an offence that has been committed is also punishable with a term of imprisonment of up to two years and/or a fine.[34]

C. When Should the FIR be Lodged?

An FIR should be lodged as soon as possible after the commission of the offence, as this allows the police to promptly begin their investigation, and allows for a more accurate account of events. The time taken to lodge an FIR will also be considered by the police when they assess the urgency of the investigation, and whether to lodge the FIR.

Should the matter proceed to trial, the courts will consider a timely FIR more reliable, and will view an unexplained delay in filing an FIR with suspicion.[35] Time taken to file the FIR will also be considered by the courts, in assessing the weight to give to the FIR, as evidence.

The courts do appreciate that in some cases a delay will inevitably exist between witnessing an offence and lodging an FIR, and the reasons for the delay, such as, distance from the police station, time of the day, and the injury suffered will be taken into consideration by the court when considering the FIR.

Examples of cases where the court accepted a delay in filing FIR
- In the case of *Krishna Pillai*,[36] a delay of twelve hours was accepted by the Supreme Court because the relatives were under shock for some time, and were mainly concerned with the treatment of the deceased.

[33] S. 202 IPC.
[34] S. 203 IPC.
[35] See for example *Ram Jag* v. *State of U.P.*, (1974) 4 SCC 201; AIR 1974 SC 606; 1974 Cr LJ 479.
[36] AIR 1981 SC 1237; 1981 Cr LJ 743; 1981 SCC (Cri) 669.

- In the case of *Harpal Singh*,[37] a delay of ten days was accepted by the Supreme Court in the rape case because victim stated that since the honour of the family was involved, its members had to decide whether to take the matter to the police or not.
- In the case of *Sone Lal and Ors* v. *State of Uttar Pradesh*,[38] the Supreme Court held that delaying until next day to file an FIR in a murder case was reasonable given the circumstances of the case, namely, that the witness' sons had just been killed, his friend abducted, and he himself faced potential reprisals from the armed assailants, had he proceeded directly to the police station.

D. What if the Police Refuse to Register the FIR?

In most circumstances, the police are legally obliged to register the FIR.[39] This is the case even if the offence was committed outside the police station's territorial jurisdiction, in which case the police are required to record the FIR and forward it to the correct police station.[40] In certain situations, the police may conduct a preliminary inquiry to establish the existence of a legitimate complaint. It is then within their powers to refuse to immediately register the FIR. In that case, they must make a general diary entry, and, depending on time constraints and the gravity of the offence, could make an on-the-spot verification.

However, the police do sometimes refuse to register an FIR. If the police refuse to register the FIR, the informant should ask the police to at least accept a copy of his or her statement. A letter on the station letterhead acknowledging receipt of the statement should be requested, which should be stamped and signed. Alternatively, the police should stamp and sign another copy of the statement and give it to the informant. The informant should also note down the name and rank of the officer who takes the statement.

While giving the police a statement is not the same thing as officially lodging an FIR, and will not necessarily result in a police investigation, it will put the commission of the offence on the public record. This means that if something happens subsequently, then there is already a government document on record relating to the crime. For example, if you give a statement to the police that someone is threatening you and the police refuses to register an FIR, and you are later assaulted, there is already a document relating to this at the police station. This not only strengthens your case, but also provides additional information to the police in their investigation.

There are also two official ways to deal with a refusal by the police to register an FIR:

First, the informant may take administrative recourse. This involves sending their statement in a letter, by post or person to the Superintendent of Police. The letter should clearly outline all the information relating to the offence, and if the Superintendent is satisfied that the

---

[37] AIR 1981 SC 361; 1981 Cr LJ 1.
[38] AIR 1978 SC 1142.
[39] *State of Haryana* v. *Bhajan Lal*, 1992 AIR 604; (1992) Cri LJ 527.
[40] *State of Andhra Pradesh* v. *Punatiramulu*, 1993 AIR SC 2644.

information discloses the commission of an offence, then he must investigate the case himself or assign the investigation to a police officer in the district.[41] Places where the Commissioner system of policing is prevalent, the communication should be addressed to the Deputy Commissioner of Police.

If the person making the complaint does send information to the Superintendent of Police by post, then he or she should make sure to get a postal receipt, either through registered post, recorded delivery, or speed post. This way, if the matter needs to be dealt with further, for example with a magistrate, then he or she will have proof of their communication with the Superintendent.

Second, the informant may take judicial recourse by lodging a complaint with a magistrate.[42] The complaint should be submitted in writing, setting out the details and context of what happened when the informant tried to lodge an FIR. A signed copy of the informant's statement, and the statements of any witnesses, should be included. The magistrate may then take cognizance of the offence,[43] or may order investigation of the offence by the police.[44] The magistrate may direct the police to file an FIR for the purpose of starting the investigation. However, even if the magistrate does not make such a direct order, it is the duty of the officer-in-charge of the police station to register the FIR in order to begin the investigation.[45]

E. What Happens to the FIR After it is Lodged?

If the officer-in-charge of the police station where the FIR is lodged believes that a cognizable offence has been committed, he or she should immediately send a report to the local magistrate and proceed to investigate the alleged crime.[46]

F. Will the FIR be used in Court?

The FIR will be presented to the court if the case goes to trial. The FIR can be placed in evidence when the informant is examined as a witness during the trial. However, the FIR cannot be used as primary or substantive evidence. This means that the FIR cannot be used as evidence to substantiate the facts stated within it. It can only be used to corroborate or contradict the information given by the informant under Ss. 157 and 145 Indian Evidence Act. However, it is still important because it conveys the earliest information regarding the offence.

---

[41] S. 154(3) CrPC.

[42] S. 200 CrPC.

[43] When a magistrate 'takes cognizance' of an offence, it means that they take judicial notice of the offence for the purpose of taking subsequent steps towards inquiry and trial: *R.R. Chari* v. *State of U.P.,* 1951 AIR 207; 1951 SCR 312; *Ajit Kumar Palit* v. *State of W.B.,* (1963) 1 Cri LJ 797, 802; AIR 1963 SC 765.

[44] Ss. 190 and 156(3) CrPC; *Madhu Bala* v. *Suresh Kumar,* (1997) 8 SCC 476; 1998 SCC (Cri) 111.

[45] *Suresh Chand Jain* v. *State of Madhya Pradesh* JT (2001) 2 SC 81; *Mohd Yousuf* v. *Afaq Jahan* (2006) 1 SCC 627.

[46] S. 157 CrPC.

G. Can you Get a Copy of an FIR that has been Filed Against You?

Yes. If you find yourself under investigation or arrested for a crime resulting from an FIR, you are entitled to a copy of the FIR, free of charge.[47] You should first request a copy at the appropriate police station. However, if the police are uncooperative, you should approach the magistrate or judge to whom your case has been assigned, and request a copy of the FIR.

H. What if a False FIR is Registered?

The first thing that a person against whom a false FIR has been lodged should do is get a copy of the FIR. If the accusations are serious, he or she should seriously consider consulting a lawyer.

It is a crime, punishable by up to two years imprisonment and/or a fine, to knowingly give false information about an offence.[48] Additionally, where a person institutes, or causes to be instituted, false criminal proceedings in an attempt to cause injury to another person, knowing that there is no just or lawful ground for doing so, they are liable to be imprisoned for up to two years and/or a fine.[49] Further, if the offence with which they falsely charge a person is punishable with imprisonment of seven years or more, life imprisonment, or death, then they will be liable to face a punishment of up to seven years in prison and/or a fine.[50] However, despite these penalties, occasionally a fake case may be lodged with the police. Sometimes the police themselves will fabricate such a report.

There are two ways in which a person can react to a false FIR:

The *first* thing he or she can do is to make a complaint to a magistrate. The complaint should be written to the Case Magistrate, setting out all of the facts regarding the false report. A copy of the FIR should be included, and a request should be made that the magistrate take action to dismiss the proceedings. The complaint should be signed by the person against whom the FIR has been lodged, and by any witness.[51]

The magistrate may then:

- Order the postponement of legal processes against the accused and either inquire into the case or direct an investigation into the matter;[52]
- Issue either a summons or warrant for the accused to be brought before a court with regards to the matter, if he or she is of the opinion that there is sufficient ground for proceeding;[53] or

---

[47] S. 207(ii) CrPC.
[48] S. 203 IPC.
[49] S. 211 ICC.
[50] S. 211 IPC.
[51] S. 200 CrPC.
[52] S. 202 CrPC.
[53] S. 204 CrPC.

- Dismiss the complaint against the accused if he or she deems there to be insufficient reason for proceeding.[54]

Secondly a petition may be made to the High Court to stop the investigation and quash the FIR.[55] If the allegations made in the FIR, taken at their face value and accepted in their entirety, do not constitute an offence, the criminal proceedings instituted on the basis of such FIR should be quashed by the High Court.[56]

However, the filing of a writ petition is expensive and most victims of false FIRs or police harassment cannot afford to take this course of action. Additionally, the Supreme Court has advised the High Court to use its power to quash an investigation very sparingly and only in rare cases.[57]

In *State of Haryana* v. *Bhajan Lal,*[58] the Supreme Court provided illustrations of cases when the High Court can use its power to quash the FIR, including:

- Where the allegations made in the FIR or the complaint, even if they are taken at their face value and accepted in their entirety, do not *prima facie* constitute any offence or make out a case against the accused;
- Where the allegations made in the FIR or complaint are so absurd and inherently improbable, on the basis of which no prudent person can ever reach a just conclusion that there is sufficient ground for proceeding against the accused; and
- Where a criminal proceeding is manifestly attended with *mala fide*, and/or where the proceeding is maliciously instituted with an ulterior motive for wreaking vengeance on the accused, and with view to spite him due to private and personal grudge.

---

[54] S. 203 CrPC.

[55] S. 482 CrPC & Art. 226, Constitution of India.

[56] *State of U.P.* v. *R.K. Srivastava,* (1989) 4 SCC 59; 1989 SCC (Cri) 713.

[57] *Talab Haji Hussain* v. *Madhukar Purshottam Mondkar* AIR 1958 SC 376.

[58] AIR 1992 SC 604: 1992 Supp 1 SCC 335: 1992 SCC (Cr) 426: 1992 Cr LJ 527.

Box 2.1   Sample of an FIR

Rajesh Das
A-12/3 Green Park
New Delhi

12 May 2003
Officer-in-Charge
Sunder Nagar Police Station
New Delhi

Dear Sir,

This is to request you to lodge a First Information Report (FIR) against Mr Sunil Roy. He lives at A-12/2 Green Park New Delhi 110 048. His phone number is 98 091 55346. The facts of the complaint are as follows:

Yesterday evening I was at home dining with my wife Ipshita. At 8.20 pm the doorbell rang and I opened the door. Mr Sunil Roy was standing at our door with his wife Mrs Vimla Roy and another man whom we do not know. Mr Roy is our landlord.

Mr Roy told me that we owed him rupees ten thousand for the electricity bill and minor repairs to be done in our apartment, specifically a broken tap, broken toilet seat, and a broken geyser. I explained that as he was the landlord he was obliged to pay for minor repairs to the apartment, and that I would not be paying the electricity bill. I had been suspecting since few months that Mr Roy had illegally rigged the electricity meter so that I also have to pay for the electricity for his apartment.

Mr Roy grew very angry, and, after a heated conversation, I told him that there was no point in arguing about it because I was not going to pay him any money. I tried to close the door, but Mr Roy punched me in the head. Mrs Roy and the other man then forcefully entered our apartment, and pushed my wife to the floor. Mrs Roy started kicking my wife on the stomach. I tried to intervene, but Mr Roy and the other man pushed me against the wall, punched me on the stomach and slapped me. During the attack, Mr and Mrs Roy had called the other man, Ravinder. That man was in his mid-twenties, was wearing a Nike hat, and had a short vertical scar on his left cheek.

Finally, before leaving, Mr Roy said 'you better pay up, or we will be back.' My wife sustained a cut on her head which was bleeding, and I suffered a black eye, a bloody nose, and sore ribs. We immediately went to Maximillan Medical Centre where, both my wife and I were admitted. The consultant, Dr Rajdeep Gupta informed that I had three broken ribs, and that my wife was in shock and was suffering internal bleeding. I was released from the hospital the next day (today). However my wife must stay in the hospital until the end of the week.

I would be grateful if an FIR is filed for criminal trespass, and serious assault. Mr and Mrs Roy and their friend must be arrested immediately.

Yours sincerely,
[signature here]
Rajesh Das

3 Investigation

This chapter describes the duties of the police and the rights of citizens during an investigation. It begins with a general overview of the investigative process, and then addresses in more detail the areas in an investigation where human rights violations are likely to occur, such as search and seizure.

3.1 INVESTIGATION OVERVIEW

An investigation is defined as all the proceedings under the CrPC for the collection of evidence, conducted by a police officer or by any person authorized by a magistrate.[1] The law relating to the investigation of all offences, both cognizable and non-cognizable, is found in Ss. 154–176 CrPC. Where there is any uncertainty as to which police station has the jurisdiction to investigate an offence, Ss. 177–189 CrPC provide guidance.

A. Who Investigates?

The principal agency with the power under law to carry out investigations is the police force. However, not all police officers have the power to investigate an offence without the order of a magistrate; only those with the rank of officer-in-charge and above may do so.[2] In some districts, an officer-in-charge is referred to as the station house officer (SHO).[3]

B. Initiation of Investigations

An investigation is generally initiated by the registration of an FIR regarding a cognizable offence.[4] However, even without an FIR, if the officer-in-charge of a police station has reason

---

[1] S. 2(h) CrPC.
[2] Ss. 156 and 36 CrPC.
[3] S. 2(o) CrPC.
[4] See Chapter 2: 'Reporting a Crime: First Information Report.'

to suspect the commission of a cognizable offence, he may investigate the offence after sending a report to a magistrate.[5] Moreover, if the police receive word of a homicide or suicide, they are obligated to investigate, unless otherwise directed by higher authorities.[6]

In some circumstances a private citizen who wishes to report a cognizable offence does not have to go to the police, but can go directly to a magistrate who may take steps to bring the accused to trial.[7] This is particularly useful where the police are, for whatever reason, indifferent to the claims of the informant, or are unwilling to register the complaint because they are in collusion with, or shielding the accused. The magistrate can then direct the police to register a case at the police station and start an investigation.[8] The magistrate has power in this situation to direct an investigation by someone other than a police officer.[9] (The appropriate procedure for filing a complaint is mentioned in the previous chapter.) After the complaint is filed, the magistrate may appoint someone to investigate the case, and this person shall have the same powers as those conferred upon an officer-in-charge by the Code, except the power of arrest without warrant.[10] Thus, the investigation of a cognizable offence may be initiated by the police themselves,[11] the order of a magistrate,[12] or by the lodging of an FIR.

If the offence is non-cognizable, the investigation may not proceed without the order of a magistrate with authority to try such a case, or commit it to trial.[13] In the case of a cognizable offence, the police are not required to wait for the order of a magistrate to investigate, and may initiate an investigation after sending the appropriate report to a competent magistrate.[14]

C. Investigation Completion and Cessation

An investigation should be completed *without* unnecessary delay.[15] The conclusion of a police investigation should be contained in a final report.[16] At the completion of an investigation, the police should submit this report with all the details of the case to a magistrate.[17] If the accused is to be prosecuted, this report is called a charge sheet or *challan*. If there is a charge sheet, it should list relevant charges along with the laws which have been contravened. After

---

[5] S. 157(1) CrPC.

[6] S. 174 CrPC.

[7] See for example, *Madhu Bala* v. *Suresh Kumar*, (1997) 8 SCC 476.

[8] See *Madhu Bala*, at p. 479.

[9] S. 202(1) CrPC.

[10] S. 202(3) CrPC.

[11] S. 156(1) CrPC.

[12] S. 156(3) CrPC.

[13] S. 155(2) CrPC.

[14] Ss. 156 and 157 CrPC.

[15] S. 173(1) CrPC.

[16] S. 173(2) CrPC.

[17] S. 173(2) CrPC.

looking at the charge sheet, the magistrate decides to either (a) proceed with the case,[18] (b) order further investigation of the case,[19] or (c) dismiss the charges against the accused.

In some circumstances, it may be possible to argue that the continuation of an investigation constitutes an abuse of law. The investigation should be carried out within the limits of the law, and without causing any harassment to the accused, or any undue or unnecessary delay.[20] If it appears that no cognizable offence in fact exists to be investigated, the High Court can quash the investigation proceedings under Article 226 of the Constitution[21] or through its inherent powers under S. 482 CrPC.[22] (See the section in Chapter 2 entitled 'What if a False FIR is Registered?' for methods of stopping an unjust investigation.)

A magistrate cannot quash an investigation. However, after the police have sent the magistrate a charge sheet of the case, the magistrate has the power to decide whether to take cognizance of the case. The magistrate also has the power to direct any further investigation.[23] A magistrate who takes cognizance has broad powers over the investigation and can dismiss a complaint against an accused person.[24] Discharging an accused is a vital function of the magistrate, whereby he can prevent the occurrence of an unfair and/or prolonged trial.

The following steps constitute a typical investigation:[25]

- The authorities will proceed to the scene of an incident.
- They will ascertain the facts and circumstances of the case.
- They will attempt to discover and arrest the suspect(s).
- They will collect evidence relating to the incident through
    a. examination of various people (including the accused), and
    b. search of places and seizure of things considered necessary for the investigation and for production at trial.
- They will form an opinion about whether the material collected forms the basis of a case to be placed before a magistrate for trial and, if so, file a charge sheet under S. 173 CrPC.

This chapter deals with the main elements of an investigation, namely search, seizure, questioning, and interrogation. Arrest receives some preliminary treatment in this chapter under interrogation, but is discussed more fully in Chapter 4—'Dealing with the Accused'.

---

[18] S. 190 CrPC.

[19] S. 156(3) CrPC.

[20] *Abhinandan Jha* v. *Dinesh Mishra*, 1967 SCR (3) 668, 673.

[21] *State of W.B.* v. *Swapan Kumar Guha*, 1982 SCR (3) 121, 139–140, and 142–143.

[22] S. 482 CrPC.

[23] S. 159 CrPC.

[24] Ss. 202 and 203 CrPC.

[25] *Rishbud* v. *State of Delhi*, 1955 SCR (1) 1150, 1157–1158; see generally Ss. 154–176 CrPC.

3.2 SEARCH

During an investigation, documents or other material objects may be needed for use during legal proceedings. Anyone who possesses such objects should produce them as required. If the accused fails to produce such objects, a competent court can pass the necessary orders to enable the police to search and seize such objects for the purpose of investigation, inquiry or trial. This section details search procedures for places and persons. It will also address the different procedures that apply when the search is conducted without written authorization, with a direct order from a police officer, with a summons from a magistrate, or with an official search warrant. The final sections detail what constitutes acceptable police conduct during a search, and what powers an individual has to resist an unwarranted search.

A. A Place

When a search is conducted of a place, this includes a house, building, tent, vehicle or vessel.[26]

Summons or Police Order

During a police investigation, the police require all documents and other items relevant to the commission of a crime. If the person in possession or power of these items does not co-operate with the police, the police may either obtain a summons for their production, or obtain a search warrant.

A summons is a court order which can be used to compel a person to appear before the court to either give testimony or produce a thing. According to S. 91 CrPC, any court or officer-in-charge of a police station, who requires a person to produce the stated document or thing at a specified time and place, can issue a summons (in the case of a court) or a written order (in the case of a police officer).[27] The summons or order is issued 'to the person in whose possession or power [a] ... document or thing is believed to be, requiring him to attend and produce it, or to produce it, at the time and place stated in the summons or order.'[28]

S. 91 CrPC does not apply to an accused person.[29] Moreover, Article 20(3) of the Constitution protects the accused from self-incrimination. This article has been interpreted to mean that the accused cannot be compelled to disclose documents which are incriminating and based on his or her knowledge.[30] Self-incrimination would imply providing of information based on the personal knowledge of the accused person and would not include the 'mechanical

---

[26] S. 2(p) CrPC.
[27] S. 91(1) CrPC.
[28] S. 91(1) CrPC.
[29] *State of Gujarat v. Shyamlal,* AIR 1965 SC 1251, 1259–1260.
[30] *State of Bombay v. Kathi Kalu Oghad,* 1962 SCR (3) 10, 11–12, 32, and 35.

process of producing documents in court which may throw a light on any of the points in the controversy.'[31] For instance, if an accused person is asked to produce a document containing his writing or thumb impression or signature so that it can be compared for the purposes of identification, it would not amount to self-incrimination.[32]

Failure to comply with a summons without any reasonable excuse may result in punishment (imprisonment or committal).[33] Failure to comply may also result in the issuance of a search warrant.[34] Furthermore, an intentional omission to produce a document is punishable under S. 175 IPC.[35] However, before a person can be punished for failure to comply with a summons, it must be proved that the conditions for issuing the summons were satisfied, and that the order was in fact served on the person.

Searching with a Search Warrant

The court can issue a search warrant during any phase of the criminal investigation or trial.[36] A search warrant is a written authority given to a police officer or other competent official to search for documents or persons wrongfully detained. Since a search constitutes a coercive invasion of privacy, courts have emphasized that the power to issue a search warrant should be exercised with great care and circumspection.[37]

Reasons to Issue a Search Warrant

- The court has reason to believe that a person issued with a summons will not or would not produce the document or thing required by the search warrant.[38]
- A document or thing is not known to be in the possession of any particular person.[39]
- The court considers that the purposes of the inquiry or trial will be served by a general search or inspection.[40]
- The court has reason to believe that the search of a place will reveal stolen property, forged documents, etc.[41]

---

[31] Article 20(2), The Constitution of India.
[32] *State of Bombay* v. *Kathi Kalu Oghad* AIR 1961 SC 1808 at 1817.
[33] S. 349 CrPC.
[34] S. 93(1) CrPC.
[35] S. 175 IPC.
[36] S. 93(1) CrPC.
[37] *Gangadharan* v. *Chellapan*, 1985 Cri LJ 1517, 1520.
[38] S. 93(1)(a) CrPC.
[39] S. 93(1)(b) CrPC.
[40] S. 93(1)(c) CrPC.
[41] S. 94 CrPC.

Box 3.1   Example of Warrant to Search after Information of a Particular Offence [See Form No. 10, Sch. 2 CrPC]

To _____ *(name and designation of police officer or other person or persons who is or are to execute the warrant).*

WHEREAS information has been laid *(or complaint has been made)* before me of the commission *(or suspected commission)* of the offence of _____ *(mention the offence concisely),* and it has been made to appear to me that the production of _____ *(specify the thing clearly)* is essential to the inquiry now being made *(or about to be made)* into the said offence *(or suspected offence);*

This is to authorise and require you to search for the said _____ *(the thing specified)* in the _____ *(describe house or place or part thereof to which the search is to be confined),* and, if found, to produce the same forthwith before this Court, returning this warrant, with an endorsement certifying what you have done under it, immediately upon its execution.

Dated, this _____ day of _____, 20 ____.

(Seal of the Court)

(Signature)

- The court has reason to believe that in any premises, any newspaper, book or document contains any matter, the publication of which is punishable for being seditious[42] or obscene;[43] for maliciously insulting religion;[44] for fostering enmity between groups;[45] or for making assertions prejudicial to national integrity,[46] in accordance with the IPC.[47]
- The court has reason to believe that a person has been wrongfully confined, or that a woman or female child has been abducted or unlawfully detained.[48]

Under S. 93(1) CrPC, the court is not bound to issue a search warrant whenever it is asked for; it may direct an investigation by the police before issuing the search warrant.[49] Before it can issue a search warrant it must make an objective determination based on careful

---

[42] S. 124(a) IPC.

[43] Ss. 292 and 293 IPC.

[44] S. 153A IPC.

[45] S. 153A IPC.

[46] S. 153B IPC.

[47] S. 95 CrPC.

[48] Ss. 97 and 98 CrPC.

[49] *Melicio Fernandes* v. *Mohan*, AIR 1966 Goa 23, 26.

deliberations.[50] Under S. 93(1)(c) CrPC, a warrant can be issued for a general search of premises, not for the purpose of finding any documents or objects in particular, but rather to make a roving inquiry to discover any documents that might involve persons in criminal liability.[51]

The police have to search in accordance with the search warrant.[52] The warrant may limit the search to particular areas of the location in question, in which case the police are only allowed to search those areas.[53]

Searching Without a Search Warrant

In exceptional circumstances, the law deems it necessary to empower certain police officers to carry out searches without first applying to the courts for authority.[54] However, the circumstances under which this may occur are restricted, and there are safeguards to prevent its abuse. The police may only search without a warrant under the circumstances outlined below.

Reasons to Search Without a Warrant

1. When the police are acting under an arrest warrant and believe that the person to be arrested has entered a place, the occupants of that place must allow the police officer access to the premises and all reasonable assistance in conducting the search;[55]

2. When an officer-in-charge of a station or an investigating officer has reasonable grounds for believing that:
   (a) A specific thing necessary for the purposes of the investigation may be found in any place within the limits of his or her police station;
   (b) That the thing cannot otherwise be obtained without undue delay,[56] and there is not time to obtain a search warrant;[57] and

3. Any magistrate may direct a search to be made in his or her presence of any place, for the search of which he or she is competent to issue a search warrant.[58]

A search under S. 165 CrPC must be for a particular thing or document and does not include a general search.[59] Before searching, the police officer must justify his or her search in writing, and specify the thing for which the search is being made.[60] A free copy of this record

---

[50] *Melicio Fernandes*, at 27.

[51] *Paresh Chandra Sen Gupta* v. *Jogendra Nath Roy*, AIR 1927 Cal 93, 94–95.

[52] S. 93(1) CrPC.

[53] S. 93(2) CrPC.

[54] *Emperor* v. *Mohd. Shah*, 48 Cri LJ 161, 163.

[55] S. 47(1) CrPC.

[56] S. 165 CrPC.

[57] *A.P. Kuttan Panicker* v. *State of Kerala*, 1963 (1) Cri LJ 669, 674.

[58] S. 103 CrPC.

[59] *Lal Mea* v. *Emperor*, 27 Cri LJ 542; *Sitaram Ahir* v. *Emperor*, AIR 1944 Pat 222, 224.

[60] S. 165(1) CrPC.

of reasons is available, on application, to the occupier of the searched premises from the nearest Magistrate.[61]

In practice, the police usually do not obtain search warrants. Sometimes they use S. 165 CrPC to claim that an accused will escape arrest, or that a search object will disappear.[62]

B. A Person

The police may search a person for two reasons.

1. Arrest: If a person is arrested (with or without warrant) on a non-bailable offence, or cannot furnish bail, the officer making the arrest may search the person and take possession of all articles, other than basic clothing, found on him or her.[63] The person should be given a receipt of all articles taken into possession by the officer.[64] Where the person arrested is a woman, the search must be made by another woman with strict adherence to decency.[65]

2. Search of a Place: While searching a place, if the police have reason to suspect that a person is concealing on his or her body any item for which the search was made, such a person may be searched.[66] Here also, women should be searched by other women with strict adherence to decency.[67] If items are found during such a body search, the searched person is entitled to a copy of a list of seized items.[68]

C. The Conduct of a Search

The conduct of all searches should be held in compliance with certain guidelines. When the police arrive and announce that they intend to search the premises, the occupant of the premises should ask to see the search warrant. The document should be read carefully; it should be checked for validity and also limits on the search area.

A warrant must carry details such as the name and designation of officers who are to execute the warrant, the offence committed or suspected to have been committed, the thing being searched for, along with mention of the place in which it is to be searched for [See 'Example of Warrant to Search after Information of a Particular Offence' at p. 32.] It must necessarily be signed by a District Magistrate or Chief Judicial Magistrate and must carry the seal of the court.

---

[61] S. 165(5) CrPC.

[62] See Sunetra Bose, *Search of a place without warrant—part of investigation*, 1997 Cri LJ 161, 165.

[63] S. 51(1) CrPC.

[64] S. 51(1) CrPC.

[65] S. 51(2) CrPC.

[66] S. 100(3) CrPC.

[67] S. 100(3) CrPC.

[68] S. 100(7) CrPC.

If a warrant is in order, or if the police are allowed to search premises without a warrant, the law requires an individual to allow the police to enter and search in accordance with the warrant.[69] Moreover, if the police are authorized to search premises but are unable to gain entry, they may enter by force.[70]

If the premises are occupied by a woman who, according to custom, does not appear in public, the police must give her the opportunity to withdraw from the house before proceeding to enter the building.[71]

Before the search of a place can begin, the police must find two local residents to witness the search. If local residents are unavailable, the witnesses may be from another area.[72] The police may issue an order requiring an unwilling witness to attend the search.[73] It is an offence under S. 187 IPC to refuse to witness a search without a reasonable excuse.[74] Generally the bodies of the search-witnesses and of the police are searched prior to their entering the premises, to make sure they do not plant evidence. While this procedure is not legally enshrined, failure to observe it gives the defence a strong argument against the credibility of evidence seized.[75] One should always ask that the search-witnesses and police be searched before a search begins. The witnesses must sign a list of any items seized and their location at the time of seizure.[76]

The occupant of the searched premises may witness the search, and is entitled to a list of seized goods signed by the search-witnesses.[77] The occupant of the searched premises is not required to sign the seizure list.[78]

D. Refusing a Search

Refusing a Search with Warrant

If a search of a place is to be made pursuant to a warrant, any person in charge of that place has a legal duty to allow free entry into it.[79] If entry is refused, the police may enter by force.[80]

---

[69] S. 100(1) CrPC.

[70] Ss. 100(2) and 47(2) CrPC.

[71] S. 47(2) CrPC.

[72] S. 100(4) CrPC.

[73] S. 100(4) CrPC.

[74] S. 100(8) CrPC.

[75] *Emperor* v. *Mehmud Ali Khan*, 1934 Cri LJ 641, 642.

[76] S. 100(5) CrPC.

[77] S. 100(6) CrPC.

[78] *Mahadeo* v. *State of Uttar Pradesh*, 1990 Cri LJ 858.

[79] S. 100 CrPC.

[80] Ss. 47(2) and 100(2) CrPC.

Refusing a Search without a Warrant

S. 165 CrPC, which governs a category of cases in which the police may conduct a search without a warrant, contains four requirements:[81]

1. The empowered officer must have reasonable grounds for believing that any thing necessary for the purpose of the investigation into an offence cannot otherwise be obtained without undue delay;

2. He or she must record in writing the grounds of his belief and also specify the thing(s) for which the search is to be made;

3. He or she must conduct the search in person, if practicable; and

4. If it is not practicable to conduct the search in person, he or she must record reasons for not doing so and must authorize a subordinate officer to conduct the search after specifying, in writing, the place of search and thing(s) for which the search is to be made.

As regards requirement (1), a police officer acts illegally if he or she does not record the grounds of his belief.[82]

Resisting a Search

During an illegal search, a person is allowed by law to resist the search.[83] However, resistance to an illegal search is only legal within the limits of the right to self-defence.[84] Therefore, if a person uses criminal force to defend his or her property against being searched, he or she could be guilty of an offence.[85] If the person resisting a search hurts a police officer, he or she is likely to face criminal charges. While the courts have found that a person is entitled to protect his or her property from an illegal search, to do so will increase the chances of police harassment and potential arrest for other offences.

If a person is the victim of an illegal search, he or she can seek either a consitutional or civil remedy.[86] He or she can petition the High Court under Article 226 of the Constitution to quash the illegal search warrant, and to return the seized documents or goods.[87] A search may be challenged on grounds such as:

- that the law authorizing the search is unconstitutional;
- that the search warrant was issued without the magistrate's judicial discretion;[88]

---

[81] *State of Rajasthan* v. *Rehman*, AIR 1960 SC 210, 212.

[82] Ibid., at 213.

[83] *Radha Kishan* v. *State of Uttar Pradesh*, AIR 1963 SC 882.

[84] See Ss. 96–106 IPC.

[85] *Shyam Lal* v. *State of Madhya Pradesh*, AIR 1972 SC 886; *Lachuman Singh* v. *Emperor*, AIR (29) 1942 Patna 281.

[86] See generally Basu, Acharya Dr Durga Das, *Criminal Procedure Code*, 1973, 3rd edn, Prentice-Hall of India, New Delhi, 1997, p. 230.

[87] *Sundaram* v. *State* AIR 1972 Mad 313.

[88] *Income-tax Officer* v. *Seth Bros.*, AIR 1970 SC 292.

- that the warrant was issued without complying with the statutory conditions;[89]
- that the power was used for a collateral purpose other than that for which it was conferred by the statute;[90] and
- that the search contravened the search-procedures laid down in Ss. 100 and 165 of the CrPC.[91]

Alternatively, the victim of an illegal search may seek a civil remedy.[92] A search contrary to law would amount to an actionable trespass by the person conducting the search. Thus, the victim of an illegal search can take the person who conducted the illegal search (and in some cases the person who authorized the illegal search, such as the magistrate in charge of issuing the warrant) to court for trespassing on his or her property.

Evidence Found in an Illegal Search

Evidence collected during an illegal search can still be used at trial, provided that no prejudice is caused to the accused. The court may choose to hold the illegally obtained evidence under greater scrutiny, and give it less weight than evidence obtained through legal methods.[93] According to S. 465 CrPC,

no finding, sentence or order passed by a Court of competent jurisdiction shall be reversed by a Court of appeal ... on account of any error, omission or irregularity in the complaint, summons, warrant, ... or other proceedings ... unless in the opinion of that Court, a failure of justice has in fact been occasioned thereby.

That is, even though a person has been searched illegally, the documents or things seized may be used against that person in court. However such evidence is viewed with caution.[94]

3.3 SEIZURE

Seizure means taking possession of property by an officer under legal process. The power of the police to search a place carries with it the power to seize items found during the search. However, the police have wider powers than just those allowing them to seize items for which the search was specifically made. The police can take any property which is suspected to be stolen, or which creates suspicion of the commission of a criminal offence.[95] A police officer can also seize articles found on a person during search on arrest where bail cannot be furnished by the person.[96]

[89] *Income-tax Officer* v. *Seth Bros.*, AIR 1970 SC 292.

[90] Ibid., AIR 1970 SC 292.

[91] *Sundaram* v. *State*, AIR 1972 Mad 313.

[92] Basu, Acharya Dr Durga Das, *Criminal Procedure Code*, 1973, 3rd edn, Prentice-Hall of India, New Delhi, 1997, p. 230.

[93] *Radha Krishan* v. *State of Uttar Pradesh*, AIR 1963 SC 822.

[94] *Harikishan* v. *State of U.P.*, 1970 All LJ 1333.

[95] S. 102 CrPC.

[96] S. 51 CrPC.

However, the police are required to give the occupant, or person searched, a copy of a list of all items seized during a search, signed by the witnesses to the search.[97] In addition, the police must report the seizure to a magistrate with jurisdiction over the case.[98] The court can also impound any documents or objects produced before it as the result of a seizure.[99]

If a person's property is seized and reported to a magistrate, and the property is not produced before a criminal court in the course of an inquiry and trial, the magistrate has powers to make an order to dispose of the property as they see fit, if the property was illegally obtained.[100] Therefore, if the person entitled to the property is known, the magistrate can order the property to be delivered to that person. If the owner is not known, the magistrate can detain the property and issue a proclamation requiring anyone with a claim to the property to appear before the magistrate and establish their claim within six months.[101]

Before deciding whether to make an order under S. 457 CrPC regarding the property, the magistrate has a duty to hear the affected party.[102] If no claimant appears within six months, and the person in whose possession the property was found is unable to show that they acquired it legally, the magistrate can order that the property be at the disposal of the State Government. They may then sell it and deal with the proceeds of the sale as they see fit.[103]

3.4 INTERROGATION/PRELIMINARY QUESTIONING

During the investigation, both the accused and witnesses are likely to be questioned by the police. If the person has been arrested and placed under police custody, this is known as interrogation. If the person is simply a witness or a suspect who has not yet been arrested, the process is known as preliminary questioning. These processes can sometimes be difficult and unpleasant.

A. Being called for Questioning

The police may order in writing that any person, who appears to be acquainted with the facts and circumstances of the case, must appear at the police station to be questioned.[104]

However, women of any age and men under the age of fifteen years should only be questioned at their own home, unless they choose to be questioned at the police station.[105]

---

[97] Ss. 100 (5), 100(7) CrPC.

[98] S. 102(2) CrPC.

[99] S. 104 CrPC.

[100] S. 457(1) CrPC.

[101] S. 457(2) CrPC.

[102] *Shyam M. Sachdev* v. *State*, 1991 Cri LJ 300 (Del HC).

[103] S. 458 CrPC.

[104] S. 160(1) CrPC.

[105] S. 160(1) CrPC.

Furthermore, if the person being questioned is female, the interview should be carried out in the presence of at least one female police officer.[106]

If a person does not agree to be questioned by the police, his or her refusal may result in prosecution for disobedience under S. 174 IPC. A refusal to furnish any information a person is *legally* bound to provide to any public servant, could result in imprisonment of up to one month, and/or a fine of up to five hundred rupees. If the information is with respect to the commission of an offence, or is required to prevent or apprehend an offender, imprisonment may be extended up to six months, and/or a fine of up to one thousand rupees.[107]

Evidentiary Value of Statement

If a person is called for questioning, and the information he or she gives during the questioning is relevant to the case, he or she may have to attend court to give testimony as a witness at the trial. If this happens, either the defence or the prosecution in the case will apply to the presiding magistrate, who will issue a summons to the witness directing them to attend.[108]

While a person is being questioned, the police may record in writing any statement that he or she makes.[109] A statement under S. 162 CrPC encompasses both oral and written statements, and can even include signs and gestures.

Statements made before the police and reduced into writing have limited evidentiary use at trial under S. 162 CrPC. They can be used by the defence to impeach the credibility of a witness of the prosecution by demonstrating that the witness made a previously inconsistent/contradictory statement.[110] However, they cannot be used by the prosecution to impeach a defence witness.[111] Furthermore, such statements may not be used to corroborate or confirm facts stated by the witness at trial. All statements made to the police must be made available to the accused before trial, whether or not the prosecution relies on those statements for their case.[112]

Do Not Sign Your Statement

A person is not legally required to, nor should he or she, sign any statement that he or she makes to the police during an investigation. In fact, the law directs that those making such statements to the police should never sign them.[113] Although the Supreme Court has ruled that statements signed at the instigation of a police officer will not always be ruled

---

[106] *Sheela Barse v. State of Maharashtra*, (1983) 2 SCC 96; see generally *D.K. Basu v. State of West Bengal*, 1997 (1) SCC 416.

[107] S. 174 IPC.

[108] S. 254(2) CrPC.

[109] S. 161(3) CrPC.

[110] S. 162(1) CrPC.

[111] *Shakila Khader v. Nauser*, 1975 Cri LJ 1105 (AP HC).

[112] *Ranjeet Singh v. State of Uttar Pradesh and Anr.*, 1998 Cri LJ 1297.

[113] S. 162(1) CrPC.

inadmissible,[114] such statements are likely to be considered to be of lesser evidentiary value.[115] This is to prevent the police from abusing or mistreating a person during questioning, in order to force him or her to sign a statement or confession.

In the course of an investigation the police are not permitted to take a person's photograph, fingerprints, or demand a sample of his or her handwriting, without permission of a magistrate, unless he or she has been arrested, or is considered a habitual offender.[116]

The police do not have the power under law to compel a person to take a polygraph test, commonly known as a lie detector test. The NHRC has stated that the use of this test by the police is 'illegal and unconstitutional unless it is voluntarily undertaken in non-coercive circumstances', and that the only occasion on which its use could be justified is where the suspect volunteers to take it without any police prompting whatsoever; for example, in order to clear his or her name.[117] As a result of this, the NHRC has laid down guidelines according to which lie detector tests may take place.

Box 3.2   NHRC Guidelines for Taking Polygraph Test

1. No test should take place without informed consent given by the accused person. Informed consent requires that they be informed of the physical, legal, and emotional implications.
2. The consent should be recorded in a hearing before a judicial magistrate where the accused is represented by his or her lawyer.
3. At this hearing the accused shall be told clearly that any statement made will not have the status of a confession but of a statement made to the police.
4. The recording of the test shall occur in an independent agency (e.g. a hospital) and conducted in the presence of a lawyer.
5. A full medical and factual narration of the information received shall be recorded.

B. Right to Legal Representation

Anyone being interrogated, whether or not charged with a crime, is allowed to consult his or her lawyer of choice.[118] This is a legal requirement under Article 22 of the Constitution and the laws of most states. However, the police are only obliged to wait for a reasonable amount of time for an arrestee's lawyer to arrive.[119] Although an arrestee may be permitted to meet

---

[114] *State of U.P. v. M.K. Anthony*, 1985 Cri LJ 493 (SC).

[115] *Zahiruddin v. Emperor*, 48 Cri LJ 679.

[116] *M.S. Syed Anwar and Ors v. Commissioner of Police, Bangalore and Anr*, 1992 Cri LJ 1606.

[117] See NHRC Guidelines relating to administration of polygraph test (lie detector test) on an accused, in *NHRC Important Instructions/Guidelines*, New Delhi, p. 59.

[118] See *Nandini Satpathy v. P.L. Dani*, AIR 1978 SC 1075.

[119] *Nandini Satpathy v. P.L. Dani*, AIR 1978 SC 1075.

his or her lawyer during interrogation, this does not mean that the lawyer can be present throughout the interrogation.[120] If for some reason a person does not have access to his or her lawyer during an interrogation, he or she should ask to be taken to a magistrate immediately after the interrogation to confirm that no torture or other prohibited behaviour was used to extract statements or other evidence. While the police are not obliged to do this, the Supreme Court has strongly suggested that police fulfill such a request.[121]

In addition to the right to an attorney, an arrestee has the right to have someone informed of his or her whereabouts when he or she is arrested.[122] For a more detailed discussion of a person's rights upon arrest, see Chapter 4: 'Dealing with the Accused.'

C. Compulsion to Answer Truthfully and Protection against Self-Incrimination

A person is required to comply with police requests for information and to answer all questions truthfully.[123] If a person refuses to answer a question, he or she may be liable under S. 179 IPC and face up to six months imprisonment and/or a fine of up to one thousand rupees.[124] Further, if a person gives an answer, which he or she either knows or believes to be false, he or she may be liable under S. 193 IPC for giving false evidence, and could face up to seven years in prison and a fine.[125]

A person is not required to answer questions that may be self-incriminating regarding the commission of an offence—whether the offence about which he or she is being questioned, or another offence.[126] This means that while being questioned or interrogated a person does not have to provide information that might indicate that he or she is guilty of a criminal offence. Suspects who are not formally charged are also entitled to this right during interrogation in custody. However, a person is still obliged to answer questions that are not self-incriminating.[127]

Abuse During Questioning

The police and authorities are clearly not allowed to make inducements (bribes), threats, or promises in the course of an investigation. The law also strictly prohibits torture or threats to

---

[120] *D.K. Basu* v. *State of West Bengal,* 1997 (1) SCC 416.
[121] *Nandini Satpathy* v. *P.L. Dani,* AIR 1978 SC 1075.
[122] *D.K. Basu* v. *State of West Bengal,* 1997 (1) SCC 416.
[123] S. 161(2) CrPC.
[124] S. 179 IPC.
[125] S. 193 IPC.
[126] S. 161(2) CrPC; Article 20(3) Constitution; *Nandini Satpathy* v. *P.L. Dani,* AIR 1978 SC 1075.
[127] *Nandini Satpathy* v. *P.L. Dani,* AIR 1978 SC 1075.

people close to a witness or an accused.[128] The police may not physically or psychologically intimidate an arrested person, or one being questioned.[129]

Police officers have been, and should be, prosecuted and punished for torturing suspects during interrogation or questioning. Confessions obtained by use of such methods should be excluded as evidence at trial.[130]

If a person is detained in custody and has suffered injury at the hands of the police, he or she has the right to, and should request, a medical examination.[131] That person should also inform the magistrate of such treatment when he or she next appears before the court.

Box 3.3   *Ram Nath* v. *Salig Ram Sharma*
AIR 1967 Allahabad 519

Facts: In the course of political tension, some students and staff of a local college ransacked a railway station. A number of students and staff were arrested and taken to the police station for interrogation. The interrogating officers asked the students to make a statement against their principal. When they refused, the Deputy Superintendent of Police assaulted them with his fists, and kicked them. They were threatened with further harm if they did not implicate their principal. They did so. Later, the students filed a complaint against the Deputy Superintendent of Police under the Indian Penal Code. The officer did not deny his actions, but said that he was acting in the discharge of his official duty and that the assault was necessary. The magistrate agreed with the Deputy Superintendent of Police and dismissed the complaint. The students then appealed to the High Court of Uttar Pradesh in Allahabad.

Held: The High Court stated that torture is not part of the job of police officers. The Court stated:

It is no part of the duty of a police officer to assault a witness or an accused in order to obtain a statement from him. It is equally no part of a police officer's duty to put a person under unlawful restraint in order to extort a confession from him. None of these acts could be said to have any connection with the official duty of the officer.

The High Court allowed the appeal and ordered the magistrate to continue to proceed against the police officer.

Confession Procedure

In order to protect the accused, a confession made by an accused person is irrelevant in a criminal proceeding if the making of the confession appears to the court to have been caused

---

[128] S. 163 CrPC; S. 24 IEA; Ss. 330–331 IPC.

[129] *Arvinder Singh Bagga* v. *State of Uttar Pradesh*, AIR 1994 SCW 4148; *Afzal and Anr* v. *State of Haryana and Ors*, 1994 Cri LJ 1240.

[130] S. 24 IEA.

[131] S. 54 CrPC.

by any inducement, threat or promise.[132] Furthermore, any confession made to a police officer cannot be used as evidence against the accused.[133]

In general, confessions must be made to, or in the presence of, a magistrate, who should ensure that the confession is made voluntarily and that the accused understands the implications of the confession.[134] The magistrate must explain to the accused that he or she is not bound to confess anything by law, and that what he or she says might be used in evidence against him or her.[135] The magistrate must question the accused as to whether he or she is making the confession voluntarily. Only if he believes that the confession is made voluntarily should he record the statement in full and ask questions.

Before the accused signs the statement, it shall be shown or read to him or her, and the accused should ask for an explanation if there is anything that he or she doesn't understand.[136] The confession is then to be signed by both the accused and the magistrate.[137] The magistrate must then forward the confession to the magistrate by whom the case is to be inquired into or tried.[138] The magistrate must comply with all the requirements of S. 164 CrPC, or else the confession could be inadmissible in court.[139]

Duration of Questioning

While the length of the questioning will depend on the police involved and the nature of the alleged crime, if a person is not under arrest, it should be within working hours. In either case, the interrogation should not be continuous—he or she should be allowed food, drink, rest and the use of appropriate facilities. While the matter of what amounts to 'excessive' interrogation depends on the circumstances, interrogation for longer than three hours without a break, may result in the court deeming statements made as 'involuntary' and the court disregarding them.[140] If the person is not being held in custody, meaning he or she has not been formally arrested, he or she may ask to leave. If the police refuse to let that person leave the station, he or she is being illegally detained, and may file a complaint with a magistrate.

If a person is harassed or intimidated during questioning, he or she should file a complaint with either the Superintendent of Police, or with a magistrate.

---

[132] S. 24 IEA.

[133] Ss. 25 and 26 IEA.

[134] S. 164 CrPC; *Shivappa* v. *State of Karnataka,* 1995 AIR 980.

[135] S. 164(2) CrPC.

[136] S. 281(4) CrPC.

[137] S. 281(5) CrPC.

[138] S. 164(6) CrPC.

[139] *Dhananjaya Reddy* v. *State of M.P.,* 2001(3) JT 395.

[140] *Amrut* v. *State of Bombay,* AIR 1960 Bom 488.

4 Dealing With The Accused

Once there are sufficient grounds to believe that a person has committed an offence, steps must be taken to ensure that he or she is present to face trial in a court of law. The presence of the accused may be secured by either serving him or her with a summons requiring his or her presence at trial, or by arresting and detaining him or her in police custody.

This chapter will briefly differentiate between summons cases and warrant cases, and then give an overview of when an individual may be arrested and what procedure the arrest must follow. After reading this chapter, the reader should be aware of when and how a person may be served with a court summons, and when he or she may be arrested and detained. Additionally, this chapter explains what a person's rights are during the detention process, and what remedies are available if and when these rights are violated.

4.1 SUMMONS CASES AND WARRANT CASES

The CrPC classifies all criminal cases into either summons cases or warrant cases. A warrant case means a case relating to an offence punishable with death, imprisonment for life or imprisonment for a term exceeding two years.[1] A summons case is defined as a case relating to an offence, not being a warrant case.[2] Thus, a warrant case relates to more serious offences with more severe punishments.

Generally speaking, where it appears to a magistrate that a case is a summons case, he will issue a court summons to ensure that the accused attends the proceedings. Whereas, if it appears to the magistrate that it is a warrant case, he will issue a warrant for the arrest of the accused.[3] This is because with warrant cases, which relate to more serious offences, there is a greater risk that the accused will abscond. There are, however, exceptions to this general rule, which are discussed as follows.

---

[1] S. 2(x) CrPC.
[2] S. 2(w) CrPC.
[3] S. 204 CrPC.

4.2 COURT SUMMONS

A summons is a court order used to compel an accused person to appear in court.

Every summons must be in writing, in duplicate, signed by the presiding officer of the court, and bear the seal of the court.[4]

Box 4.1	Sample Summons to an Accused Person [See Form 1, Schedule II CrPC]

To _____ (*name of accused*) of _____ (*address*)

WHEREAS your attendance is necessary to answer to a charge of _____ (*state shortly the offence charged*), you are hereby required to appear in person (*or by pleader, as the case may be*) before the (*Magistrate*) of _____ on the _____ day of _____. Herein fail not.

Dated, this _____ day of _____, 20 ____.

(*Seal of the Court*)

                                         (*Signature*)

A. Service of a Summons

Every summons must be served on the accused person by either a police officer, an officer of the court issuing it, or a public servant.[5] The summons should, if practicable, be served personally on the person summoned, by delivering one of the duplicates of the summons.[6] However, if the accused, despite the exercise of due diligence by authorities, cannot be found, then a duplicate of the summons can be left with an adult male member of the accused's family who resides with the accused.[7]

When a summons is served on a person, he or she may be required to sign a receipt confirming that he or she received it.[8] Likewise, if the summons is served in the accused's absence, the family member with whom the summons is left must sign the duplicate as confirmation of receipt.[9]

[4] S. 61 CrPC.
[5] S. 62(1) CrPC.
[6] S. 62(2) CrPC.
[7] S. 64 CrPC.
[8] S. 62(3) CrPC.
[9] S. 64 CrPC.

If the summons cannot be delivered by personally serving it upon the accused or a member of his or her family, the summons can be served by the serving officer affixing a duplicate of the summons to some conspicuous part of the accused's normal residence.[10] This method is known as substituted service, and it may only be used in exceptional circumstances where the methods of personal service have failed.

An accused may refuse to accept service of a summons which has been delivered, but in most cases the summons will still be considered to have been properly delivered. Only in certain circumstances will a person be able to properly refuse service of a summons without incurring a penalty. Examples include where the court has no power to issue the summons,[11] or where the essential requirements are not observed in the issuing of a summons. However, the defect must be essential in nature and not a mere error, omission, or irregularity.[12]

B. Summons for Witnesses

A summons may also be issued to a witness to attend the trial and give evidence for the prosecution or for the defence. A summons to a witness can be served by the same methods described above for the serving of a summons on the accused, or also by issuing a summons by registered post, addressed to the witness at his or her place of residence or business.[13]

C. Penalties for Failure to Comply

Absconding to avoid being served with a summons to attend in Court, failing to obey a summons by failing to attend Court, and preventing service of a summons to attend Court, intentionally or otherwise, are all offences punishable by a prison term of up to six months, and/or a fine of up to one thousand rupees.[14]

D. Issuing a Warrant of Arrest in a Summons Case

Generally speaking, where it appears to a magistrate that a case is a summons case, he will issue a court summons to ensure that the accused attends the proceedings.[15] However, a court may instead issue a warrant of arrest in a summons case if, prior to the date fixed for the accused's appearance, the court has reason to believe that the accused has absconded, or will otherwise not obey the summons.[16] A court may also issue a warrant if the accused, after being properly served with a valid summons, fails to appear in court at the scheduled time

---

[10] S. 65 CrPC.

[11] *McLennan v. State*, AIR 1968 Cal 195; 1968 Cri LJ 482.

[12] *Rishbud v. State*, AIR 1955 SC 196; (1955) 1 SCR 1150; 1955 Cri LJ 526.

[13] S. 69 CrPC.

[14] Ss. 172–174 IPC.

[15] S. 204 CrPC.

[16] S. 87(a) CrPC.

and has offered no reasonable excuse for this failure.[17] In any instance where a warrant is issued for a summons case, the court must record the reasons for issuing the warrant in writing.

4.3 ARREST

An arrest is the deprivation of an individual's personal liberty by a legal authority. It may be used to secure the attendance of the accused at trial, or to stop the commission of an offence. However, arresting an accused person is not mandatory during or after investigation, and in order to ensure that an accused is not arrested arbitrarily or capriciously, the arrest procedure should follow the safeguards set forth by the law.

A. Circumstances of Arrest

In practice, an arrest is usually made by a police officer. However it is also possible, although unusual, for a magistrate or private person to make an arrest.[18] The CrPC provides that, in making an arrest, the police officer shall 'touch or confine the body of the person to be arrested', unless the person being arrested submits to the police officer's custody by word or by action.[19]

An arrest may be made with or without an arrest warrant depending upon the circumstances of the offence alleged.

i. Arrest Without a Warrant

Normally a warrant for the arrest of the accused must be procured before taking an individual into custody. However, S. 41 CrPC provides that the police may arrest a suspect without a warrant (and without an order from a magistrate) when:

- The reported crime is a cognizable offence, provided that the information leading to the arrest is reasonable or credible;
- A person is found with tools for house-breaking, without lawful excuse;
- The person has been proclaimed an offender by the State Government or under the CrPC;
- A person is found in possession of anything that might reasonably be considered stolen, and the person may reasonably be suspected to having stolen it;
- A person obstructs the actions of a police officer in the course of duty, or when a person has escaped or attempts to escape from legal custody;
- A person is suspected of being a deserter from any of the Indian Armed Forces;

---

[17] S. 87(b) CrPC.
[18] Ss. 41, 43 & 44 CrPC.
[19] S. 46(1) CrPC.

- A person is reasonably suspected of having committed an offence outside India which would be punishable by law if committed in India, and for which the person is liable to be extradited to or apprehended in India;
- A released repeat offender fails to notify the court of a change in residence;
- Another police officer requests the arrest, and specifies the person to be arrested and the offence in question, and when the police officer making the request would seemingly be able to make the arrest without a warrant if acting alone; or
- A person has been deemed either a habitual offender, or someone who is trying to hide and is likely to commit a cognizable offence, by an executive magistrate under Ss. 109 & 110 CrPC. Such an arrest can only be made by an officer-in-charge of a police station.

A person who has committed a non-cognizable offence, but refuses to give the police his name and address, or gives a name and address which the police believe to be false, may also be arrested without a warrant.[20] The CrPC also provides the police with the power to make an arrest without a warrant in order to prevent the commission of cognizable offences.[21] Furthermore, according to Section 34 of the Police Act, 1861, where the police witness a variety of trivial offences in public places, for example, slaughtering cattle, cruelty to animals, or indecent exposure, it is also lawful for the police to arrest the offender without a warrant.

The power to arrest without a warrant can be exercised only after a reasonable satisfaction is reached, after some investigation, as to the genuineness of a complaint and a reasonable belief as to both the person's complicity as well as the need to effect arrest.[22]

ii. Arrest With a Warrant

If the case is a warrant case, the magistrate may issue a warrant for the arrest of the accused.[23] An arrest warrant will not necessarily be issued for every warrant case. The CrPC gives a judicial officer the discretion to determine whether the particulars of a case require the issuance of an arrest warrant or a court summons.

An arrest warrant is a written order bearing the signature and seal of the court, usually the local magistrate, commanding and authorizing a police officer to arrest the accused named in the warrant. A valid arrest warrant must be in writing, signed by the presiding officer of the court, and bear the seal of the court.[24] As can be seen from the sample on the next page, a warrant of arrest must clearly identify the person who is to be arrested, state the offence with which he or she is charged, and contain the name and designation of the person who is to execute the warrant.

---

[20] S. 42 CrPC.

[21] S. 151 CrPC.

[22] *Joginder Kumar v. State of U.P. and Ors,* AIR 1994 SC 1349.

[23] S. 204 CrPC.

[24] S. 70 CrPC.

Box 4.2   Sample Warrant of Arrest
              [See Form 2, Schedule II CrPC]

To _____ (*name and designation of the person or persons who are about to execute the warrant*).

Whereas (*name of accused*) of (*address*) stands charged with the offence of _____ (*state the offence*), you are hereby directed to arrest the said _____, and to produce him before me. Herein fail not.

Dated, this _____ day of _____, 20 ____.

(*Seal of the Court*)

(*Signature*)

A warrant of arrest is ordinarily executed by one or more police officers. However, if the court requires the immediate execution of the warrant and no police officer is immediately available, they can direct any other person or persons to execute the warrant.[25] A Chief Judicial Magistrate or magistrate of the first class may also issue a warrant to any person within his local jurisdiction for the arrest of any escaped convict, proclaimed offender, or any other person accused of a non-bailable offence and evading arrest.[26]

iii. Illegal Arrest

If a person is arrested pursuant to a warrant, and its contents are not disclosed to him or her, the arrest is unlawful. If a person is arrested without a warrant and the circumstances outlined above under 'Arrest Without a Warrant' are not met, the arrest is illegal.

Illegal arrests are a serious problem in India. In the Third Report of the National Police Commission, it was revealed that 60 per cent of arrests were either unnecessary or unjustified.[27] It has been stressed that the mere existence of the power to arrest, does not in itself justify the exercise of that power.[28] However, despite courts condemning illegal arrests, they continue to occur.

iv. Time of Arrest

In the case of *Christian Community Welfare Council of India and another* vs. *State of Maharashtra & Another*[29] the Bombay High Court directed the State Government to 'issue instructions

---

[25] S. 72 CrPC.

[26] S.73(1) CrPC.

[27] See discussion in *Joginder Kumar* v. *State of Uttar Pradesh and Ors*, AIR 1994 SC 1349, 1352.

[28] *Joginder Kumar*, at 1353.

[29] 1995 (3) Cri LJ 4223.

immediately in unequivocal and unambiguous terms to all concerned that no female person shall be detained or arrested without the presence of lady constable and in no case, after sun set and before sun-rise.' On appeal, the Supreme Court was of the view that there may be circumstances where arrest is necessary and delay that may arise in trying to secure a female constable may hamper investigation. The court was of the view that in such a situation, the police officer can arrest a female at any time of the day or night and even in the absence of a female constable after recording reasons for such an arrest or doing so immediately after the arrest.[30]

The Code of Criminal Procedure (Amendment) Act, 2005 retains a part of the above as it allows for arrest of women after sunset and before sunrise in exceptional circumstances.[31] The arrest can, however, be made only by a woman police officer after she has prepared a report in writing and obtained permission from a Judicial Magistrate of the first class, in whose jurisdiction the offence has been committed or the arrest is to be made.

Remedies Available

A trial will not necessarily be invalidated because an arrest was made irregularly or illegally.[32] So even if a person was arrested illegally or not according to the correct procedure, he or she can still be tried and convicted of a criminal offence. However, if a person is arrested illegally, he or she may bring a civil suit for damages and compensation against the person who made the arrest.[33] The remedies available to a person whose rights have been violated are discussed further below.

B. Rights When Arrested

Since arrest will deprive a person of his or her right to personal liberty, the law will only allow arrest to take place in circumstances prescribed by law,[34] as described above. In addition to these restrictions as to when a person can be legally arrested, there also exist other protections which a person is entitled to enforce after arrest and while in custody.

i. Rights at Time of Arrest

When apprehended, a person has the right to be informed of the grounds for the arrest.[35] The person being arrested should be informed precisely of the act done by him or her that has constituted a crime, not merely the law that he or she has allegedly broken. In order for the constitutional requirements to be sufficiently complied with, the arresting officers should inform him or her of the grounds for the arrest in a language which he or she understands.[36]

---

[30] *State of Maharashtra v. Christian Community Welfare Council of India*, AIR 2004 SC 7.

[31] S. 46(4) CrPC.

[32] *Muhammad Yusaf v. Queen Empress*, (1897) 24 IA 137 (PC).

[33] *Anwar Hussain v. Ajoy Kumar Mukherjee*, AIR 1965 SC 1651; (1965) (2) Cri LJ 686.

[34] Article 21, Constitution of India; Article 9 ICCPR.

[35] Ss. 50(1), 55 & 75 CrPC, Art. 22(1) Constitution.

[36] *Harikishan v. State of Maharashtra*, AIR 1962 SC 911, 914; 1962 (1) Cri LJ 797.

At the time of the arrest, the arresting officer should prepare a memo of arrest, stating the date and time of arrest, signed by at least one witness, and countersigned by the arrested person. During the arrest the officer should also bear accurate, visible, and clear identification tags with his or her name and designation.[37]

A person who is arrested under a warrant has the right to be informed of the substance of the warrant and to be shown the warrant.[38] An arrest is unlawful if the substance of the warrant is not notified to the arrested person.[39] Upon arrest, the arrested person should be told whether the offence for which he or she is accused is bailable or non-bailable, in order to arrange for pre-trial release. A police officer is obliged to inform an arrested person of his or her right to be released on bail.[40]

An arrested person may be eligible to be released from custody by either paying a bond with sureties or a personal bond, depending on the type and circumstances of the offence for which he or she is arrested. For a more detailed explanation of the bail process, including explanations on when a person may be released for a bailable offence, a non-bailable offence, and under anticipatory bail, see Chapter 5: 'Bail.'

A person who has been arrested has the right to have a friend, relative or other person informed of his or her arrest and the place of detainment. The police should advise the arrested person of this right when he or she arrives at the police station. If they do not, then the arrested person should ask to contact someone. The police should record the name of the person informed in the police station diary. These requirements flow from Articles 21 and 22 of the Constitution.[41] These requirements have been incorporated into the Criminal Procedure Code in Section 50A by the amendment in 2005. Further, duty has been imposed on the Magistrate before whom an arrested person is produced to ensure that the police have conveyed the right to inform a friend and details of the person informed have been recorded.[42]

The arrested person should be informed of his or her right to have access to a lawyer of his or her choice.[43] If the accused cannot afford a lawyer, he or she should be informed of his or her right to free legal aid. (See Chapter 8: 'Legal Aid and Compensation'). Non-compliance with this requirement will vitiate the trial.[44]

The right to legal representation can be superceded by the provisions of the specific Act under which the accused is apprehended. For example, the accused's rights to legal representation are conditional if he or she is arrested under the NSA.[45]

[37] *D.K. Basu* v. *State of West Bengal*, AIR 1997 SC 610, 623 at para 36.

[38] S. 75 CrPC.

[39] *Abdul Gafur* v. *Queen Empress*, ILR 23 Cal. 896.

[40] S. 50(2) CrPC.

[41] *Joginder Kumar* v. *State of Uttar Pradesh*, AIR 1994 SC 1349; *D.K.Basu* v. *State of West Bengal*, AIR 1997 SC 610.

[42] S. 50A(4) CrPC.

[43] Article 22(1), Constitution of India, S. 303 CrPC; *D.K. Basu* v. *State of West Bengal*, AIR 1997 SC 610.

[44] *Suk Das* v. *Union Territory of Arunachal Pradesh*, 1986 SCC (Cri) 166; (1986) 2 SCC 401; 1986 Cri LJ 104 (SC).

[45] *A. K. Roy* v. *Union of India*, AIR 1982 SC 710.

Appropriate Restraint

The most common method of restraint is handcuffing and fettering in custody. While this is common practice, the courts have set very strict limitations on the use of handcuffs. The Supreme Court has described handcuffing as inhuman, unreasonable, over-harsh and arbitrary, and in the absence of fair procedure and objective monitoring, is repugnant to Article 21 of the Constitution of India.[46]

Proper Use of Handcuffs

The Supreme Court has held that a person in custody should only be handcuffed if there is a clear and present danger of escape and breaking out of police control. This is the only determinant, and the nature of the accusation is not the criterion.[47]

There must be no other reasonable way to prevent the accused person from escaping in the given circumstances. The police officers subjective satisfaction of likely escape, if fetters are not fitted on the prisoner is not enough. There must be no alternative or less cruel means available, such as more guards or a close watch by armed policemen.[48]

Procedural Safeguards When Handcuffs are Used

The Supreme Court has also set out procedural safeguards that should be observed by police when, in extreme circumstances, handcuffs have to be put on the prisoner:

- The detailed reasons for imposing the handcuffs must be recorded contemporaneously;
- The escorting officer must show the reason for handcuffing to the judge and get his or her approval; and
- Once the court directs that handcuffs shall be off, no escorting authority can overrule the judicial discretion.[49]

As the Supreme Court has been quite clear on the specific circumstances in which handcuffing is allowed, officers who handcuff persons illegally may be charged with contempt of court and face disciplinary action. A person who is illegally restrained at the time of his or her arrest, may also pursue civil damages from the delinquent officer.

Resisting Arrest

Resistance to comply with a warrant, or obstruction of an arrest of another person, is an offence punishable by imprisonment.[50] If a person forcibly resists arrest, the officer may use 'all means necessary to effect the arrest.'[51] These means may legally result in a person's death, if the crime he or she is being charged with may be punishable by death or life imprisonment.[52]

---

[46] *Prem Shanka Shukla* v. *Delhi Administration*, AIR 1980 SC 1535, 1541.

[47] *Prem Shankar Shukla* v. *Delhi Administration*, AIR 1980 SC 1535, 1544.

[48] *Prem Shankar Shukla,* 1542.

[49] *Prem Shankar Shukla,* 1543.

[50] Ss. 225, 225B IPC.

[51] S. 46(2) CrPC.

[52] S. 46(3) CrPC.

However, the officer may not use more force than necessary to obtain the arrest.[53] An arrest warrant stays in force until it is executed or cancelled by the court which issued it.[54] Therefore a person will not avoid liability for obstructing the execution of a warrant by arguing that it has expired.

ii. Rights During Detention

If a person is in custody waiting to be brought before a magistrate on formal charges, or awaiting trial and unable to secure bail, he or she is said to be in detention. A person can only be legally detained in specific circumstances established by law.[55]

Appearance Before a Magistrate

An arrested person has the right to be taken before a magistrate without delay whether or not the arrest was made under a warrant.[56] Moreover, an arrested person has the right not to be detained for more than 24 hours without appearing before a magistrate.[57] The Supreme Court has strongly urged the State and its police authorities to see that this constitutional and legal requirement must be scrupulously observed.[58]

If this right is violated, the arrested person may sue the arresting officer under the common law tort of 'wrongful imprisonment.' The delinquent officer may also be subject to criminal charges.

Length of Detention

There are set limits on the length of time a person may be detained before being brought to trial to face the charges against him or her. Unfortunately, these limits are regularly flouted in India and detainees awaiting trial, known as 'undertrials', may occasionally spend more time in detention awaiting trial, than the length of their punishment had they been convicted. For more detailed information about the limits placed upon detention prior to trial, see Chapter 6: 'Detention.'

Search and Interrogation

An arrest will generally be followed by the interrogation of the arrested person and other witnesses, and often will result in a charge being laid. The charge officially initiates legal proceedings against an arrested person. If the arrested person is not granted bail, or is otherwise unable to furnish bail, the police have the right to search him or her for investigative purposes. For more detailed information, see Chapter 3: 'Investigation.'

---

[53] S. 49 CrPC.

[54] S. 70(2) CrPC.

[55] Article 21, Constitution of India.

[56] Ss. 56 & 76 CrPC.

[57] Article 22(2), Constitution of India; Ss. 57, 76 CrPC.

[58] *Khatri (II)* v. *State of Bihar*, 1981 1 SCC (Cri) 228; (1981) 1 SCC 627.

Medical Examination

A person who is arrested may request to be examined by a medical practitioner if he or she believes that a medical examination would help his or her defence, or would show that someone has caused him or her injury during the arrest.[59] The accused has the right to undergo a medical examination as soon as he or she is arrested, and if any injuries are present on his or her body, they must be recorded at that time. An 'inspection memo' must then be signed by both the arrested person and the police officer effecting arrest, and a copy provided to the arrested person.[60]

A medical examination may be requested when the accused appears before a magistrate or at any time during detention in custody.[61] The magistrate must inform the accused of this right when the accused appears before him.[62] The magistrate should grant the examination provided that the request is believed to be genuine, and not one intended to merely delay the process or defeat the ends of justice.[63] On completion of examination, the registered medical practitioner must give a copy of the report to the arrested person or his/her nominee.[64]

Where the alleged crime is one which may result in evidence on or inside the body of the arrested person, the police may require the person to be examined by a medical practitioner.[65] Such medical examinations are only available in relation to crimes where bodily evidence may be important, for example murder, rape, assault, and some drug offences. A medical examination under S. 53 CrPC permits the use of reasonable force for the taking of samples in relation to such crimes.

Section 53A introduced by the CrPC (Amendment) Act, 2005 provides for examination of a person accused of rape or attempt to commit rape by a registered medical practitioner if such examination is likely to result in evidence pointing to the commission of rape. If such a medical practitioner is not present within 16 kms of the place where the offence has occurred, a police officer not below the rank of a sub-inspector can request another medical practitioner to conduct the examination.[66]

Examination has been defined to include the 'examination of blood, blood stains, semen, swabs in case of sexual offences, sputum and sweat, hair samples and finger nail clippings by the use of modern and scientific techniques including DNA profiling and such other tests which the registered practitioner thinks necessary in a particular case.'[67]

---

[59] S. 54(1) CrPC.

[60] *D.K. Basu* v. *State of West Bengal*, AIR 1997 SC 610, 623.

[61] S. 54(1) CrPC.

[62] *Sheela Barse* v. *State of Maharashtra*, (1983) 2 SCC 96, 104.

[63] S. 54(1) CrPC.

[64] S. 54(2), CrPC.

[65] S. 53 CrPC.

[66] S. 53A(1) CrPC.

[67] Explanation inserted in Section 53 defining the term 'examination' as it appears in Sections 53, 53A and 54, CrPC.

The Code also provides for medical examination of victims of rape by a registered medical practitioner attached to a Government hospital.[68] The examination must be conducted within 24 hours of receiving information of the commission of rape. If no registered medical practitioner in a Government hospital is available, any other registered medical practitioner can conduct the examination after obtaining the victim's consent.[69]

On examining either an accused or a victim of rape, the medical practitioner is required to prepare a report of examination without delay containing necessary details such as the name, address, age, marks of injury, materials taken for DNA profiling, reasons for arriving at conclusions, and exact time of commencement and completion of the examination.[70] The examination report of a victim of rape must specifically state that her consent or consent on her behalf for the examination was obtained.[71] It is likely that an examination held without the victim's consent would be held unlawful. The medical examination report must be forwarded to the investigating officer who, in turn, must forward it to the Magistrate along with his report.[72]

While in police custody, the arrested person should be examined every 48 hours by a trained medical practitioner on a panel of approved doctors appointed by the Director of Health Service of the State concerned.[73]

Box 4.3   Additional Rights of Arrested Women

1. A female shall only be allowed to be examined by, or under the supervision of, a female registered medical practitioner;[74]
2. If a female is to be searched, the search must be made by another female with strict regard to decency;[75]
3. Female suspects should be kept in different police lock-ups than male suspects;[76] and
4. Female suspects should only be interrogated in the presence of female police officers.[77]

---

[68] S. 164A(1) CrPC.

[69] S. 164A(1) CrPC.

[70] S. 53A(2, 3, and 4) and S. 164A(2, 3, and 5) CrPC.

[71] S. 164(4) CrPC.

[72] S. 53A(5) and S. 164A(6) CrPC.

[73] *D.K. Basu* v. *State of West Bengal*, AIR 1997 SC 610, 623.

[74] S. 53(2) CrPC.

[75] S. 51(2) CrPC.

[76] *Sheela Barse* v. *State of Maharashtra*, (1983) 2 SCC 96.

[77] *Sheela Barse* v. *State of Maharashtra*, (1983) 2 SCC 96.

4.4 REMEDIES AVAILABLE WHEN A PERSON'S RIGHTS HAVE BEEN VIOLATED

A person whose rights have been violated while being arrested or held in custody may pursue several legal remedies. These include:

- Seeking a writ of *habeas corpus* for release of a person who has been illegally detained;
- Seeking compensation under the Constitution for the violation of fundamental constitutional rights;
- Seeking civil damages from the arresting officer for illegal arrest, false imprisonment, illegal confinement, etc;
- Pursing criminal charges against the police officers; and
- Making a complaint to the NHRC.

A. Petitions Protesting Illegal Arrest/Detention

Writ of *Habeas Corpus*

If a person is arrested or detained illegally, he or she may petition the Supreme Court under Article 32 of the Constitution, or the High Court under Article 226 of the Constitution. Under these Articles, a petitioner may ask the court to issue a writ for enforcement of his or her fundamental rights, under Part III of the Constitution. In particular, the Court has the power to issue a writ of *habeas corpus*. See Chapter 6: 'Detention.'

For a more detailed discussion about the writ of *habeas corpus*, see Chapter 6: 'Detention.'

B. Compensation for Violation of Constitutional Rights

In an effort to curb illegal police conduct, the courts have awarded compensation to victims of human rights violations at the hands of the police, and to the victims' families. For example, in the case of *Rudul Sah* v. *State of Bihar*,[78] the petitioner was released from jail after he was detained illegally for more than fourteen years after he was acquitted. The Supreme Court held that compensation for deprivation of a fundamental right can be granted under Article 32 of the Constitution. The petitioner was awarded thirty-five thousand rupees in compensation from the government.

Similarly in the case of *Nilabati Behera* v. *State of Orissa*,[79] the body of the Petitioner's son was found on a railway track after he had been taken into police custody. The Supreme Court held that it had power under Article 32, or the High Court under Article 226 of the Constitution, to award monetary compensation where the human rights and fundamental freedoms have been violated by the state and its agencies. This is a remedy available in public law, based on strict liability for contravention of the guaranteed basic and indefeasible rights of the citizen. The State of Orissa was ordered to pay the petitioner Rs 1,50,000.

[78] AIR 1983 SC 1086; 1983 SCR (3) 508; 1983 SCC (4) 141.
[79] 1993 AIR 1960; (1993) 2 SCC 746; 1993 SCR (2) 581.

For a more detailed discussion on compensation, see Chapter 8: 'Legal Aid and Compensation.'

C. Civil Damages

If a person is arrested illegally, he or she may bring a private, civil suit for damages against the person who made the arrest.[80] Under the common law of torts, the arrested person may be able to sue the delinquent officer for false imprisonment, assault, or wrongful death, depending on the specific circumstances of the case. The same act may be both a civil wrong and a criminal act. Pursuing civil damages will not absolve the delinquent officer from the criminal charges stemming from the act in question.

Problems in Practice

Although the law of torts does exist in India, court cases are often subject to lengthy time delays. A civil case may take a number of years before a final judgement is reached, with additional delays in the enforcement of the judgement being common. Due to the prevalence of delays, and the cost of seeking damages under tort law, even if a person files a civil suit against the officers who have violated his or her rights, he or she may also wish to pursue criminal charges.

D. Criminal Charges

Along with being liable for the payment of civil damages, delinquent officers may also be subjected to criminal charges. Any public servant who has the authority to make an arrest, and knowingly exercises this authority in contravention of the law to effect an illegal arrest, can be prosecuted under S. 220 IPC. A police officer or other person who makes an illegal arrest is guilty of wrongful confinement, and could be punished with a prison term of up to three years and or a fine.[81] A police officer who uses violence against any person in his custody may be charged for offences under the IPC relating to criminal force, and will also liable to punishment under S. 29 of the Police Act, 1861. A person who causes a police officer to arrest another person without sufficient grounds, may be ordered to pay compensation, not exceeding one hundred rupees, to the person arrested.[82]

If an arrested person's rights are violated while in custody, he or she may file a complaint when brought in front of the magistrate. Additionally, criminal proceedings against the delinquent officer(s) may be commenced by the filing of an FIR at a police station. If the police officer-in-charge of the station where the FIR was filed fails to act on it, the complainant may contact the Superintendent of Police or the District Magistrate and request both an enquiry and additional legal action against the police officer.[83]

[80] *Anwar Hussain* v. *Ajoy Kumar Mukherjee*, AIR 1965 SC 1651; (1965) (2) Cr LJ 686.

[81] Ss. 340, 342–344 IPC.

[82] S. 358 CrPC.

[83] See Chapter 2—'Reporting a Crime.'

E. Filing a Complaint with the NHRC

Another avenue that a person may pursue in bringing charges against police officers who have violated his or her rights is by filing a complaint with the National Human Rights Commission (NHRC). The NHRC was created under the Protection of Human Rights Act 1993, and has been charged with investigating and intervening in cases involving the violation of human rights, including abuses committed by public servants.

A complaint to the NHRC may be written in Hindi, English, or any language included in the Eighth Schedule of the Constitution. There is no fee involved in filing a complaint.

Box 4.4   Complaints *Not* Entertained by NHRC[84]

1. Complaints about events that have occurred over one year prior to the date of the filing of the complaint;
2. Complaints related to matters which are already under some level of judicial consideration;
3. Complaints that are vague, anonymous, or pseudonymous;
4. Complaints which are of a frivolous nature; and
5. Complaints which pertain to service matters.

Upon receipt of the complaint, the Commission may inquire into the complaint on its own, request an investigation into the complaint to be executed by the Central or State Government, or choose to not proceed with the complaint and inform the person making the complaint accordingly.

After completion of the inquiry, the Commission may:

1. Recommend prosecution by the concerned government against the delinquent officer(s);
2. Approach the Supreme Court or the High Court concerned for such directions, orders or writs as that Court may deem necessary; or
3. Recommend to the concerned Government or authority for the grant of such immediate interim relief to the victim or the members of his family, as the Commission may consider necessary.

---

[84] National Human Rights Commission, Frequently Asked Questions (available at *http://nhrc.nic.in/faq.htm*).

5 Bail

5.1 INTRODUCTION

One of the aims of detaining an accused person following his or her arrest, is to ensure that he or she attends trial and, if he or she is found guilty, is present to receive a sentence. However, since arrest and detention are serious infringements of the right to personal liberty, the presence of the accused at the trial should, where possible, be ensured through methods other than pre-trial detention.

A fundamental principle of the criminal justice system is that all defendants are innocent until proven guilty; accordingly, the granting of bail should be the rule rather than the exception.[1] Pre-trial detention may be justified in some circumstances, for example, to prevent the accused from absconding, committing another offence, tampering with evidence or intimidating witnesses before the trial. Unnecessary pre-trial detention subjects the accused to the stigmatizing effects of detention, including inability to prepare an effective defence, without any proper justification in law.[2] The CrPC governs pre-trial detention through the system of bail.

Bail is a monetary amount or precondition for pre-trial release from custody.[3] It is designed to ensure that the accused will return for subsequent proceedings, and is granted by the execution of a bail bond. A bail bond is a written document that states that (a) the accused will appear at a designated proceeding when attendance is required, and (b) failure to do so will require payment to the court, money in the amount specified in the order fixing bail.

A bail bond can be executed by the accused or his or her surety. A surety is someone who assumes responsibility for the appearance of the accused at designated proceedings. The surety may be required to pay money to the court if the accused fails to attend court, or is declared by the court to have absconded. To be a surety, a person must have the capacity, control, and competence to ensure that the accused will appear in court or pay the amount of the bail bond. The surety will therefore usually be a family member or close friend. The

[1] *State of Rajasthan* v. *Balchand*, 1978 SCR (1) 535, 536.

[2] See *Moti Ram* v. *State of M.P.*, 1979 SCR (1) 335, 341.

[3] For definitions, see *Black's Law Dictionary*, 6th edn, West Group, St. Paul, 1990.

surety must make a declaration before the Court stating the number of persons (including the accused) for whom he or she may have stood as surety along with other relevant details.[4]

Box 5.1   Bond and Bail Bond after Arrest[5]

I, _____ (name), of _____, being brought before the District Magistrate of _____ (or as the case may be) under a warrant issued to compel my appearance to answer to the charge of _____, do hereby bind myself to attend in the Court of _____ on the day of _____ next, to answer to the said charge, and to continue so to attend until otherwise directed by the Court; and, in case of my making default herein, I bind myself to forfeit, to Government, the sum of rupees.

Dated, this _____ day of _____, 20 ____.

(Seal of the Court)

(Signature)

I do hereby declare myself surety for the above-named _____ of _____, that he shall attend before _____ in the Court of _____ on the day of _____ next, to answer to the charge on which he has been arrested, and shall continue so to attend until otherwise directed by the Court; and, in case of his making default therein, I bind myself to forfeit, to Government, the sum of rupees.

Dated, this _____ day of _____, 20 ____.

(Signature)

The amount of bail should be reasonable, not excessive or beyond the financial capacity of the accused.[6] This ensures that the right to be released on bail is not nullified by a bail amount that is too high. If necessary, the High Court or the Court of Session can direct that the amount of bail be reduced.[7] Moreover, if the accused is poor and unable to post bail, he or she may still be released on a personal bond.[8] (See below section 5.3 'Release on Personal Bond'). If the accused is unable to give bail within a week of arrest, he or she will be considered 'indigent' and should be released on a bond without sureties.[9]

---

[4] S. 441-A CrPC.

[5] Form No. 3, CrPC.

[6] See S. 440(1) CrPC.

[7] S. 440(2) CrPC.

[8] See *Hussainara Khatoon* v. *State of Bihar*, AIR 1979 SC 1360, 1360–1363.

[9] Proviso (a), S. 436(1) CrPC (See section 5.3).

As soon as the bail bond has been executed, the accused should be released.[10]

If the investigation cannot be completed or if the charge sheet cannot be filed with the court within sixty to ninety days, and the accused is being held in detention, then 'even in serious and ghastly types of crimes the accused will be entitled to be released on bail.'[11] Also, if trial before a magistrate cannot be completed within sixty days after the first date fixed for taking evidence, then the accused, if not previously released from custody during this period, may be released.[12]

Sureties may apply to the court for the discharge of a bail bond; when a surety is discharged, the court will issue a warrant for the arrest of the accused.[13]

If a police officer arrests someone without a warrant for a bailable offence, the police officer must inform the arrested person of entitlement to bail.[14] If the police fail to do this, the arrested person should ask about the availability of bail. (See also Chapter 4; 'Rights When Arrested'.)

5.2 BAILABLE AND NON-BAILABLE OFFENCES

All criminal offences under the IPC have been categorized as either bailable or non-bailable.[15] A bailable offence is one which is shown as bailable in the First Schedule of the CrPC, or which has been made bailable by any other law. All other offences are categorized as non-bailable. In relation to offences under laws other than the IPC, which have not been listed under the Schedule, there is a general rule that more serious offences will be classified as non-bailable, while less serious offences will be classified as bailable.

Bailable offences are generally less serious offences, for which being granted bail is a right.[16] If someone is accused of a bailable offence, and arrested and detained without a warrant, such a person can be released either after the execution of a bail bond, or on a personal bond. The courts as well as the police can grant bail for bailable offences.

Non-bailable offences are generally serious offences (punishable by imprisonment for three or more years), for which bail may be granted only at the discretion of the court. Therefore, in case of such an offence, the granting of bail is not a matter of right, but only a privilege to be granted at the discretion of the court.

[10] S. 442 CrPC.

[11] *Natabar Parida* v. *State of Orissa*, 1975 SCR 137, 143; *see also* CrPC S. 167(2).

[12] S. 437(6) CrPC.

[13] S. 444(2) CrPC.

[14] S. 50(2) CrPC.

[15] S. 2(a) CrPC.

[16] See S. 436 (1) CrPC.

In deciding whether to exercise discretion and grant bail for a non-bailable offence, the court will consider the following factors:[17]

- Nature and seriousness of charge;
- Character of evidence supporting the charge;
- Circumstances peculiar to the accused;
- Reasonable possibility of presence of accused not being secured at trial;
- Reasonable apprehension of witnesses being intimidated or influenced;
- Larger interest of public and state; and
- Other considerations, which the judge may weigh up from case to case. (These may include the previous convictions and criminal record of the accused, as well as the likelihood of the repetition of prior offences by the accused person if released on bail.)[18]

The court is not permitted to grant bail to a person accused of a non-bailable offence where:

- There are reasonable grounds for believing that the accused has been guilty of an offence punishable with death or life imprisonment,[19] or
- The alleged offence is a cognizable offence and the person has previously been convicted of an offence punishable with death, life imprisonment or imprisonment for seven years or more; or the person has previously been convicted on two or more occasions of 'a cognizable offence punishable with imprisonment for three years or more but not less than seven years'.[20]

These limitations may be overlooked by the court if the accused is under the age of sixteen, a woman, is sick, or if the court is satisfied that it is just and proper for any other special reason. This is because these groups are thought to be less likely to abscond or interfere with the investigation.[21] However, not every sickness will entitle an accused to bail under S. 437(1); only a life-threatening sickness will suffice.[22] The Public Prosecutor must be given an opportunity of hearing before bail can be granted to a person accused of an offence punishable with death, life imprisonment or imprisonment for seven years or more.[23] If the court does take these factors into consideration when deciding whether to grant bail, it must record in writing its reasons for doing so.[24] Only the court may grant bail in these circumstances, not a police officer.

---

[17] See *State* v. *Jagjit Singh (Capt.)*, 1962 SCR (3) 622, 624; *Gurcharan Singh* v. *State (Delhi Admn)*, 1978 SCR (2) 358, 367.

[18] See *Sagri Bhagat* v. *State of Bihar*, 52 Cri LJ 657, 658.

[19] S. 437(1) CrPC.

[20] S.437(1)(ii) CrPC.

[21] See *Nirmal Kumar Banerjee* v. *State*, 1972 Cri LJ 1582, 1583.

[22] See *State* v. *Sardool Singh*, 1975 Cri LJ 1348, 1349.

[23] Proviso 4, S. 437(1) CrPC.

[24] S. 437(4) CrPC.

In the context of a non-bailable offence, if the magistrate or judge grants or refuses an application for bail, his or her reasons must be recorded.[25] This requirement enables higher judicial authorities to check whether judicial discretion was properly exercised. The exercise of discretion in the granting of bail in such cases 'must not be arbitrary, vague and fanciful, but legal and regular.'[26] The mere fact that the accused may be required for identification by witnesses during the investigation is not sufficient ground for refusing to grant bail, if the accused would otherwise be entitled to be released on bail.[27] In general, the scope of the discretion in granting bail depends on considerations such as:

- The gravity of the crime. As the gravity increases, discretion to release on bail decreases;
- Whether a police officer or judicial officer is granting bail. Judicial officers have a wider discretion;
- Which class of judicial officer is granting bail. High Courts and Courts of Sessions have a wider discretion than other courts.

5.3 RELEASE ON PERSONAL BOND

The Supreme Court has held that the Indian system of bail causes a great deal of injustice to the poorer sections of Indian society by emphasizing monetary bonds, which many accused persons cannot afford to post.[28] Often they will also not know anybody else with sufficient security to post the bond and act as surety for them. The full extent of this problem was revealed in the *Hussainara Khatoon* case.[29] The Court learned that a large number of men and women who had been unable to post excessive monetary bail bonds were being held in detention for months or even years, including those who were only charged with offences carrying minor punishments.[30] Consequently the Supreme Court held that the risk of monetary loss is not the only deterrent against fleeing from justice, and that in appropriate cases the accused should be released on a personal bond.[31]

In *Moti Ram* v. *State of M.P.*, a poor mason was asked to furnish ten thousand rupees and sureties from the same district as the Court.[32] The Supreme Court found it unfair to ask an indigent person to deposit such a high amount of bail bond and upheld *Hussainara Khatoon*, ruling that bail covers release on one's own bond, with or without sureties. The holding in *Moti Ram* has been codified by section 436 of CrPC. Section 436, amended by the Code of

---

[25] S. 437(4) CrPC.

[26] Lord Mansfield, in *Gudikanti Narasimhulu* v. *Public Prosecutor A.P.*, 1978 SCR (2) 371, 373.

[27] S. 437(1) CrPC.

[28] See comments of Bhagwati, J. in *Hussainara Khatoon* v. *State of Bihar*, AIR 1979 SC 1360, 1362–3.

[29] *Hussainara Khatoon* v. *State of Bihar*, AIR 1979 SC 1360, 1362.

[30] Ibid., at 1361.

[31] Ibid., at 1360.

[32] 1979 SCR (1) 335.

Criminal Procedure Amendment Act 2005, now mandates that a person unable to furnish bail within a week of arrest must be released on a personal bond without sureties.[33]

In the case of an accused who cannot afford to post bail, the following factors should be considered in assessing whether to release him or her on personal bond:[34]

- Length of residence in the community;
- Employment status, history, and financial condition;
- Family ties and relationships;
- Reputation, character, and monetary condition;
- Prior criminal record including prior releases on recognizance or on bail;
- Identity of responsible members of the community who would vouch for him;
- Nature of the offence charged, and the apparent probability of conviction, and the likely sentence in-so-far as they are relevant to the risk of non appearance; and
- Other factors indicating ties of the accused to the community or bearing on the risk of wilful failure to appear.

These considerations should prevail over bail bonds to ensure that the bailee does not flee justice.

5.4 OTHER INSTANCES WHERE BAIL MUST BE GRANTED

In addition to bail being granted for the commission of a bailable offence, an accused person has the right to be granted bail if the investigation is not completed within the prescribed number of days. (See 'Length of Detention' in Chapter 6)

It is extremely important to note that once the given time has elapsed, the right to bail is absolute. The Supreme Court has ruled that even in cases dealing with ghastly and serious types of crimes, the accused will be entitled to be released on bail.[35] Not only is this right absolute, but bail granted pursuant to S. 167(2) CrPC shares the property of bail granted pursuant to Ss. 437 and 439 CrPC in that, it cannot be cancelled except through the powers conferred upon the court in Ss. 437(5) CrPC and 439(2) CrPC.[36] Therefore, once bail has been granted, it cannot be cancelled for the sole reason that a charge sheet has been filed.[37] However, if a charge sheet is filed after the sixty or ninety-day period, and the accused has not exercised the right to bail, the court may actually deny bail; and so, it is extremely important that the accused exercise this right as soon as the mandated period has expired.[38]

---

[33] Proviso (a), S.436(1) CrPC.

[34] 1979 SCR (1) 335.

[35] See *Natabar Parida* v. *State of Orissa*, 1975 SCR 137, 143.

[36] See *Aslam Babulal Desai* v. *State of Maharashtra*, AIR 1993 SC 1, 7.

[37] See *Ajit Singh* v. *State of Punjab*, 1994 Cri LJ 2342, 2344.

[38] See *Dara Singh* v. *State of Haryana*, 1996 Cri LJ 1430.

It should also be noted that if the accused is presented to an executive magistrate, that magistrate can only authorize detention for an additional period of seven days total.[39]

In the context of non-bailable offences, bail should be granted if the trial is not over within 60 days from the first day fixed for taking evidence, if the accused is in custody during the whole of period.[40] This limitation does not apply to cases that are tried before a court of session. Moreover, a magistrate may decide not to release the accused on bail if the magistrate records her reasons for doing so.[41]

5.5 WHEN BAIL MUST BE GRANTED DUE TO REASONABLE BELIEF OF INNOCENCE

The police and the courts are required to grant bail for non-bailable offences if there are reasonable grounds for believing that the accused did not commit the crime.[42] While further investigation is being completed, the accused must be released on bail.[43] Also, if at the conclusion of the trial, but before judgement is delivered, the court is of the opinion that there are reasonable grounds for believing that the accused is not guilty of the offence, the accused should be released on personal bond.[44]

If a judicial or police officer grants an application for bail for any reason under Ss. 437(1) or 437(2) CrPC, their reasons must be recorded in writing.[45] This requirement ensures that the higher judicial authorities can check whether the discretion was properly exercised. The exercise of discretion in the granting of bail in such cases 'must not be arbitrary, vague, and fanciful, but legal and regular'.[46] The mere fact that the accused may be required for identification by witnesses during the investigation is not sufficient ground for refusing to grant bail if the accused would otherwise be entitled to be released on bail.[47]

5.6 CONDITIONAL BAIL

Where a person is accused or suspected of the commission of an offence punishable with imprisonment for seven years or more, the Court may impose any conditions on the bail

---

[39] See S. 167(2A) CrPC.

[40] S. 437(6) CrPC.

[41] S. 437(6) CrPC.

[42] See S. 437(2) CrPC.

[43] See S. 437(2) CrPC.

[44] See S. 437(7) CrPC.

[45] S. 437(4) CrPC.

[46] Lord Mansfield, in *Gudikanti Narasimhulu* v. *Public Prosecutor, A.P.*, 1978 SCR (2) 371, 373.

[47] S. 437(1) CrPC.

which it considers necessary.[48] The CrPC grants the power to impose conditions only to the Court, not to a police officer. The power to impose conditions may also be exercised where:[49]

- The offence is one under Chapter VI (offences against the State), Chapter XVI (offences against the human body), or Chapter XVII (offences against property) of the IPC; or
- The offence is one of the abetment of, or conspiracy to, or attempt to commit any such offence as mentioned above.

The possible conditions which can be imposed upon bail are designed to prevent the accused from escaping, repeating the offence, tampering with evidence, or threatening witnesses.[50] However, a condition which has the effect of altogether denying the accused access to bail, such as a large sum of money demanded as bond for a poor person, will not be authorized by law.[51] Nor can a condition be imposed which derogates from or violates any fundamental right of the accused under the Constitution. Similarly, a condition that the accused must aid the police in their investigation in order to be granted bail would be in violation of the right of the accused against self-incrimination, and would thus be invalid.[52]

Where anticipatory bail is granted, it is also likely that conditions will be placed on the grant of bail.[53]

5.7 ANTICIPATORY BAIL

There may be cases in which a person anticipates arrest for some specific reason, for example, an acquaintance or friend has already been arrested. If someone has reason to anticipate arrest for an alleged non-bailable offence, they may apply to the High Court or Court of Session for anticipatory bail.[54] If such bail is granted, an individual will be released immediately upon arrest, possibly with conditions attached by the Court.[55] It should be noted that the granting of anticipatory bail is not a matter of right, but a discretionary power exercised by the court in each case.[56] It occurs rarely and in exceptional circumstances.[57]

In order to secure anticipatory bail, the accused must demonstrate a reasonable apprehension of arrest for a non-bailable offence; mere fear of an accusation is insufficient.[58] Moreover, it is not necessary for an FIR to have been filed against the accused. The Court

[48] S. 437(3) CrPC.

[49] S. 437(3) CrPC.

[50] S. 437(3) CrPC.

[51] See *Mohd. Tariq* v. *Union of India,* 1990 Cri LJ 474.

[52] *Shaik Layak* v. *State,* 1981 Cri LJ 954, 957–8.

[53] See S. 438(2) CrPC.

[54] S. 438(1) CrPC.

[55] See S. 438 CrPC.

[56] See *Gurbaksh Singh Sibbia* v. *State of Punjab,* 1980 SCR (3) 383 at 388.

[57] *Balchand Jain* v. *State of Madhya Pradesh,* 1977 SCR (2) 52, 55–6.

[58] *Gurbaksh Singh* at 417.

must be able to determine on objective grounds whether the applicant has good reason to believe that he or she may be arrested.

There is no restriction on granting anticipatory bail, even where the alleged offence is punishable by death or life imprisonment.[59] It is also immaterial for the purposes of S. 438(1) CrPC whether an offence is cognizable or non-cognizable,[60] or whether it is an offence under the IPC or another law.[61] As long as the offence is a non-bailable one, the possibility of anticipatory bail will be available.[62]

The courts have a wide discretion to consider all of the circumstances of the case when deciding whether to grant anticipatory bail. However, the Supreme Court has listed the following factors for consideration of an application:[63]

- Nature and seriousness of the proposed charges;
- The context of the events likely to lead to the making of the charges;
- The criminal history of the applicant;
- The reasonable possibility of the applicant absconding;
- The reasonable apprehension of witnesses or evidence being tampered with; and
- Any interests of the public or state that may be affected.

In 2005, Section 438(1) was amended to incorporate the above factors laid down by the Supreme Court. The Court may grant anticipatory bail if it appears that accusations have been levied to humiliate 'the applicant by having him arrested'.[64] Based on the above factors, the Court may either reject the application or pass an interim order granting anticipatory bail. If an interim order is granted, the Court must serve a minimum of seven days notice to the Public Prosecutor and the Superintendent of Police so as to afford them 'a reasonable opportunity of being heard' at the final hearing.[65] If the Public Prosecutor makes an application and the Court considers it 'necessary in the interest of justice', the applicant may be required to be present in Court at the final hearing.[66]

If the High Court or the Sessions Court does not pass an interim order or rejects the application, an officer-in-charge of a police station can arrest the applicant without warrant based on the accusations contained in the bail application.[67]

Owing to widespread protests against the above provision, the Code of Criminal Procedure (Amendment) Amending Act, 2006 was passed, allowing the Central Government to appoint

---

[59] *Gurbaksh Singh* at 407–10.

[60] See *Suresh Vasudeva* v. *State*, 1978 Cri LJ 677, 683.

[61] *E. Joseph* v. *Asst Collector of Customs, Tuticorin*, 1982 Cri LJ 559 at 564.

[62] See ibid.

[63] See *Gurbaksh Singh*, at 416.

[64] S. 438(1)(iv) CrPC.

[65] S. 438(1A) CrPC.

[66] S. 438(1B) CrPC.

[67] Proviso to Section 438(1), CrPC.

different dates for the coming into effect of different provisions of the Amendment Act [*Code of Criminal Procedure (Amendment) Amending Act, 2006 at http://indiacode.nic.in/ fullact1.asp?tfnm=200625*]. The amendment to Section 438 is yet to come into force [*Ministry of Home Affairs Notification No: SO923(E) Date of Notification : 21.06.2006*].

Anticipatory bail must be specific in its scope; it may not order the release of an accused every time that person is arrested. In other words, S. 438 CrPC does not contemplate or allow a 'blanket order' of anticipatory bail. The Supreme Court has held that a court that grants anticipatory bail must take care to specify the particular offence in relation to which the anticipatory bail is to be granted.[68]

The grant of anticipatory bail in no way affects the right of the police to fully investigate the case.[69] Indeed, a grant of anticipatory bail under S. 438 CrPC generally carries conditions, including:

- That the accused be available for interrogation by the police when required;[70]
- That the accused in no way make any inducement, threat, or promise to anyone acquainted with the case, with a view to impeding the investigation;[71] and
- That the accused person should not leave India without the prior permission of the Court.[72]

The foregoing conditions mentioned in S. 438 (2) CrPC are not exhaustive, and the court may impose other conditions in order to strike a balance between the individual right to personal liberty, and the police duty to investigate offences.[73]

Section 438 CrPC does not make clear whether the order granting anticipatory bail can be cancelled even before regular bail has been granted. It seems likely that the order of anticipatory bail would be effective until the conclusion of the trial, as it would be if granted under S. 437 (1) CrPC.[74] However, it has been held that a court making an order for anticipatory bail is entitled to cancel the order upon appropriate consideration.[75]

5.8 REMEDIES

If the accused is denied release on bail for a non-bailable offence, this does not necessarily preclude him or her from filing another application on a later occasion, or from appealing a refusal of bail in the higher courts, including the Supreme Court, if there are grounds for

---

[68] See *Gurbaksh Singh*, at 418–9.

[69] *Chain Singh Dhakad* v. *Hargovind*, 1991 Cri LJ 33, 37–8.

[70] S. 438(2)(i) CrPC.

[71] S. 438(2)(ii) CrPC.

[72] S. 438(2)(iii) CrPC.

[73] S. 438(2)(iv) CrPC.

[74] See *Ramsewak* v. *State of M.P.*, 1979 Cri LJ 1485, 1490–1.

[75] See *State of Maharashtra* v. *Vishwas Shripati Patil*, 1978 Cri LJ 1403, 1405.

appeal, or new circumstances arise.[76] However, the continuous filing of bail applications may be considered an abuse of process by the court.[77] The accused is only entitled to file a fresh application if a substantial change of the facts and circumstances is revealed.[78]

If the accused is denied bail, he or she can file a complaint with the court or an administrative agency, petition the High Court under S. 482 CrPC, claim an abuse of law, and/or contact the press. The accused can also ask a higher court to review the decision under S. 397 CrPC.

5.9 BAIL DURING APPEAL AND REVISION

Bail can also be granted during appeal and revision. During appeal, the appellate or High Court may, by written order, suspend a sentence and order the convicted person to be released on bail.[79] If a convicted person notifies the court that he or she intends to appeal, the judge must order that the convicted person be released on bail, unless there are special reasons for refusing.[80] During this time, the convicted person's prison sentence will be suspended.[81] While the trial court can only exercise the power of suspension of sentence and granting of bail when the person convicted has been given a sentence of less than three years, or when the offence is a bailable one, there is no limitation on the type of cases where an appellate court can exercise this power.[82]

If the High Court or Court of Session believes that a lower court decided a case in error, it has the power to direct that any sentence or order be suspended, and if the accused is in confinement, that he or she be released on bail or their own bond pending the examination of the record.[83] However, once an application for revision has been made to either the High Court or the Court of Sessions, another application by the same person shall not be entertained by the other.[84]

5.10 AFTER RELEASE ON BAIL

As soon as the bail bond is executed, the accused should be discharged from custody.[85] After being released on bail, the accused is mostly free to carry on with life. However, the accused

---

[76] See *Babu Singh* v. *State of U.P.,* 1978 SCR (2) 777, 779.

[77] See *State of Maharashtra* v. *Buddhikota Subha Rao,* AIR 1989 SC 2292, 2292–2293.

[78] See ibid., at 2292.

[79] See Ss. 389(1) and 401 CrPC.

[80] S. 389(3) CrPC.

[81] S. 389(3) CrPC.

[82] See *Bhaskaran* v. *State of Kerala,* 1987 Cri LJ 1588, 1590.

[83] See *Bhaskaran* v. *State of Kerala,* 1987 Cri LJ 1588, 1590.

[84] S. 397(3) CrPC.

[85] S. 442(1) CrPC.

must attend court at the time and place specified in the bail bond.[86] During this time, the accused should not in anyway interfere with the investigation of the case or attempt to abscond; doing so may result in cancellation of bail.

The surety who posted the accused person's bond may apply to the Court to discharge the bond.[87] If this happens, the court will issue a warrant for the accused person's arrest.[88]

5.11 NON-APPEARANCE

In the event that the bailed person does not appear for trial, the bail money is forfeited by the surety and kept by the court, and a warrant for re-arrest will be issued. When the person is re-arrested, he or she is generally denied bail for the same offence.

If the accused cannot be traced for a long period, and the Court believes that it will not be possible to trace them, then the court will issue a warrant for arrest under Ss. 82, 83 CrPC Upon completion of this process the accused will be declared a 'proclaimed offender.'

5.12 CANCELLATION OF BAIL

Once bail has been granted it can be cancelled, either by the court that granted the bail, or, if the bail was granted by a police officer, by the High Court or Court of Session.[89] The power to cancel bail lies with the courts, not with police officers.

While the law provides for the cancellation of bail, overwhelming circumstances are needed to succeed in a cancellation application.[90] It is much harder for a court to cancel bail granted in a non-bailable case, than it is for that court to simply reject the application for bail in the first place.[91] This is because cancellation of bail will involve a review of the decision previously made to grant bail.

Bail may be cancelled if the accused:[92]

- Misuses the bail by indulging in similar criminal activity;
- Interferes with the course of investigation;
- Attempts to tamper with evidence of witnesses;
- Threatens witnesses, or in other ways hampers the smooth conduct of the investigation;
- Is likely to flee the country;

---

[86] See CrPC S. 441(1).

[87] S. 441(1) CrPC.

[88] S. 441(2) CrPC.

[89] Ss. 437(5) and 439(2) CrPC.

[90] See *Dolat Ram v. State of Haryana,* 1995 SCC (1) 349, 350.

[91] *State (Delhi Admn.) v. Sanjay Gandhi,* 1978 SCR (3) 950, 957.

[92] See S. 37 CrPC; *Dolat Ram,* at 350–1.

- Attempts to go underground or become unavailable to the investigation agency; or
- Attempts to place him or herself beyond the reach of the surety.

In all of the above, a strong case needs to be presented to the court for cancellation of bail.[93] In some circumstances, it may be possible for bail to be cancelled if the bail was granted illegally or improperly by a wrong or arbitrary exercise of judicial discretion.[94]

An order for anticipatory bail can, similarly, be cancelled by the court upon appropriate consideration.[95]

---

[93] See *Dolat Ram*, at 350.

[94] See *State of Maharashtra* v. *Anand Chintaman Dighe*, 1990 SCR (1) 73, 75–76.

[95] See *Chain Singh Dhakad* v. *Hargovind*, 1991 Cri LJ 33, 37–38.

6 Detention

6.1 INTRODUCTION

When a person is in custody and his or her personal liberty is taken away, except as a result of conviction for an offence, he or she is said to be in detention. This may be because the person is waiting to be brought before a magistrate on formal charges, or is waiting for a trial and is unable to secure bail.

A sound understanding of the law governing detention is imperative because the majority of torture and ill-treatment in the Indian criminal justice system occurs during the first stage of detention in police custody. The National Human Rights Commission (NHRC) received intimation of one hundred and thirty-six cases of custodial death from State Governments in the period 2004–2005.[1]

The CrPC contains several provisions guaranteeing the basic rights of the accused. Section 50 CrPC requires that a police officer arresting without a warrant 'shall forthwith communicate to [the accused] full particulars of the offence for which he [or she] is arrested.' Thus, the grounds of an arrest must be disclosed to the accused at the time of arrest, and he or she shall not be detained 'without warrant for a longer period than under all the circumstances of the case is reasonable,' and shall be produced before the magistrate within 24 hours after the arrest.[2] A special order of a magistrate may extend the period of detention, but this too is limited to situations when 'it appears that the investigation cannot be completed within the period of twenty-four hours ... and there are grounds for believing that the accusation or information is well-founded.'[3]

It is important to be mindful of the basic protections guaranteed by the Constitution, which permit detention only under specific circumstances prescribed by law.[4] It is highly

---

[1] National Human Rights Commission, Annual Report 2004–2005, Annexure 1, NHRC, New Delhi, 2005 at p. 211.

[2] S. 57 CrPC. The 24 hours requirement can be exceeded with a special order of a magistrate under S.167 and it excludes the travel time to the court.

[3] S. 167 CrPC.

[4] See Article 21, Constitution of India: no person shall be deprived of his life or personal liberty except according to procedure established by law.

advisable for individuals to know their legal rights upon arrest and detention and actively demand them, rather than relying on police to inform and uphold such rights.

Many issues in this chapter are closely linked to preceding chapters. In particular, the rights of a detenu may be best understood when studied with Chapter 4: 'Rights When Arrested' and Chapter 5: 'Bail.'

6.2 LENGTH OF DETENTION

As a rule, an investigation should be completed within twenty-four hours, and the detenue must be released within twenty-four hours.[5] This period can be extended for up to fifteen days by a magistrate, if he or she is satisfied that the remand is necessary for the investigation.[6] This process can be repeated, but the total period of detention must not exceed 90 days where the offence is punishable by death, life imprisonment, or a sentence of 10 years or more;[7] or 60 days for any other offence.[8] The accused must be produced at each hearing for the extension of the period of custody.[9] On the expiry of this extension period, the detenu should be granted bail and be released, once the bail is furnished.[10]

It is not uncommon for those who are detained to spend four or five years awaiting trial for a crime when they would have served a much shorter sentence had they been convicted. This often occurs where those awaiting trial ('undertrials') cannot afford the bail bond, despite the fact that the Supreme Court has stated that accused persons who cannot afford to post large amounts of money for bail should, in most cases, be released on a personal bond instead.[11] This kind of prolonged detention of undertrials is illegal under the Indian criminal law and in violation of the accused's human rights.

In light of rampant violations, the Common Cause, a civil rights group, petitioned the Supreme Court to provide general directions for pending criminal cases under Article 32 of the Constitution.[12] The Supreme Court in response declared the following directions in order 'to protect and effectuate the right to life and liberty of the citizens ... [and] to ensure that these criminal prosecutions do not operate as engines of oppression.'[13] It held that an undertrial:

---

[5] Ss. 57, 167 CrPC.

[6] S. 167(2) CrPC. In Punjab—'15 days' should read '30 days.'

[7] S. 167(2)(a)(i) CrPC. In Gujarat—'90 days' should read '120 days.'

[8] S. 167(2)(a)(ii) CrPC.

[9] S. 167(2)(b) CrPC.

[10] See Chapter 5: Bail.

[11] See *Hussainara Khatoon and Ors* v. *Home Secretary, State of Bihar,* (1980) SCC (1) 81.

[12] *'Common Cause'* v. *Union of India,* JT 1996 (4) S.C. 701; 1996 AIR 1619.

[13] Ibid., at 703.

- accused of an offence punishable with imprisonment for up to three years, who has been in jail for a period of six months or more, and whose trial has been pending for at least a year, should be released on bail;
- accused of an offence punishable with imprisonment for up to five years, who has been in jail for a period of six months or more, and whose trial has been pending for at least two year, should be released on bail;
- accused of an offence punishable with imprisonment for up to seven years, who has been in jail for a period of one year, and whose trial has been pending for two years, should be released on bail;
- accused of a traffic offence whose trial has been pending for more than two years may be discharged;
- accused of an offence that is compoundable with the permission of the court whose trial has been pending for more than two years shall be discharged after hearing the public prosecutor;
- accused of a non-cognizable and bailable offence whose trial has been pending for more than two years shall be discharged or acquitted by the court;
- accused of an offence punishable with only a fine and not of a recurring nature, whose trial has been pending for a year shall be discharged or acquitted;
- accused of an offence punishable with imprisonment of up to one year and whose trial has not commenced within a year shall be discharged or acquitted; and
- accused of an offence punishable with imprisonment of up to three years whose trial has been pending for more than two years in the criminal courts shall be discharged or acquitted and the case against them closed by the court.[14]

With a view to minimize the number of undertrial prisoners in India, the Amendment Act of 2005, introduced Section 436-A which mandates release on personal bond with or without sureties of a person who has undergone detention during investigation, inquiry or trial, for 'one-half of the maximum period of imprisonment specified for that offence'.[15] This cannot, however, be invoked by a person accused of offences punishable with the death penalty like murder.[16] The Court has the discretion to order continuation of detention after hearing the Public Prosecutor and recording the reasons for passing such an order in writing.[17] Under no circumstances should the period of detention of an undertrial exceed the maximum period of imprisonment provided for the offence.[18] The computation of the period of detention for the purposes of granting bail will not include delays caused by the accused, while in detention.[19]

---

[14] Ibid., at 703–05. Taken from NHRC Special Rapporteur Sankar Sen letter to all Inspector Generals of prisons regarding undertrial prisoners (29 April 1999) in NHRC Important Instructions/Guidelines, at *http://nhrc.nic.in/sec-5.pdf*.

[15] S. 436A CrPC.

[16] S. 436A CrPC.

[17] Proviso 1 to S.436A CrPC.

[18] Proviso 2 to S.436A CrPC.

[19] Explanation to S.436A CrPC.

Furthermore, the Supreme Court responded to the endemic problem of custodial death in *D.K. Basu* v. *State of West Bengal*,[20] and issued the following set of requirements applicable to 'all cases of arrest or detention till legal provisions are made in that behalf to prevent custodial violence':[21]

- Police officers conducting an arrest or interrogation 'should bear accurate, visible, and clear identification and name tags with their designations.'
- Police officers conducting arrest should produce a memo of arrest at the time of arrest, with at least one witness, and countersigned by the arrestee.
- An arrestee or detenu is entitled to inform his or her friend or relative, 'as soon as practicable.' (S.50A(1) CrPC)
- 'The time, place of arrest, and venue of custody of an arrestee must be notified by the police, where the next friend or relative of the arrestee lives outside the district or town through the Legal Aid Organisation in the District and the police station of the area concerned telegraphically within a period of eight to twelve hours after the arrest.'
- The arrestee must be informed of his or her right to inform someone of the arrest. (S.50A(2) CrPC)
- The records of the arrest, the name of the next friend, and the police officers holding custody must be made at the place of detention. (S.50A(3) CrPC)
- The arrestee should be entitled to an examination of his or her injuries at the time of arrest and any injuries be recorded.
- The arrestee should get a medical examination every forty-eight hours of detention by a trained doctor.
- 'Copies of all the documents including the memo of arrest, referred to above, should be sent to the Magistrate for his record.'
- 'The arrestee may be permitted to meet his/her lawyer during interrogation.'
- Police officers should be able to make the information regarding the arrest available at a police control room.[22]

6.3 CONDITIONS IN CUSTODY

The conditions in which accused persons are held in India are very poor in general, and they vary greatly depending on the circumstances of detention. Some are held in police lock-ups, and others are detained in prisons. In fact, over 70 per cent of India's over-crowded prison population are undertrials, who are yet to face trial.[23] While it is common for undertrials to

---

[20] AIR 1997 SC 610.

[21] S. 229 CrPC.

[22] *Ram Kumar* v. *State of Uttar Pradesh*, 1998 Cri LJ 1267, 1270.

[23] National Human Rights Commission, Annual Report 2001–2002, NHRC, New Delhi, 2002, at 42.

be held in prison with convicted prisoners due to the lack of space in detention facilities, the Prisons Act, 1894 provides that 'unconvicted prisoners shall be kept apart from convicted criminal prisoners.'[24] The law is based on the need to protect possibly innocent people from the potentially harmful effects of being housed with convicted criminals.

Furthermore, juvenile detenus should be held in detention facilities separate from those holding adult detenus,[25] and female detenus should be held separately from male detenus.[26] While some Southern states are beginning to have all-female police stations for holding female detenus, many other states do not have such facilities yet.

In the landmark case of *Sheela Barse* v. *State of Maharashtra*,[27] the Supreme Court treated a letter from a journalist as a writ petition concerning alleged assaults on women in police lock-up in Bombay, and issued the following directions:

- Female suspects should be kept in different police lock-ups from male suspects and be guarded by female constables.
- Female suspects should only be interrogated in the presence of female police officers.
- As soon as a person is arrested, he or she should be apprised of the grounds of arrest and his or her rights.
- The police must immediately inform a nominated friend or relative of the accused, of the fact and place of detention.
- Judges should make surprise visits to police lock-ups.
- When an accused is brought before a Magistrate, the Magistrate should ask if he or she has been tortured or maltreated while in police custody, and advise on the right to a medical examination.
- Lawyers from the District Legal Aid Committee should be advised of the fact of detention, and be allowed to meet with the detenu.[28]

The fact that a person is detained as an undertrial does not mean that the person has forfeited his or her basic rights.[29] The Indian courts have affirmed that even convicted prisoners retain all of their human rights, except the right to freedom of movement.[30]

---

[24] S. 27(3) Prisons Act, 1894; see also U.N. GA Resolution 43/173, Principles for the Protection of All Persons under Any Form of Detention or Imprisonment, Principle 8 (1988) [hereinafter Principles for the Protection of All Persons].

[25] U.N. GA Resolution 45/113, UN Rules for Protection of Juveniles Deprived of their Liberty, Section III, 17 (1990)[hereinafter Rules for Protection of Juveniles].

[26] *Sheela Barse* v. *State of Maharashtra*, 1983 SCR (2) 337.

[27] *Sheela Barse* v. *State of Maharashtra*, 1983 SCR (2) 337.

[28] *Hussainara Khatoon* v. *State of Bihar*, AIR 1979 SC 1360, 1361, 1362.

[29] For example, the Supreme Court ordered a release and compensation to a prisoner who had been detained in jail for 14 years after his acquittal in *Rudul Sah* v. *State of Bihar*, 1983 AIR 1086.

[30] See generally discussion of cases in Dr B. Hydervali, *Regulating the Treatment of Criminal Defendants: Trends, Issues and Challenges*, 1996 Cri LJ 57, 59; See also Chapter 4: 'Dealing With the Accused.'

6.4 TORTURE IN CUSTODY

Custodial violence by police is a widespread problem in India. Both domestic law and international human rights instruments impose strict parameters for police's handling of detenus. The Supreme Court has been trying to protect the rights of victims through court decisions, yet torture and ill-treatment of detenus continue to pose a serious problem in India.

Torture and ill-treatment of detenus of any kind, whether physical or psychological, and deprivation or other attempts to induce statements or confessions, is strictly prohibited. The Indian Government is also committed to follow the provisions of the ICCPR, which prohibits torture or cruel, inhuman or degrading treatment or punishment.[31] India has signed the Convention Against Torture and Other Cruel, Inhuman, and Degrading Treatment or Punishment, which proffers a thorough guideline in order to effectuate the universal ban on torture.[32]

The Supreme Court of India has also laid down guidelines on treatment of those in custody, to protect them from abuse. For example, the Supreme Court provided procedural safeguards by holding that handcuffing of prisoners is cruel and degrading treatment under Article 5 of the Universal Declaration of Human Rights.[33] Solitary confinement of detenus was also denounced by the Court as an unsuitable form of detention, that should be avoided.[34]

The Supreme Court also went further to award compensation to victims of custodial violence who suffered physical and psychological torture, and ordered prosecution of police officers responsible for such crimes.[35] For instance, in *Arvinder Singh Bagga* v. *State of U.P.*, the Supreme Court awarded compensation of rupees ten thousand to the abused wife and husband each 'who were illegally detained and humiliated for no fault of theirs,' and ordered 'the State of Uttar Pradesh [to] take immediate steps to launch prosecution against all the police officers involved in [the] sordid affair.'[36]

The NHRC has also been making an effort to reduce the custodial violence by issuing a guideline that any incident of custodial death or rape must be informed to the NHRC within 24 hours of occurrence.[37] Furthermore, the NHRC has directed the police, in a case of death in custody, to submit a post-mortem report, videography report on the post-mortem examination, an inquest report, a magisterial enquiry report, and a chemical analysis report in order to prevent the police from distorting evidence relating to the death.[38]

---

[31] Article 7 ICCPR.

[32] U.N. Convention Against Torture and Other Cruel, Inhuman or Degrading Treatment or Punishment [*signed on* 14 Oct. 1997].

[33] *Sunil Batra* v. *Delhi Administration* (I), 1979 SCR (1) 392, 396.

[34] *Sunil Batra* v. *Delhi Administration* (II), 1980 SCR (2) 557, 560.

[35] *Arvinder Singh Bagga* v. *State of U.P.*, 1994 SCC (6) 565.

[36] S. 219 CrPC.

[37] National Human Rights Commission, Annual Report 2001–2002, NHRC, New Delhi, 2002, at 32.

[38] Ibid., yet, the recommendation of requiring video-filming of post-mortem examination has not be complied with in some states such as Manipur, Uttar Pradesh, and Maharashtra.

Finally, it should be noted that despite earnest attempts by the Supreme Court to curb torture and deaths in custody, these crimes are still very prevalent in India. Thus, it is crucial for individuals to be aware of all their rights while in custody and to actively demand them, particularly those mentioned in Chapter 4: 'Rights When Arrested.'

6.5 WRIT OF *HABEAS CORPUS*

When a person is detained, and if there is some reason to suspect that he or she is unsafe in custody or there are no legal grounds for the person's detention, one can file a petition with the appropriate High Court or the Supreme Court of India for a 'writ of *habeas corpus*'.[39] A writ of *habeas corpus* is an order from the court demanding that the detaining officer present the detained person before the court, and inform the court of the grounds of the detenu's confinement. If it is revealed that there are no lawful grounds for the detainment, the detenu should be released. Otherwise, the detention is sustained, and the regular bail procedure should be followed.

When the detenu is presented before the court by means of the *habeas corpus* writ, the court can also ascertain whether or not the detenu has been tortured or mistreated by the police or anyone else while in detention.

A writ of *habeas corpus* can be filed either by the detained person or by a relative or friend on his or her behalf. The application for a writ of *habeas corpus* must be accompanied by a report stating the circumstances of the imprisonment. A writ of *habeas corpus* need not be a formal document. It may be a letter or telegram to the court setting out the circumstances of the detention.[40] An advantage of a telegram is that it is an officially timed and dated document. If the police later claims that the person was not arrested, or was arrested at a later date, the telegram can effectively be used as evidence of the details of the detention.

While there is no limitation period on petitioning the court for a writ of *habeas corpus*, the sooner the petition is lodged, the greater is its chances of success.[41] When filing a writ, the petitioner should always keep a copy of the request for *habeas corpus*.

The *habeas corpus* writ has long been used as a method of preventing and discovering illegal detentions, and also as a vital checking mechanism to ensure that the detenu has not been abused. It provides an instant determination as to the legality of an existing detention, and, if exercised, protects detenus from incommunicado and indefinite detention by unscrupulous police officers. For these reasons, it is important to be fully aware of the existence of and procedures relating to the exercise of the *habeas corpus* writ petition.

---

[39] Articles 32 (Supreme Court) and 226 (High Court) Constitution.
[40] *Sunil Batra Kishore Singh* v. *State of Rajasthan*, AIR 1981 SC 625.
[41] *P.S. Sadasivaswamy* v. *State of Tamil Nadu*, 1975 SCR (2) 356, 357.

Box 6.1   Example—Writ of *Habeas Corpus*

Lachuman Singh
Sardar Patel Bhawan
Sansad Marg
New Delhi 110 001

14 January 2003

The Honourable Chief Justice
High Court of Delhi
New Delhi

Dear Sir,

I write to you as a petition of *habeas corpus*. At 11.20 pm on 8 January 2003, my husband, Ranjit Singh was arrested at our home by Police Sub-Inspector Madhu Limaye of Sansad Marg Police. His badge number was SI 483320. Sub-Inspector Madhu said that my husband is involved in a conspiracy against a public official and that he is under arrest. Three other police officers entered our home and dragged my husband out, kicking and abusing him. I have not heard from him since. That was six days ago.

My husband is a taxi driver. Ranjit has never been in any trouble with the police and is a law-abiding citizen. There is no way that he was involved in any conspiracy. I do not know where my husband is being detained. I do not even know if he is alive.

I ask that you issue a writ of *habeas corpus* and order the Delhi Police to produce my husband before a court, and state the charges with which he has been charged. Please contact me should you require further information.

Yours respectfully,

Lachuman Singh

6.6 PREVENTIVE DETENTION

Preventive detention is the holding of a person in custody based on a suspicion or reasonable probability that the person will commit an illegal act, in light of his or her past behaviour.[42] Preventive detention is not intended to punish past offenders, but is rather a precautionary measure against future crimes.[43] Article 22(4) to (7) of the Constitution provide protection against preventive detention, yet those provisions allow the central and state governments to prescribe their own laws regarding preventive detention.

The courts have held that preventive detention laws should only be exercised in rare cases, where the larger interests of the state demand restrictions on the potential future activities

---

[42] *A.K. Gopalan v. State of Madras*, 1950 SCR 88, 249–50.
[43] *A.K. Gopalan v. State of Madras*, 1950 SCR 88, 249–50.

of citizens.[44] However, there is a multitude of preventive detention laws in India at both the union and state levels, and they are exercised broadly by the empowered authorities.

Rights of Persons under Preventive Detention

A person who has been preventively detained has the following rights:

- To be informed of the grounds of arrest.[45] This right extends to being furnished with sufficient particulars of the grounds of detention as soon as possible to enable the detenu to make a representation against the charge.[46] For instance, under the National Security Act 1980, the detenu should ordinarily find out the grounds for detention within five days, or within ten days in exceptional circumstances.[47] The Courts decide what constitutes a reasonable length of time.[48]

- To be given the earliest possible opportunity to make a representation against the order.[49] Any unexplained delay in securing representation may result in the quashing of the detention.[50]

- To be reviewed by an Advisory Board within three months of preventive detention.[51]

- While in custody 'the restrictions placed on a person preventively detained must, consistently with the effectiveness of detention, be minimal.'[52]

- While in detention, detenus should be permitted to wear their own clothing, eat their own food, receive visits from their family members at least once a week, and have reasonable reading and writing materials.[53] However, this right may be restricted in the case of hardened criminals.

- Detenus should be segregated from convicted offenders and separately lodged.[54] Furthermore, females detenus must be kept separate from male detenus,[55] and juvenile detenus should be held separately from adult ones.[56]

---

[44] *Sakeenal Beevi and Ors* v. *State of Karnataka*, 1997 Cri LJ 1583.

[45] Article 22(5), Constitution of India; S. 50 CrPC.

[46] *K.M.Agrawale v. Union of India* (1975) 4 SCC 481.

[47] S.8 National Security Act, 1980 (NSA).

[48] M.P. Jain, Indian Constitutional Law; 5th edition, volume I (New Delhi: Wadhwa and Company, Nagpur, 2003) at 1345–9. Detention orders have been quashed as a result of delay, see e.g. *Pritam Nath Hoon* v. *Union of India*, AIR 1981 SC 92; *Mangalbhai Motiram* v. *State of Maharashtra*, AIR 1981 SC 510: (1980) 4 SCC 470.

[49] Article 22(6), Constitution of India. Article 22(5).

[50] See *State of Andhra Pradesh* v. *Balajangam Subbarajamma*, 1988 SCR Supl. (3) 620, 631.

[51] Constitution of India. Article 22(4), amend. 44, S. 3.

[52] *Sampat Prakash* v. *State of Jammu and Kashmir*, 1969 SCR (3) 574, 580.

[53] *A.K. Roy* v. *Union of India*, 1982 SCR (2) 272, 278.

[54] *A.K. Roy* v. *Union of India*, SCR (2) 272, 278.

[55] See *Sheela Barse*.

[56] Rules for Protection of Juveniles, *supra* note 24.

- The relatives of the detenu have a right to be informed in writing of the fact and place of detention. They should also be advised of any transfer of the detenu during the course of the detention.[57]

Representation and Advisory Board

One of the fundamental rights of a detenu is to be permitted to make a representation to the detaining authority. Upon representation, the government authority can then either release the detenu or send the case to an Advisory Board.

An Advisory Board is generally comprised of present or past High Court judges or those qualified to be a judge of the High Court.[58] While it is not a judicial body, therefore not bound by the procedure of the courts, a mandatory review by an Advisory Board is one of the important protections provided by the Constitution.

To better safeguard a detenu's constitutional right to representation, in *Jayanarayan Sukul v. State of West Bengal*,[59] the Supreme Court set out the following four principles:

- The representation should be heard and considered by the appropriate government authority as soon as possible. The appropriate authority should be the authority that ordered the detention.
- The consideration of the detenu's representation by the appropriate authority is independent of any action by the Advisory Board, including the consideration of the representation of the detenu by the Advisory Board.
- There should not be any delay in the consideration of the representation.
- The appropriate authority should exercise its opinion and judgement on the representation before sending the case, along with the detenu's representation, to the Advisory Board.[60]

After representation, the government may release the detenu without sending the matter to the Advisory Board, or the government may not release the detenu and send the case, along with the detenu's representation, to an Advisory Board. No reasons are required to be given for rejecting the detenu's representation.[61]

Before an Advisory Board, a detenu has the right to offer oral and documentary evidence stating his or her case, although there is no right to cross-examine in the proceedings.[62] Also, unlike a trial, the proceedings of the Board are not open to the public.[63]

---

[57] *D.K. Basu*, 1997 SC 610, 611.

[58] Article 22(4), amend. 44 Constitution of India.

[59] *Jayanarayan Sukul* v. *State of West Bengal*, 1970 SCR (3) 225, 232.

[60] *Jayanarayan Sukul* v. *State of West Bengal*, 1970 SCR (3) 225, 232.

[61] *Bhut Nath Mete* v. *State of West Bengal*, 1974 SCR (3) 315, 326.

[62] *A.K. Roy* v. *Union of India*, 1982 SCR (2) 272, 278.

[63] *A.K. Roy* v. *Union of India*, 1982 SCR (2) 272, 278.

A detenu can request the aid of a lawyer, but he or she does not have a right to be represented by a lawyer before the Board.[64] However, if the detaining authority has legal representation before the Board, then a detenu should also be allowed representation.[65] On the other hand, a detenu is always entitled to assistance by a friend who is not a legal practitioner,[66] but he or she must make a request to the Board to allow this, rather than expecting these rights to be offered as a matter of course.

If the Board is not consulted within two months of the detention, the detention becomes illegal and the detenu is entitled to be released.[67] Furthermore, the remedy of *habeas corpus* is available for preventive detention cases.[68]

Upon the Advisory Board's review of a preventive detention case, if the Board finds that there are no grounds for detention, the detenu should be released immediately, or he or she is otherwise eligible for compensation.[69] If the Advisory Board reports that the detention is justified, then the detaining authority may decide the period of detention, as the Advisory Board has no power to determine the appropriate length of detention.[70] The period of detention, however, may not be longer than the maximum period prescribed by an act of Parliament for the given class of detenus.[71]

A person may not be preventively detained for longer than three months unless:

- the Advisory Board holds before the expiration of the three months that there is sufficient cause for the detention; or
- he or she is detained under any preventive detention law made by Parliament.[72]

The Parliament may make laws specifying circumstances in which a class of people may be detained for a period longer than three months without obtaining an opinion of the Advisory Board.[73] The Parliament may be either that of the central government, or a state legislative assembly,[74] and there are no limits to the maximum period of detention that may be set by Parliament, except for the requirement of reasonableness in the circumstances.[75] For instance, under the Jammu and Kashmir Public Safety Act, based on the confirmation by the Advisory Board, a person can be detained for one year for 'acting in any manner prejudicial to the

---

[64] *Hussainara Khatoon* v. *State of Bihar*, AIR 1979 SC 1360, 1361, 1362; see also *Phillipa Anne Duke* v. *State of Tamil Nadu*, 1982 SCR (3) 769.

[65] *A.K. Roy* v. *Union of India*, 1982 SCR (2) 272, 344–345.

[66] Ibid., at 345. *Hussainara Khatoon* v. *State of Bihar*, AIR 1979 SC 1360, 1361, 1362.

[67] *Abdul Latif* v. *B.K. Jha*, 1987 SCR (2) 203, 207.

[68] See Section 5: Writ of *Habeas Corpus*.

[69] *Pramod Kumar Garg* v. *Union of India and Ors*, 1994 Cri LJ 3121.

[70] *Puranlal Lakhanpal* v. *Union of India*, 1958 SCR 460, 466.

[71] Article 22(4)(b), Constitution of India.

[72] Article 22(4), Constitution of India.

[73] Article 22(4), Constitution of India. Article 22(7)(a).

[74] *State of West Bengal* v. *Ashok Dey*, 1972 SCR (2) 434, 440.

[75] See *Fagu Shaw* v. *State of West Bengal*, 1974 SCR (2) 832, 855.

maintenance of public order or indulging in smuggling of timber;' and for a period of two years for 'acting in any manner prejudicial to the security of the State.'[76] The preventive detention laws that the union and state governments enacted include the following:

- Union Government Acts—Preventive Detention Act 1950; Maintenance of Internal Security Act (MISA) 1971; Conservation of Foreign Exchange and Prevention of Smuggling Activities Act 1974; National Security Act 1980; Prevention of Black Marketing and Maintenance of Supplies of Essential Commodities Act 1980; Prevention of Illicit Traffic in Narcotic Drugs and Psychotropic Substances Act 1988; Prevention of Terrorism Act 2002.

- State Government Acts—Andhra Pradesh Prevention of Dangerous Activities of Bootleggers, Dacoits, Drug Offenders, Goondas, Immoral Traffic Offenders and Law Grabbers Act 1986; Assam Preventive Detention Act 1980; Bihar Control of Crimes Act 1981; Chhattisgarh Special Public Security Act 2005; Gujarat Prevention of Anti-Social Activities Act 1985; Jammu and Kashmir Public Safety Act 1978; Jammu and Kashmir Prevention of Illicit Traffic in Narcotic Drugs and Psychotropic Substances Act 1988; Jammu and Kashmir Public Safety Act 1978; Karnataka Prevention of Dangerous Activities of Bootleggers, Drug-Offenders, Gamblers, Goondas, Immoral Traffic Offenders and Slum-Grabbers Act 1985; Maharashtra Prevention of Communal, Anti-Social and other Dangerous Activities Act 1980; Maharashtra Prevention of Dangerous Activities of Slumlords, Bootleggers and Drug-offenders Act 1981; Tamil Nadu Prevention of Dangerous Activities of Bootleggers, Drug-Offenders, Goondas, Immoral Traffic Offenders and Slum-Grabbers Act 1982; Rajasthan Preventive Detention Act 1970.

NSA

The National Security Act (NSA) 1980, is presently the most extensive and widely abused of these preventive laws, providing for the detention of individuals who are deemed to pose a threat to national security, public order, and the maintenance of supplies and services essential to the community.[77] This previously also applied to the Prevention of Terrorism Act 2002, which was repealed in October 2004. However, many of the provisions of POTA have been replicated in the Unlawful Activities Prevention (Amendment) Ordinance 2004.

Under the NSA, individuals can be detained for up to a year by local authorities without charges, trial or any of the other rights usually afforded to accused persons.[78]

A detenu's constitutional right for a prompt notification of the grounds of the preventive detention is also undercut by the NSA. It allows the authorities to take up to five days, or in exceptional circumstances ten days, to disclose the grounds of detention, hindering the detenu's

[76] S. 18 Public Safety Act.
[77] S. 3(2) NSA; S. 3(1)(a) POTA.
[78] S. 13 NSA.

ability to formulate representations against the detention and exercising the right to form an adequate defence.[79]

Violation of ICCPR Provisions

India is one of the few countries in the world whose constitution allows for preventive detention during peacetime without basic safeguards to protect fundamental human rights. Yet, India has ratified the ICCPR, which explicitly proscribes preventive detention.[80]

Article 4 of the ICCPR permits derogation from guaranteeing certain personal liberties during a state of emergency. However, the Indian Government has not invoked this privilege, nor could it, as the current situation in India does not satisfy the standards set forth in Article 4. Nonetheless, preventive detention is an executive act, and this decision is only to be reviewed by an Advisory Board, which too is an executive body. This results in excluding the judiciary from the decision-making process and contravenes a detenu's right to 'fair and public hearing' and to appear before an 'independent and impartial tribunal' under Article 14(1) of ICCPR.

While India's laws and policies directly violate Article 9 of ICCPR, which bans arbitrary arrest or detention and requires the grounds of arrest to be communicated at the time of arrest, India had made a reservation to Article 9 of ICCPR, stating that this article will only be applied in consonance with the section of Article 22 of the Indian Constitution.[81]

---

[79] S. 8(1) NSA.

[80] See Article 9, ICCPR.

[81] Liesbeth Lijnzaad, *Reservations to UN-Human Rights Treaties: Ratify and Ruin?*, International Studies in Human Rights Treaties, Martinus Nijhoff, Dordrecht, 1995, p. 206.

7 Trials

7.1 THE TRIAL SYSTEM

A trial is the process by which a court decides on the innocence or guilt of an accused person. The procedure for trials is found in the Code of Criminal Procedure 1973, the Indian Penal Code 1860, and the Indian Evidence Act 1872. The broader principles underlying the trial process are also found in international law,[1] and in the Constitution of India.[2]

Like many countries of the Commonwealth, India follows the adversarial system of trial. In the adversarial system, the prosecution, on behalf of the State, accuses the defendant of the commission of a crime, and must convince an independent judge of the person's guilt beyond a reasonable doubt. The accused person is then given a fair opportunity to defend himself or herself. Cases are not judged by juries in India. Trials are heard by a single judge or magistrate only. Appeals are often heard by more than one judge. The judge plays an active role[3]— examining witnesses, refereeing motions, and deciding on the guilt of the accused by weighing the facts, evidence presented, and relevant law.

The judge also plays an active role in protecting both the public interest and the human rights of the accused person. For example, only the court can frame the charge against the accused, taking into account all of the circumstances of the case.[4] Likewise, certain offences cannot be compounded without the consent of the court.[5] The court also has the power to summon and examine any person as a witness, even if that person has not been called by

---

[1] ICCPR, Articles 14, 15.

[2] Article 20 of the Constitution provides: 1. No person shall be convicted of any offence except for violation of law in force at the time of the commission for the act charged as an offence, nor be subjected to a penalty greater than that which might have been inflicted under the law in force at the time of the commission of the offence. 2. No person shall be prosecuted and punished for the same offence more than once. 3. No person accused of any offence shall be compelled to be a witness against himself.

[3] *Ram Chander v. State of Haryana*, (1981) 3 SCC 191.

[4] Ss. 228, 240 CrPC.

[5] S. 320 CrPC.

either party as a witness,[6] and to examine the accused at any time to get explanations from him or her.[7]

The adversarial system is based on the idea that the truth will emerge from the disputed facts through effective and constant challenges. In order for the truth to emerge from the adversary system, its three main components, namely, the prosecution, the defence, and the courts must perform their roles.

A. Prosecution

Cases are prosecuted either by or under the direction of public prosecutors. Cases before the Court of Sessions must be tried by a public prosecutor.[8] Generally, cases that have been instituted by a police report and not in the Court of Sessions, are tried by an assistant public prosecutor. Cases that have been instituted by a private complaint are either conducted by the complainant or by complainant's counsel. The rationale is that the state will represent itself with a public prosecutor when there has been a crime against society at large, but not for private wrongs. The court can still appoint a public prosecutor in a case instituted by a complaint if the case involves public interest.[9]

B. Defence

The accused is the one who is on trial for the commission of an offence. The accused has the right to a pleader of his choice to defend him in the Court.[10] Provisions in the code also provide for counsel for indigents (see Chapter 8: 'Legal Aid and Compensation').

C. Courts

The court and the type of trial are determined by the severity of the offence and the competence of judicial authority to try the offence. A warrant case is one relating to an offence punishable with death, imprisonment for life, or imprisonment for a term exceeding two years.[11] A summons case is any case which is not a warrant case.[12] Thus, under the CrPC there are four modes of trial (listed here from those that handle the most severe offences to the least):

1. Court of Sessions trial;
2. Magistrates' Warrant Cases;

---

[6] S. 311 CrPC.
[7] S. 313 CrPC.
[8] S. 225 CrPC.
[9] *Mukul Dalal* v. *Union of India*, (1988) 3 SCC 144.
[10] S. 303 CrPC.
[11] S. 2(x) CrPC.
[12] S. 2(w) CrPC.

3. Magistrates' Summons Cases;
4. Summary trials.

Although the different types of trials share many common features, they have significant differences as well. These differences will be discussed in section 'Separate Trial Procedures' later in this chapter.

In most cases, the High Courts and the Supreme Court will be courts of appeal only.

Jurisdiction of the Courts

Two types of jurisdiction apply to court cases: subject matter jurisdiction and territorial jurisdiction.

Subject matter jurisdiction means that a particular court is empowered to try a case of a particular nature. Such jurisdiction can easily be ascertained using S. 26 CrPC and the First Schedule. This Schedule lists the type of court that is eligible to try a particular offence. If a magistrate who is not empowered to try a case does so in violation of S. 26 CrPC, the trial proceedings will generally be void upon review.[13]

Territorial jurisdiction means that a court is in the correct location to try a case. The rules regarding territorial jurisdiction are flexible and are covered by Ss. 177–189 CrPC. The general rule is that a court will have jurisdiction if an offence was committed within its local jurisdiction.[14] When the appropriate court cannot be determined by S. 177 CrPC, special rules of jurisdiction apply.[15]

Should a court take territorial jurisdiction of a case in error, the trial will not be vitiated unless it can be shown that it has somehow resulted in a failure of justice.[16] However, this should not be used as an excuse by a court to go forward with a case, when it is aware that it has taken jurisdiction over a case in error.[17]

The court has the power to investigate people within its local jurisdiction, even if they are suspected of having committed a crime outside that jurisdiction. The magistrate is further empowered to send the suspect to the appropriate magistrate.[18] With the permission of the central government, the court's jurisdiction can also extend to Indian citizens regardless of whether or not the offence is committed in India.[19]

---

[13] S. 461 CrPC.

[14] S. 177 CrPC.

[15] Ss. 178–84 CrPC.

[16] S. 462 CrPC.

[17] *Sukhdev Singh* v. *Sukhvinder Kaur*, 1974 Cri LJ 229 (P&H HC); *Ramnath Sardar* v. *Rekharani Sardar*, 1975 Cri LJ 1139.

[18] S. 187(1) CrPC.

[19] S. 188 CrPC.

Moving a Trial

When a state government feels that it would be in the public interest to move a trial, the state government has the power to move a case to any Sessions Division as long as the High Court or Supreme Court does not disapprove.[20] In cases where two courts have taken cognizance of the same crime, the High Court has the power to decide which court will handle the case. When the two courts are not in the jurisdiction of the same High Court, the court who first took cognizance of the case shall be the only court to continue the proceedings.[21]

7.2 RIGHTS GUARANTEED FOR A FAIR TRIAL

The right to a fair trial is a fundamental human right to which all accused persons are entitled. The major objective of the laws governing criminal procedure is to provide for fair trial, and consequently the concept of fair trial is pervasive throughout the Code.

A. Presumption of Innocence

The criminal justice system presumes that an accused is innocent until the prosecution has proven the person's guilt beyond reasonable doubt.[22] The burden of proof lies on the prosecution to show that the accused is guilty—the defence must only attempt to disprove the contentions made by the prosecution.[23]

The presumption of innocence is at the heart of a fair trial process. It also underlies other areas of criminal procedure, such as the right to be released on bail. In this context, the presumption of innocence provides the basis of the rule that the accused person should not be detained until he or she is proven guilty by a court of law. This has had the practical effect of ensuring that pre-trial detention is the exception and that bail is granted in most cases. As the Supreme Court noted in *State of Rajasthan* v. *Balchand*,[24] 'bail not jail is the rule.'

One notable exception to the presumption of innocence is in cases of dowry death under S. 304B of the IPC. Under S. 113B of the IEA, if a person is suspected of committing the dowry death of a woman and he or she is shown to have subjected the woman to cruel or harassing treatment in connection with a demand for dowry before her death, the accused is presumed to be guilty. This exception was created due to the difficulty of obtaining evidence against the accused.

---

[20] S. 185 CrPC.

[21] S. 186 CrPC.

[22] *Babu Singh* v. *State of Punjab*, (1964) 1 Cri LJ 566; *K.M. Nanavati* v. *State of Maharashtra*, 1962 1 Cri LJ 521, 533.

[23] *Kali Ram* v. *State of H.P.*, (1973) 2 SCC 808: 1973 SCC (Cri) 1048, 1059: 1974 Cri LJ 1, 9.

[24] AIR 1977 SC 2447.

B. Independent, Impartial, and Competent Judges and Courts

The Code provides for this aspect of a fair trial by ensuring that the Judiciary is separate from the Executive, and operates free from any executive control or influence.[25] This is necessary because these branches compose two of the three components of the adversary system. This principle has been codified in Article 50 of the Constitution. Article 50 has been enacted in S. 479 CrPC, which states that no magistrate shall try or commit for trial in any case, which he is personally involved without the permission of the court to which appeal would lie.

The judge or magistrate overseeing a trial must not be connected with or have any personal interest in the prosecution.[26]

The court is also forbidden from trying offences that it has initiated or which have occurred in its presence.[27] These offences generally consist of contempt and false production of evidence and are specifically enumerated in S. 195 CrPC. The only exceptions to this are found in Ss. 344, 345, 349, and 350 CrPC and consist of summary procedure for trial for giving false evidence, procedure in certain cases of contempt, summary procedure for punishment of a person refusing to answer or produce documents, and summary procedure for non-attendance by a witness in obedience to summons.

Furthermore, the courts are empowered to transfer cases where it appears that a fair and impartial inquiry cannot be had in the current court. The power to transfer varies with the level of the court.[28] In cases where the magistrate is not empowered to give an appropriate sentence, he can transfer the case to the appropriate official.[29] In cases where the magistrate finds that he is either unable to dispose of the case or that the case should be committed to the Court of Sessions, the magistrate is also empowered to transfer the case to the appropriate authority.[30]

C. Right to a Public Trial

During a trial, the public should be allowed free access to the courtroom, to the extent that the courtroom can hold people.[31] This is to guarantee public scrutiny of the trial process and assure a fair trial, which is considered 'the first imperative of the dispensation of justice.'[32]

---

[25] S. 6 CrPC.

[26] S. 479 CrPC.

[27] S. 352 CrPC.

[28] Ss. 406–408 CrPC.

[29] S. 325 CrPC.

[30] Ss. 322–323 CrPC.

[31] S. 327 CrPC.

[32] Confirmed in *Commissioner of Police Delhi and Anr* v. *Regional Delhi High Court, New Delhi*, 1997 Cri LJ 90.

However the right to a public trial is qualified by several exceptions

- Where the trial should be closed in the public interest;[33]
- Where a public trial would result in prejudice to the accused;
- Where the judge or magistrate thinks that the public generally, or a particular person should not have access to, or remain in the room.[34] For example, this may occur when obscene matters are being canvassed during a trial.[35]
- Where the trial is of an offence involving rape.[36] This exception is to encourage women who have been raped to testify against the perpetrators. In India, as in many societies, a great deal of social shame is attached to being raped. Holding trials for this crime in open court would only further discourage women from coming forward and testifying against rapists. Therefore, trials for rape are not open to the public. However, it has yet to be explicitly legislated that cases where the victim is a child who has suffered abuse, sexual or otherwise, should always be held *in camera*. Therefore, whether such cases are held in public or *in camera* is still a matter of discretion left to individual judges. However, where the child is a juvenile, the case will be held in open court, but in a special juvenile court separate from the trial of adults.
- The Unlawful Activities Prevention (Amendment) Ordinance allows trials to be conducted *in camera* at the order of the court, and allows the proceedings of such trials to remain unpublished.

D. Speedy Trial

Courts have interpreted Article 21 of the Constitution to guarantee the right to a speedy trial.[37] The requirement of swift justice applies to all stages of the criminal process—investigation, inquiry, trial, appeal, revision, and retrial.[38] Once the examination of witnesses has begun, it shall continue day to day until all the witnesses in attendance have been examined, unless the Court finds the adjournment to be necessary for reasons that must be recorded.[39]

The right to a speedy trial is particularly vital to the protection of the accused person's human rights where they have not been granted bail and are awaiting trial in pre-trial detention. In this context, the right of the accused to be released on bail if the trial is not completed within sixty days under S. 437(6) of the CrPC is relevant.

---

[33] *Naresh Shridar Mirajkar* v. *State of Maharashtra*, 1996 SCR (3) 744 at 804.

[34] S. 327(1) CrPC.

[35] *In re: M.R. Venkataraman*, AIR 1950 Mad 441 at 442.

[36] S. 327(2) CrPC.

[37] *Hussainara Khatoon* v. *Home Secretary, State of Bihar*, AIR 1979 SC 1369.

[38] *Abdul Rehman Antulay and Ors* v. *R.S. Nayak and Anr*, 1992 (1) S.C.C. 225; AIR 1992 SC 1701.

[39] S. 309(1) CrPC.

The court should consider the following factors when assessing whether a trial has been unacceptably delayed:[40]

- Whether the accused is responsible for the delay.
- Whether the accused is prejudiced by such delay in any manner, recognizing that in some cases the delay may itself amount to prejudice; and
- The nature of the offence with which the accused is charged.

What is 'too long' depends on the circumstances of the case and the above factors. However, courts have found that anything from two years to eighteen years constitutes a sufficient delay to necessitate release.[41]

Once the court finds that the constitutional guarantee of a speedy trial has been violated, the accused may be unconditionally released.[42] However, the Supreme Court has held that the appropriate response to an excessive delay in trial will depend on what is 'just and equitable in the circumstances of the case.'[43]

In its latest decision in this regard, that of *P. Ramachandra Rao* v. *State of Karnataka*,[44] the court has, while upholding the right to speedy trial, emphasized that the this does not entail the mandatory termination of cases once a particular period of time has lapsed. This was in recognition of the fact that there could be no strict time period after which a case would terminate, the decision on whether a case had been delayed so as to become oppressive on the accused would have to be evaluated by the judges, taking into account all relevant factors.

There are some situations where the continuation of a trial is an abuse of the law. One such circumstance is if a trial is lengthy and/or adjourned on flimsy grounds, particularly if the defendant is in pre-trial detention that is prolonged because of such adjournment. For example, in a group criminal trial, if even one of the accused is not present for trial, the case may be adjourned on this account alone. This leaves the other accused vulnerable, particularly if they are in pre-trial detention.

E. Right of the Accused to Know the Accusation

Under the CrPC, an accused person must be informed of the particulars of the offence when brought before the court for trial.[45] This right is essential to the conduct of a fair trial because unless the accused person is aware of and understands the offence with which he or she is accused, he or she will not have an adequate opportunity to formulate a defence.

---

[40] See *State of Maharashtra* v. *Champalal Punjabi Shah*, (1981) 3 S.C.C. 610.

[41] Hasan J in *State* v. *Maksudan Singh and Ors*, AIR 1986 Parna 38; *Mehmood Mirza* v. *The Assistant Collector of Customs (Preventive), Bombay*, 1997 Cri LJ 181 at 183.

[42] *State* v. *Muksudan Singh and Ors*, AIR 1986 Patna 38 at 41.

[43] *Abdul Rehman Antulay and Ors* v. *R.S. Nayak and Anr*, 1992 (1) SCC 225; AIR 1992 SC 1701.

[44] AIR 2002 SC 1856.

[45] See, for example, Ss. 228, 240, 246, 251 CrPC.

In addition, before the accused is brought to trial, he or she should be provided with the FIR, all police reports, any recorded confession, and all of the witness statements.[46] All copies of these documents should be provided, not just those upon which the prosecution intends to rely.[47]

F. Right of the Accused to be Present at Trial

An important element of a fair trial is that the accused be present at trial, during the taking of evidence.[48] As discussed above in Chapters 4 and 5, it is vital that the accused is present at the trial to be able to formulate for himself or herself a proper defence against the charges. This is because the presence of the accused throughout the trial enables him or her to understand the details of the prosecution case against them as it unfolds, and thus prepare rebuttals of the relevant evidence.[49] This also means that evidence in the trial must also only be taken in the presence of the accused.[50]

The only exception to this general rule is where the judge or magistrate is satisfied that the personal attendance of the accused is either unnecessary or would disrupt the court proceedings.[51] In this event the judge or magistrate must record their reasons for so deciding.[52] In the event that the accused is unable to attend the trial, his or her advocate is entitled to attend.[53]

G. Right of the Accused to Cross-examine Prosecution Witnesses

Cross-examination is seen as a fundamental aspect of the right to a fair trial, because evidence which has been tested under cross-examination is generally thought to be more reliable than evidence which is not. Therefore, a criminal trial which denies the accused person the right to cross-examine prosecution witnesses is considered an illegality that not even consent can cure and the trial should be vitiated.[54]

H. The Right Against Self-Incrimination

The accused may be called as a witness and can give evidence under oath to disprove the charges. However, the accused can only be called as a witness if he chooses to do so.[55] If the

---

[46] Ss. 207, 208, 238 CrPC.

[47] *Ranjeet Singh* v. *State of Uttar Pradesh and Anr*, 1998 Cri LJ 1297, 1299.

[48] S. 273 CrPC.

[49] S. 273 CrPC

[50] S. 273 CrPC.

[51] S. 317 (1) CrPC.

[52] S. 317 (1) CrPC.

[53] S. 273 CrPC.

[54] *Sukanraj* v. *State of Rajasthan*, AIR 1967 Raj 267; 1967 Cri LJ 1702.

[55] S. 315 CrPC.

accused does not give evidence, this cannot be held against him or her, and should not be commented on by parties to the trial.[56] This is in order to uphold the right of the accused against self-incrimination. Alternatively or additionally, the accused can present a written statement to the court, which the magistrate must file with the record of the proceedings.[57]

I. Doctrine of 'Autrefois Acquit' and 'Autrefois Convict'

If a person is tried and acquitted or convicted of an offence by a competent court, he or she cannot then be tried again for the same offence, or on the same facts for any other offence. This is to avoid malicious and unnecessary prosecutions, which would cause unfairness and harassment of the accused. Article 20(2) of the Constitution of India prohibits prosecution and punishment for the same offence more than once. This protection cannot, however, be availed by an accused who has been acquitted a significant limitation on the right. However, Section 300 of the CrPC extends the protections to person who may have been acquitted.

7.3 COMMENCEMENT OF PROCEEDINGS

A. Cognizance

Trial proceedings commence after a magistrate takes cognizance of an offence pursuant to S. 190 CrPC. This section allows for a magistrate to take cognizance of an offence for one of three reasons: (1) upon receiving a complaint of facts which constitute an offence; (2) upon a police report of such facts; or (3) upon his own knowledge, howsoever acquired, that such offence has been committed.[58] The decision to take cognizance of a crime is the magistrate's, and while the magistrate should review the police recommendation, if any, the magistrate is not bound by it.[59]

If a magistrate takes cognizance of a crime through knowledge that he has acquired on his own, as detailed in S. 190(1)(c) CrPC, several restrictions will apply. First, if it can be shown that the magistrate did not have jurisdiction or was not empowered to act in that case, the proceedings will be vitiated.[60] The proceedings will not be vitiated if a magistrate erroneously takes cognizance pursuant to Ss. 190(1)(a) and 190(1)(b) CrPC as long as it can be shown that the magistrate was genuinely mistaken and acted in good faith.[61] Secondly, a magistrate taking cognizance pursuant to S. 190(1)(c) CrPC must inform the accused that he or she has the right to choose a new magistrate who will be chosen by the Chief Judicial Magistrate.[62]

---

[56] S. 315 CrPC.

[57] S. 233(2) CrPC.

[58] S. 190(1) CrPC.

[59] *Harihar Chaitanya* v. *State of U.P.*, 1990 Cri LJ 2082, 2084.

[60] S. 461(k) CrPC.

[61] *Purshottam Jethanand* v. *State of Kutch*, AIR 1954 SC 700; 1954 Cri LJ 1751.

[62] S. 191 CrPC.

A magistrate cannot take cognizance of certain offences unless the complaint is either filed by the aggrieved party or the appropriate authority gives authorization. These restrictions are meant to protect the government and private parties from frivolous and embarrassing complaints. Examples of such offences include those against public justice,[63] offences against the state,[64] and the offence of defamation.[65]

B. Summons

If after taking cognizance of an offence a magistrate is satisfied that there are sufficient grounds for proceeding, he or she will issue process to ensure the presence of the accused at the trial. Depending on the type of offence, the magistrate will either issue a warrant for the arrest of the accused or a summons.[66] Before issuing a warrant or a summons, the magistrate must wait for the prosecution to file a witness list.[67] For a more detailed discussion of this process, see Chapter 4: 'Dealing with the Accused.' At this stage, the magistrate need only be *prima facie* satisfied that there are grounds for proceeding.

The power of a superior court to quash the process of a magistrate is limited, as the magistrate need only make a *prima facie* showing of evidence. However, the Supreme Court did lay out some grounds for the quashing of process in *Nagawwa* v. *Veeranna*,[68] holding that process could be quashed where the complaint is not properly formed; where the allegations made in the complaint are patently absurd; where the discretion of the magistrate was exercised capriciously; and where the complaint suffers from fundamental legal defects, such as being proffered by an unauthorized party. To quash process, a petition should be filed to the High Court pursuant to S. 482 CrPC.

When a magistrate issues a summons, he may also decide that the accused may appear at the trial through his pleader.[69] In fact, a magistrate may find that the accused may be represented by his pleader at any stage of the trial so long as the presence of the accused is not necessary for the interests of justice or the accused is a persistent nuisance at the trial.[70] The general rule is that for cases involving moral depravity, the presence of the accused will be required at the trial. However, when the case is of a technical nature or is punishable by a fine, an accused can generally be represented by his pleader. In deciding whether the presence of the accused is required, the court should take into consideration the hardship that a court appearance will place upon the accused.

---

[63] Ss. 193–196, 199, 200, 205–11 IPC.

[64] Ss. 121–130, 153-A, 153-B, 295-A, 505 IPC.

[65] Ss. 499–502 IPC.

[66] S. 204(1) CrPC.

[67] S. 204(2) CrPC.

[68] AIR 1976 SC 1947; (1976) 3 SCC 736; 1976 Supp. SCR 123; 1976 Cri LJ 1533.

[69] S. 205(1) CrPC.

[70] S. 317 CrPC.

C. Special Summons in Cases of Petty Offence

Section 206 of CrPC allows the accused to enter a plea of guilty and pay the fine amount without appearing in court if:

- The offence is either:
    a. Punishable by a fine of less than one thousand rupees;
    b. Compoundable under S. 320 CrPC; or
    c. Punishable with imprisonment for less than three months;
- The fine amount specified on the summons is no greater than one hundred rupees,
- The magistrate is of the opinion that the case may be summarily disposed of under S. 260 CrPC, which provides for summary trials; and
- The offence is not already covered by existing legislation that provides for expedited process.

If the accused qualifies for this procedure, the accused need only remit a plea of guilty to the court along with the fine amount on the specified date.[71]

D. Document Production and Information to the Accused

Without delay and free of cost, the accused has a right to certain documents. The accused must have access to the list of prosecution witnesses that must be filed in court before the issuance of service process.[72] In a case instituted by the complaint, a copy of the complaint must be issued with the service process.[73]

The magistrate may decide that certain documents are too voluminous to be reproduced for the accused, and instead of providing the accused with a copy, provide the accused with an opportunity to review the documents.[74]

In a case instituted by a police report, the accused should receive a copy of the following:[75]

- The police report;
- The first information report recorded under S. 154 CrPC;
- The statements recorded under sub-section (3) of S. 161 CrPC of all persons whom the prosecution proposes to examine as its witnesses;
- The confessions and statements, if any, recorded under S. 164 CrPC; and
- Any other document or relevant extract thereof forwarded to the magistrate with the police report under sub-section (5) of S. 173.

---

[71] S. 206 CrPC.
[72] S. 204(2) CrPC.
[73] S. 204(3) CrPC.
[74] S. 207 CrPC.
[75] S. 207 CrPC.

A police officer may request that certain evidence not be provided to the accused under S. 173(6) CrPC; however, in accordance with S. 207 CrPC the magistrate has the final say in this matter.

Whereas S. 173(7) allows the police to provide the accused with copies of relevant documents at their convenience, S. 207 CrPC requires a magistrate to provide the accused with copies of the relevant documents without delay.

In a case not instituted by a police report but exclusively triable by the Court of Sessions:[76]

- The statements recorded under Ss. 200, 202 CrPC of all persons examined by the magistrate;
- The statements and confessions, if any, recorded under Ss. 161, 164 CrPC; and
- Any documents produced before the magistrate on which the prosecution proposed to rely.

To find out if a case is exclusively triable by the Court of Sessions, the First Schedule should be consulted.[77]

A magistrate's failure to ensure that documents are produced for the accused pursuant to Ss. 207 and 208 CrPC, is a serious irregularity that could vitiate the trial. However, the trial will only be vitiated if the error has prejudiced the accused in his defence so as to result in a failure of justice.[78] For the purpose of determining if there has been reversible error, the court must examine the police record.

E. The Charge

Charge is the formal accusation made against the accused. The main provisions regarding the charge are contained in Ss. 211–224, 464 CrPC (Chapter XVII). The court is in all cases responsible for framing the charge, and the charge shall be in the language of the court.

Section 211 CrPC lists the details of framing the charge. Once the magistrate issues a charge, it indicates that the accused is suspected of every legal condition required by law to constitute such offence. The charge must specify the offence with which the accused is charged. If the offence already has a specific name, it should be identified as such and if it does not, then a definition should be given such that the accused will receive notice of the matter with which he is charged. The law and section of the law against which the offence has been committed should be mentioned as well. If any previous conviction is to be held against the accused this must also be contained in the charge, but can be appended onto the charge at any time before the sentence is passed. The charge must mention the time, place, and/or object of the offence, except in the case of breach of trust in which case this requirement is relaxed.[79] When the aforementioned provisions are not sufficient to inform the accused about

---

[76] S. 208 CrPC.
[77] S. 26 CrPC.
[78] S. 465 CrPC.
[79] S. 212 CrPC.

the manner of the offence, the charge shall also contain such particulars so as to properly inform the accused of the offence.[80]

The general rule is that for every distinct offence with which any person is charged, there should be a separate charge, and every such charge should be tried separately.[81] However, there are many exceptions to this rule. If the accused commits up to three offences of the same kind within the span of one year, the accused may be tried together for all of them.[82] When the accused commits many offences in the course of one transaction, he may be tried together for those offences.[83] The Supreme Court has defined one transaction as several acts which show a unity of purpose or design.[84] When it is unknown what offence the accused has committed from a series of related offences, the accused may be charged jointly for any or all of them.[85]

A charge can also be levelled at more than one accused when the offence was committed together, when the accused is being charged with those who aided and abetted the offence, when an offence was committed jointly and pursuant to S. 219 CrPC, or when the offences occurred in the course of the same transaction, including theft, extortion, cheating, criminal misappropriation, receiving or harbouring stolen property or counterfeit property.[86]

In cases of criminal conspiracy, the Supreme Court has stated that the court that has local jurisdiction to try the crime of criminal conspiracy is empowered to try all offences committed in pursuance of that conspiracy, even if they should occur outside of the local jurisdiction of that court.[87] When joinder of charges into one trial is permissible, the court has the final say as to whether joinder will occur.[88]

The court not only has the power to frame the charge, but also the power to alter the charge once the case has begun at any time before the judgement.[89] However, the court cannot frame a charge for an entirely new offence, and must give the accused a fair chance to respond to the amended charge.[90] If the new charge is likely to prejudice the case, the court may

[80] S. 213 CrPC.

[81] S. 218 CrPC.

[82] S. 219 CrPC.

[83] S. 220(1) CrPC.

[84] *State of A.P.* v. *Cheemalapati Ganeswara Rao*, AIR 1963 SC 1850; (1963) 2 Cri LJ 671, 682; *State of Bihar* v. *Simranjit Singh Mann*, 1987 Cri LJ 999 (Pat HC); 1987 Pat LJR (HC) 417.

[85] S. 221 CrPC.

[86] S. 223 CrPC.

[87] *Purushottam Dalmia* v. *State of W.B.*, AIR 1961 SC 1589, 1593; (1961) 2 Cri LJ 728.

[88] *Ranchhod Lal* v. *State of Madhya Pradesh*, AIR 1965 SC 1248; (1965) 2 Cri LJ 253.

[89] *Kantilal Chandulal Mehta* v. *State of Maharashtra*, (1969) 3 SCC 166; 1970 SCC (Cri) 19, 23; 1970 Cri LJ 510, 514.

[90] *Kantilal Chandulal Mehta* v. *State of Maharashtra*, (1969) 3 SCC 166; 1970 SCC (Cri) 19, 23; 1970 Cri LJ 510, 514.

adjourn and direct a new trial as necessary.[91] If the court does amend a charge, it also has the power to call new witnesses as needed to adjudicate the matter.[92]

The accused may also be convicted of an offence for which he has not been formally charged. The accused can be convicted of a minor offence without being formally charged when it is a component of a major offence for which he has been charged.[93] The accused may also be convicted of an attempt to commit the crime he has been charged with, even if not specifically charged with attempt.[94] Finally, the accused may be convicted of a crime when it is unclear whether the accused committed the crime, even if the accused was not formally charged.[95]

The court and the prosecution with the assent of the court may withdraw charges if the accused is convicted of one or more other charges.[96] As with most other aspects of the criminal justice system, an omission or defect in the charge will not vitiate the proceedings, unless it can be shown that undue prejudice has been caused to the accused.[97]

7.4 SHARED FEATURES OF THE TRIAL PROCESS

As discussed above, there are four different types of trials in the criminal justice system. The type of trial that an accused will be given varies with the severity of the offence that he or she has committed. Although differences exist, the four different types of trials share some common rules of evidence, language, examination, and argument presentation.

A. Special Rules of Evidence

If the court finds that it requires the testimony of a witness who cannot attend court, it may order the examination of that witness by a commission.[98] A commission should only be used sparingly, for example, when the examination of the witness in court would involve undue amount of delay, expense or inconvenience.[99]

Normally, testimony is admitted only when it has either been given under oath or the where the opposing party has the opportunity to cross-examine the witness. However, there are certain forms of evidence for which an administration of oath or cross-examination is not necessary. These are in cases of a deposition by a medical witness, evidence from officers in

---

[91] S. 216(4) CrPC.

[92] S. 217(b) CrPC.

[93] Ss. 222(1), 222(2) CrPC.

[94] S. 222(3) CrPC.

[95] S. 221(2) CrPC.

[96] S. 224 CrPC.

[97] Ss. 215, 464 CrPC.

[98] S. 284(1) CrPC.

[99] *Dharmanand Pant* v. *State of U.P.*, AIR 1957 SC 594, 598; 1957 Cri LJ 894, 898–9.

the mint, report of certain government scientific experts, certain documents, affidavits in proof of certain matters, and proof of previous conviction or acquittal.[100]

B. Language of Trials

According to Article 348(1) of the Constitution, unless Parliament provides otherwise, all proceedings before the High Courts and the Supreme Court are to be held in the English language. However, under Article 348(2) of the Constitution, the State Governor may authorize the use of Hindi, or another language used for the official purposes of that state, in proceedings in the High Court (except with regard to any judgement, decree, or order passed or made by such High Court). The state government determines what shall be the language of all the lower courts (i.e. all except the High Court) within the state.[101] The accused and any witnesses may give their statement or evidence in a language different from that of the court.[102]

The court should take proper measures to ensure that all parties to the trial understand the proceedings. Where evidence is given in a language not understood by the accused (or his or her lawyer), it too should be interpreted in a language he or she understands.[103] If the record of the evidence is in a language different from the language it was given in, and the witness does not understand the language of the record, then the record must be interpreted for him or her.[104] If the accused does not understand the language in which the record is written, the record should be interpreted to him or her in a language he or she understands.[105] Finally, while the judgement should be recorded in the language of the court,[106] the court is required to give the accused a translation of the judgement free of cost if it is requested.[107]

C. Examination Powers of the Court

The court has significant powers of examination over both witnesses and the accused. The court can summon and examine any person as a court witness if the person's evidence appears to be essential to the just decision of a case.[108] What is essential in a particular case depends on the facts and circumstances of that particular case.[109] The court also has an obligation to examine the accused to allow them to explain themselves. The court may examine the accused

---

[100] Ss. 291–298 CrPC.

[101] S. 272 CrPC.

[102] S. 277 CrPC.

[103] S. 279(1) CrPC.

[104] S. 278(3) CrPC.

[105] S. 281(4) CrPC.

[106] S. 354(1)(a) CrPC.

[107] S. 363(2) CrPC.

[108] S. 311 CrPC.

[109] *Mukti Kumar* v. *State of W.B.*, 1975 Cri LJ 838, 840 (Cal HC).

at any point during the trial, without warning, and is required to examine the accused after the witnesses for the prosecution have been examined, unless it is a summons case, in which case this requirement is waived.[110] During this questioning, no oath shall be administered to the accused.[111] Furthermore, the accused shall not be punished for refusing to answer or answering falsely any questions.[112] However, the testimony of the accused may be used as evidence against him or her in any inquiries or trials to which he or she is party.[113]

D. Oral and Written Arguments

A side may present oral arguments after they have finished presenting their evidence. Before the conclusion of these oral arguments, the side may also submit a memorandum, which forms part of the record, to the court setting forth its arguments in support of his case.[114]

E. Contempt

The court has the power to hold a party in contempt if disrespect is shown to the court. There are five main reasons that a court will hold a party in contempt—intentional omission to produce a document; refusal to take an oath when required; refusal to answer questions by one who is legally bound to state the truth; refusal to sign a statement made to a public servant when legally required to do so; and intentional insult or interruption of a public servant sitting in judicial proceedings. These are codified in Ss. 175, 178, 179, 180, 228 IPC respectively.

The court has much leeway in punishing parties for contempt. It is empowered to punish the offending party with a fine not exceeding two hundred rupees, and in default, simple imprisonment for up to one month.[115] However, if the court finds that this punishment will not suffice, it is further empowered under S. 346 CrPC to send the offending party to a magistrate, who can then handle the case as he or she sees fit.

A witness who fails to obey a court summons to appear before a criminal court can also be punished by the court. The court can punish the offending witness with a fine not exceeding one hundred rupees.[116]

Someone who has been convicted of contempt or failure to appear for a summons may appeal the decision.[117]

---

[110] S. 313(1) CrPC.
[111] S. 313(2) CrPC.
[112] S. 313(3) CrPC.
[113] S. 313(4) CrPC.
[114] S. 314 CrPC.
[115] S. 345 CrPC.
[116] S. 350 CrPC.
[117] S. 351 CrPC.

7.5 SEPARATE TRIAL PROCEDURES

A. Court of Sessions Trial

The trial in a Court of Sessions is tried by a judge and prosecuted by a Public Prosecutor.[118]

The trial begins with the prosecutor describing the charge and giving a brief summary of the evidence he or she will use to prove the guilt of the accused.[119] After considering this statement, the record and the documents submitted, the judge may discharge the case if he or she feels there are insufficient grounds for proceeding.[120] If the judge decides to proceed, he or she will frame, or formally state in writing, the charge,[121] and then read and explain the charge to the accused.[122] If necessary, the judge may interrogate the accused to ensure that he or she fully understands the charge and the implications of making a plea.[123]

If the accused pleads guilty, the judge may exercise discretion to convict.[124] However, while a judge may convict on the basis of the plea, where the offence is serious, the court should proceed to take evidence, deciding on this basis whether the accused is guilty.[125]

If the accused pleads guilty, the trial proceeds. The prosecution calls witnesses and gives evidence to support its case,[126] and these witnesses may be cross-examined by the defence and re-examined by the prosecutor.[127] At the conclusion of the prosecution evidence, the judge is required to ask questions to the accused, so that he or she may explain his or her situation.[128] After this examination, the judge may order the acquittal of the accused.[129]

If the accused is not acquitted, the defence will present its case.[130] Like the prosecution's case, this involves calling of witnesses who may be cross-examined by the prosecutor and may be recalled by the defence.[131] Alternatively or additionally, the accused can present a written statement to the court, which the magistrate must file with the record of the proceedings.[132]

---

[118] S. 225 CrPC.

[119] S. 226 CrPC.

[120] S. 227 CrPC.

[121] S. 228(1)(b) CrPC.

[122] S. 228(2) CrPC.

[123] *Kesho Singh* v. *Emperor*, (1917) 18 Cri LJ 742.

[124] S. 229 CrPC.

[125] *Ram Kumar* v. *State of Uttar Pradesh*, 1998 Cri LJ 1267, 1270.

[126] S. 231(1) CrPC.

[127] S. 231(2) CrPC.

[128] S. 313(1)(b) CrPC.

[129] S. 232 CrPC.

[130] S. 233(1) CrPC.

[131] S. 138 IEA.

[132] S. 243(1) CrPC.

After the defence has examined its witnesses, the prosecutor will sum up the case against the accused and the defence will reply.[133] The judge will then give a judgement in the case.[134] If the accused is convicted, the judge will ask to hear submissions regarding the sentencing of the accused and then pass sentence according to the law.[135]

B. Trial of a Warrant Case by a Magistrate

When a magistrate tries a warrant case, the steps in the process vary depending on whether the case was instituted by a police report or otherwise. The steps below outline the procedure in a warrant case instituted by a police report, as they tend to be more common.

The case will once again begin with the prosecution's statement. After considering it and the pre-trial evidence both, and examining the accused, the magistrate may discharge the accused if he or she considers the charge against the accused to be groundless.[136] If the magistrate chooses not to discharge the accused, he or she will frame a charge and the accused must enter a plea.[137]

The magistrate can convict on the basis of the plea[138] or proceed to trial.[139] At the trial, the prosecution and then the defence make their cases, subject to the same procedural requirements (cross-examination and re-examination) as in a Court of Sessions trial.

After the close of the defence reply, the magistrate will give a judgement in the case,[140] and if the accused is convicted, the judge will ask to hear submissions regarding sentencing.[141]

In a case instituted by means other than a police report, the magistrate will first hear the prosecution's case before deciding whether to discharge the accused or frame a charge against him.[142]

C. Trial of a Summons Case

Summons cases are less formal than warrant cases. When the accused appears before a magistrate, he or she will be told the particulars of the alleged offence, and will be asked whether he or she pleads guilty, or has a defence to make.[143] Unlike other trials, no formal

---

[133] S. 234 CrPC.
[134] S. 235(1) CrPC.
[135] S. 235(2) CrPC.
[136] S. 239 CrPC.
[137] S. 240 CrPC.
[138] S. 241 CrPC.
[139] S. 242(1) CrPC.
[140] S. 248 CrPC.
[141] S. 248(2) CrPC.
[142] S. 246 CrPC.
[143] S. 251 CrPC.

charge is framed by the judge.[144] However, the magistrate should still state the particulars of the offence in order to inform and explain the charges to the accused.[145]

If the accused pleads guilty, the magistrate may convict on the basis of the plea.[146] If the magistrate decides to do so, he should call evidence to decide the question of sentence.[147]

If the accused does not plead guilty or the magistrate decides not to convict, the prosecution will make its case.[148] At the close of the prosecution's case, the magistrate should question the accused generally about the case presented against him, for the purpose of explicating his situation.[149] The defence will then present its case.[150]

At the end of both the prosecution and defence cases, the magistrate will either convict or acquit the accused.[151] If the accused is convicted, the magistrate will either release the offender on probation of good conduct,[152] or pass sentence on the offender, after consideration of his character and the circumstances of the offence.[153]

D. Summary Trials

Summary trials may only be tried by senior magistrates for petty crimes. The trial follows the format of the trial of a summons case, although slightly abridged.

The procedure in summary trials is the same as the procedure in trials of summons cases, except for the following:

- The maximum sentence that can be passed is three months.[154] However there is no restriction on the amount of fine that might be imposed.
- If at any time during the summary trial the magistrate believes that the case should no longer be tried summarily, the magistrate should recall any witnesses and proceed to try the case in the requisite manner.[155]
- The judgement should contain a brief statement of the reasons for the finding.[156]

---

[144] S. 251 CrPC.

[145] *State of Mysore* v. *Shivanna*, 1972 Cri LJ 1146, 1147–8.

[146] S. 252 CrPC.

[147] *Emperor* v. *Janardan Kashinath Abhyankar*, AIR 1931 Bom 195; (1931) Cri LJ 66, 68.

[148] S. 254(1) CrPC.

[149] S. 313(1)(b) CrPC.

[150] S. 254(1) CrPC.

[151] S. 255(1) CrPC.

[152] S. 360 CrPC.

[153] S. 255(2) CrPC.

[154] S. 262(2) CrPC.

[155] S. 260(2) CrPC.

[156] S. 264 CrPC.

7.6 PLEA BARGAINING

Plea-bargaining has been defined by the Law Commission of India to mean 'pre-trial negotiations between the defendant, usually conducted by the counsel and the prosecution, during which the defendant agrees to plead guilty in exchange for certain concessions by the prosecutor.'[157] The Criminal Law (Amendment) Act, 2005 has introduced Chapter XXIA on plea-bargaining within the CrPC. Plea bargaining can be resorted to only in cases involving offences that are not punishable by death, life imprisonment or imprisonment for more than seven years. Apart from the above punishment threshold, plea bargaining cannot be invoked if the 'offence affects the socio-economic condition of the country or has been committed against a woman, or a child below the age of fourteen years.'[158]

Under the Amendment legislation, [159] the only means of initiating the plea bargaining process is through a written application by the accused detailing the facts of the case. The application must be presented in the Court before whom the trial is pending.[160] The accused must also submit an affidavit stating that having understood the 'nature and extent of punishment provided under the law for the offence'; he or she has voluntarily agreed to submit the application.[161] The affidavit must also clarify that the accused has not been convicted earlier for the same offence. The statement of facts made by the accused in such an application cannot be used for any other purpose other than plea-bargaining.[162]

After receiving the application, the Court shall issue notice to the Public Prosecutor or complainant and the accused. On the date of the hearing, the Court 'shall examine the accused in camera' to ascertain whether the application has been made voluntarily.[163] If the Court is satisfied, the Public Prosecutor or complainant and the accused shall proceed to devise a 'mutually satisfactory disposition of the case which may include giving to the victim by the accused compensation and other expenses during the case…'.[164]

Section 265C sets out the guidelines for a 'mutually satisfactory disposition':

- In cases instituted on a police report, notice must be issued to the Public Prosecutor, the investigating police officer, the accused (with or without his or her pleader), and the victim in order for them to meet in order to work out the disposition
- In cases instituted other than a police report, notice will be issued only to the accused and the victim and they shall meet, to work out a disposition.

---

[157] Law Commission of India, *142nd Report on Concessional Treatment for Offenders who on their own initiative choose to plead guilty without any Bargaining, 1991*, PP–5; *http://lawcommissionofindia.nic.in/101–169/Report142.pdf.*

[158] S. 265A(1)(b) CrPC.

[159] S. 265B(2) CrPC.

[160] S. 265(1) CrPC.

[161] Supra n. 159.

[162] S. 265K CrPC.

[163] S. 265B(3) and (4) CrPC.

[164] S. 265B(3)(a) CrPC.

The Court has been vested with the responsibility of ensuring the voluntary nature of plea-bargaining meetings between the accused and the authorities.[165] If a satisfactory disposition has been reached, the Court must order compensation to the victim.[166] The Court must then proceed to hear the parties on the course of action that may be adopted in relation to the accused person—the quantum of punishment, whether he or she must be released on probation of good conduct or after admonition or dealt with under the Probation of Offenders Act, 1958.[167]

The Law Commission of India suggested that an independent authority in the form of a specially designated plea judge should assess applications for plea-bargaining.[168] However, the amendment legislation allows for the same judge who assesses a potential plea agreement for the accused, to later preside over a trial if the plea-bargaining application is not successful.[169] This has the potential to unfairly prejudice the judge against the accused from the outset, and affect the right of the accused to receive a fair and impartial trial.

7.7 STOPPING A TRIAL

The accused can escape conviction without going through the entire trial process. The accused can enter a plea before the start of the trial to bar the trial, or the trial can be stopped once it has started.

Barring a Trial

There are certain motions that an accused can file before a trial that can bar a trial from beginning: (1) jurisdictional; (2) time limitation; and (3) double jeopardy.

1. Jurisdictional questions can be of two types—subject matter and territorial. As discussed above, subject matter jurisdictional questions are more important than territorial issues, as a trial by a court without proper subject matter jurisdiction will be vitiated.[170] While territorial jurisdictional issues do not have this bite, if they are taken up before the start of a trial, a court must honour a legitimate objection and cannot hide behind the shield of S. 462 CrPC, which states that a trial will not be vitiated for issues of territorial jurisdiction unless they can be shown to have caused a failure of justice.[171]

---

[165] Proviso, S. 265C CrPC.

[166] S. 265E(a) CrPC.

[167] S. 265E(a) CrPC.

[168] Law Commission of India, 142nd Report on Concessional Treatment for Offenders who on their own initiative choose to plead guilty without any Bargaining [Law Commission 142nd Report], at 24; http://lawcommissionofindia.nic.in/101–169/index101–169.htm5.

[169] S.265B(4)(b) CrPC.

[170] S. 461 CrPC.

[171] *Sukhdev Singh* v. *Sukhvinder Kaur*, 1974 Cri LJ 229, 230 (P&H HC).

2. A case may also be barred on the ground that the case has been dormant for too long, and that the time period during which prosecution could have occurred has expired. The provisions regarding the limitation period are contained in Ss. 467–473 CrPC. The limitation periods are as follows—an offence that is punishable only with a fine has a limitation period of six months; an offence that is punishable with up to one year in prison has a limitation period of one year; and an offence that is punishable with up to three years in prison has a limitation period of three years.[172] The limitation period begins on the date that the offence is committed, or where knowledge of the offence is obtained.[173]

Courts have not made a conclusive statement as to when the offence is no longer affected by the limitation period. The Delhi High Court has ruled that the period of limitation should be understood with regards to the date the magistrate takes cognizance of the offence.[174] However, as this would unduly penalize a punctual complainant, other courts have ruled that in cases of complaints, the statute of limitation stops running once the complaint has been filed.[175]

3. A case can also be barred on grounds of double jeopardy, or *autrefois* acquit and *autrefois* convict.

Sometimes a trial may end even though the entire trial process has not been completed. There are five reasons that a trial may end prematurely.

1. Where the Offence is Compounded

Compoundable offences are those which are essentially of a private and non-serious nature. If an offence is compoundable, it means that the aggrieved party has the power to acquit the accused of all charges. Certain offences are compoundable only with the permission of the court. A list of compoundable offences, along with a list of the aggrieved parties who may compound such offences, is found in S. 320 CrPC.

2. Where the Prosecution Withdraws

A trial may also be prematurely halted at the behest of the prosecutor and the consent of the court. If the prosecutor withdraws the case before a charge has been framed by the court, the accused shall merely be discharged; if however, the prosecutor withdraws the case after the framing of the charge, the accused shall be acquitted of those offences. Certain charges against the Central Government which are listed as provisos to S. 321 CrPC cannot be withdrawn without the express permission of the Central Government. Generally, offences should be withdrawn when it is in the public interest to do so, or it appears that the charges are false.

---

[172] S. 468 CrPC.

[173] S. 469 CrPC.

[174] *Oriental Bank of Commerce* v. *Delhi Development Authority*, 1982 Cri LJ 2230, 2237–38 (Del HC).

[175] *Basavantappa Basappa Bannihalli* v. *Shankarappa Marigallappa Bannihalli*.1990 Cri LJ 360, 362 (Kant HC); *Anand R. Nerkar* v. *Rahimbi Shaikh Madar*, 1991 Cri LJ 557, 562 (Bom HC).

3. Where the Complaint is Withdrawn

There does not seem to be any provision in the code for a withdrawal of a complaint in a warrant case. However, in summons cases, the complaint may be withdrawn with the permission of the court.[176] Upon the withdrawal of the complaint, the accused shall be acquitted of the charges against him.

4. Where the Court Issues a Conditional Pardon

The court may end a trial prematurely by tendering pardon to the accused. This should only be done to gain evidence against another offender. A pardon can be tendered for offences that are triable exclusively by a Court of Sessions or by a Court of Special Judge appointed under the Criminal Law Amendment Act 1952, or where the offence is punishable with imprisonment which may extend to seven years or more with a more severe sentence.[177] The court is further empowered to give another person with similar standing a conditional pardon at any stage of the trial process before judgement is passed.[178] If the conditions of a tendered pardon are broken, the court can try the person for the offence for which pardon was given and for the offence of giving false evidence. However, the court must prove that the accused has violated the terms of his conditional pardon.[179]

5. Where the Court Orders the Termination of the Trial

The court may also order the termination of a summons case instituted otherwise than by a complaint at any stage of the proceedings. If the stoppage is made after the principal witnesses have presented evidence, the accused shall be acquitted, otherwise, he shall be discharged. The magistrate is to record his reasons for stopping a trial.[180]

7.8 JUDGMENT AND SENTENCING

After the court has passed its judgment it will be recorded pursuant to S. 354 CrPC: the judgment shall be written in the language of the court; shall contain the rationale for the decision; and shall specify the offence for which the accused is either convicted or acquitted. Metropolitan magistrates and summary trials may have abridged judgments pursuant to S. 355 CrPC.

In warrant cases, the accused has a right to be heard before sentencing.[181]

If the accused is found guilty, the court or magistrate shall hear the accused on the question of sentence and then pass sentence on him according to law. The word 'hear' has

[176] S. 257 CrPC.
[177] S. 306 CrPC.
[178] S. 307 CrPC.
[179] S. 308 CrPC.
[180] S. 258 CrPC.
[181] Ss. 235(2), 248(2) CrPC.

been used to give an opportunity to the accused to place before the court or magistrate the various circumstances bearing on the sentence to be passed against him. The hearing contemplated by Ss. 235(2) and 248(2) is not confined merely to hearing of oral submissions, but it is also intended to give an opportunity to the prosecution and the accused to place before the court facts and material relating to various factors bearing on the question of sentence, including evidence relating to contested matters.[182]

The non-compliance with the provisions of S. 235 (2) or of S. 248 (2) amounts to bypassing an important stage of the trial so that the trial, can no longer be said to be that contemplated under the Code. Such non-compliance would be considered as vitiating the order of sentence, particularly in those cases where the accused is deprived of the chance to get a lesser sentence due to absence of such a hearing.

The court shall then pass a sentence upon the accused according to law. Criminal courts have limitations as to what type of punishments they can pass on the accused. If an accused is acquitted on the grounds that he is mentally unsound, he will either be detained in safe custody or released to the custody, of a relative or friend after acquittal.[183]

7.9 PROBATION

It is possible, and often preferable, for the courts to release offenders on probation. Release on probation means the court may order that instead of being immediately sentenced, for a period of up to three years the convicted may be released on probation, with the condition that he or she maintains good behaviour during this period.[184] This means that the accused will not have to serve a prison sentence unless he or she violates the condition(s) of good behaviour. In the event that the person on probation commits a crime, he/she will likely be sent to jail.

Probation may be ordered where the courts think that the offender can be reformed and rehabilitated, without subjecting him or her to the damaging effects of serving a prison sentence in jail. Section 360 of the Code specifies that offenders who may be released on probation must satisfy any of the following criteria:

- A person over twenty-one years who is convicted of an offence punishable with only a fine or imprisonment of seven years or less.
- A person under twenty-one years of age who is convicted of an offence not punishable with death or life imprisonment.
- A woman who is convicted of an offence not punishable with death or life imprisonment.
- The offender has no previous convictions.

---

[182] *Santa Singh* v. *State of Punjab*, (1976) 4 SCC 190; 1976 SCC (Cri) 546.
[183] S. 335 CrPC.
[184] S. 360 CrPC.

- It appears to the court with regard to the age, character or antecedents of the offender, and with regard to all the circumstances of the case, that he or she should be released on probation of conduct.

The Probation of Offenders Act states that for offenders under twenty-one years of age, probation is to be the rule and imprisonment the exception.[185] This is clearly in order to prevent young persons from being exposed to the harsh conditions of jail life and to hardened criminals who may have a bad influence on them. It may also be thought that first time young offenders can be more easily rehabilitated and are less of a risk if released into society.

7.10 APPEALS AND REVISION

Although there is no automatic right of appeal, under Chapter XXIX of the Code, it is possible to appeal against a conviction in certain cases where this right is provided in law.[186] An appeal is a petition to a superior court regarding an alleged injustice or error by an inferior court. The appeal calls upon the superior court to reverse or correct the judgment or decision of the lower court.[187] The right of appeal carries with it the right to appeal the application of law, not re-hear the facts or the evidence.

The appeals system is an integral aspect of the right to a fair trial and the judicial protection of human rights. It provides a system to review court decisions and thereby ensures that any mistakes or injustices can be rectified. Where the offences in question are serious ones which would stigmatise the offender, and particularly where loss of liberty is involved, it is vital that any decision made by a court is subject to scrutiny.

An appeal is made in the form of a petition in writing to the court, accompanied by a copy of the judgement or order appealed against.[188] If the offender is in jail, the petition of appeal and copies of the accompanying documents can be given to the officer-in-charge of the jail, who should then forward these documents to the proper appellate court.[189]

The person presenting the appeal has the right to be given reasonable opportunity to be heard by the court.[190] However, if the court has good reason to believe that there are no grounds for the appeal, it may summarily dismiss it.[191] If the court dismissing the appeal is a Court of Sessions or that of the Chief Judicial Magistrate, then the court must record its reasons for dismissing the appeal.[192] This is in case the High Court comes to examine or

---

[185] S. 6, Probation of Offenders Act, 1957.

[186] *H. Parvathamma Hiremath* v. *State of Mysore*, 1966 Cri LJ 555.

[187] *Black's Law Dictionary*, 6th edn, p. 96.

[188] S. 382 CrPC.

[189] S. 383 CrPC.

[190] S. 384(1)(b) CrPC.

[191] S. 384 (1) CrPC.

[192] S. 384(3) CrPC.

revise the summary dismissal. For the same reasons, the High Court should also record its reasons for summarily dismissing a case, in case this decision comes to be examined by the Supreme Court later.

In order to appeal a conviction, legal representation is highly desirable, as appeals are conducted on the basis of the law applied in a trial, rather than on the basis of the facts of the case. Legal aid is as much a right in appeal cases as it is in other trials (see Chapter 8—'Legal Aid and Compensation').

Appeal is not possible in the following circumstances:[193]

- Where a High Court passes a sentence of imprisonment for a term not exceeding six months or a fine not exceeding rupees one thousand or both;[194]
- Where a Court of Session or Metropolitan Magistrate passes a sentence of imprisonment for a term not exceeding three months or a fine not exceeding rupees two hundred or both;[195]
- Where a first class magistrate passes only a sentence of a fine not exceeding one hundred rupees;[196]
- Where, in a case tried summarily, a magistrate passes only a sentence of fine not exceeding two hundred rupees;[197] and
- Where an accused person has pleaded guilty and been convicted on this plea, if the conviction is by a High Court, Court of Session, Metropolitan Magistrate or Magistrate of the first or second class. In this case, although the conviction cannot be appealed, the sentencing term can be appealed.[198]

The rationale underlying S. 375 is that a person who deliberately pleads guilty cannot then complain of being convicted. However, if the guilty plea is not 'real', that is it is not genuinely and voluntarily made, or has been obtained by trickery, then it does not constitute a guilty plea barred under S. 375.[199] Even if the guilty plea is genuine, this does not mean that the person has accepted the accompanying punishment irrespective of its nature or legality. For this reason the convicted person is still able to appeal the sentence if not the conviction itself. The only exception is where the High Court has passed the sentence, since it is assumed that the High Court would not make a serious error in relation to the extent or legality of the sentence.[200]

---

[193] S. 375 CrPC.

[194] S.376(a) CrPC.

[195] S. 376(b) CrPC.

[196] S. 376(c) CrPC.

[197] S. 376(d) CrPC.

[198] S. 375 CrPC.

[199] *Profulla Kumar Roy* v. *Emperor*, AIR (31)1944 Cal 120; 45 Cri LJ 517.

[200] S. 31.11, 41st report, Law Commission of India, 1969.

The above restrictions apply to all appeals, whether they occur in the Supreme Court, High Court, or Court of Sessions.

In rare circumstances, it may be possible to make an appeal to the Supreme Court. Subject to the restrictions listed above, these include:

- Where any person is convicted in a trial held by a High Court in its criminal jurisdiction, they may appeal to the Supreme Court.[201]
- Where the High Court has, on appeal, reversed an order of acquittal of an accused person and convicted and sentenced them to death, imprisonment for life or for more than ten years, this person has a right to appeal to the Supreme Court.[202]
- Where the High Court certifies any judgement, decree or final order in a case before it involves a substantial question of law as to the interpretation of the Constitution, there is a right of appeal to the Supreme Court under the Article 132(1) of the Constitution. Even where the High Court refuses to give such a certificate, where the Supreme Court is satisfied that there is a substantial question of law in relation to the Constitution it may grant special leave to appeal.[203] If leave is granted by either the High Court or the Supreme Court, then any party in the case may appeal on the ground that the law has been wrongly decided.[204]
- In some cases where the High Court has made a sentence of death, it may be possible to appeal this sentence before the Supreme Court.[205]
- Where the Supreme Court exercises its discretion under the Constitution to grant special leave to appeal from any judgement, sentence or order by any court or tribunal, except for those made by any court or tribunal constituted under any law relating to the armed forces.[206]

In some circumstances it is also possible to appeal to the High Court. This is where a person has been convicted by a Sessions Judge or Additional Sessions Judge, or where he/she or any co-accused was sentenced to seven or more years imprisonment.[207] In this situation the judgement can be suspended pending the outcome of the case.[208]

Appeal to the Court of Sessions may occur in the following circumstances under S. 374(3) CrPC:

- Where a person is convicted by a Metropolitan Magistrate, or Assistant Sessions Judge, or a Metropolitan Magistrate of the first or second class.

---

[201] S. 374(1) CrPC.

[202] S. 379 CrPC.

[203] Article 136(1), Constitution of India.

[204] Article 132 (3), Constitution of India.

[205] Article 134(1)(a), Constitution of India.

[206] Article 136, Constitution of India.

[207] S. 374(2) CrPC.

[208] *Sundararamireddi* v. *State*, 1990 Cri LJ 167; *S.M. Malik* v. *State*, 1990 Cri LJ 1919 (Delhi HC).

- Where a person is sentenced under S. 325 CrPC.
- Where an order or sentence has been passed under S. 360 by any magistrate.

In cases where a person is convicted along with a number of other co-accused, and one or more of these co-accused is granted a right to appeal, all those convicted in the case will have the same right of appeal.[209]

Occasionally, an appeal may be made against an acquittal, or by the state government against the length of a sentence.[210] However, appeal against acquittal is extremely rare because it would be akin to an attempt to put the person on trial again even after the presumption of his or her innocence had not been rebutted by the prosecution in the original trial.

[209] S. 380 CrPC.
[210] Ss. 377–378 CrPC.

8 Legal Aid and Compensation

8.1 INTRODUCTION

One of the essential elements of a fair trial is the right of the accused to be defended by a competent and qualified legal practitioner of his or her choice. The right to a fair trial cannot be realized where the accused does not have equal access to legal resources in comparison with the prosecution. Without adequate legal services, the accused will not have the means or expertise to rebut the evidence presented by the prosecution.[1]

Many people in India cannot afford a lawyer when they are accused of a crime. As a result, they are essentially denied any meaningful access to the criminal justice system.

For this reason, both international and Indian domestic law have established that an accused person who cannot procure a lawyer with his or her own resources is entitled to free legal aid at the State's expense. This right is enshrined in the ICCPR and Articles 22(1)[2] and 39(A)[3] of the Constitution of India. Through these provisions, free legal aid should be provided to ensure that access to justice is not limited by economic disadvantage.

---

[1] Legal Aid Committee (Report), (1971), p.10, para 2 (1.15).

[2] Article 22(1) confers the Right to be defended by a lawyer of his own choice. Article 22(1) reads as follows: 'No person who is arrested shall be detained in custody without being informed, as soon as may be, of the grounds for such arrest nor shall he be denied the right to consult, and to be defended by, a legal practitioner of his choice.'

[3] Article 39-A Equal Justice and Free Legal Aid reads as follows: 'The State shall secure that the operation of the legal system promotes justice, on a basis of equal opportunity, and shall, in particular, provide free legal aid, by suitable legislation or schemes or in any other way, to ensure that opportunities for securing justice are not denied to any citizen by reason of economic or other disabilities.'

It Must Always be Remembered that Legal Aid is a Right and not a Matter of Charity

Repeatedly, the Indian courts have stated that legal aid is vital for India's legal system.[4] Many judicial rulings have helped shape the rules regarding legal aid in India. In *Hussainara Khatoon*, the Supreme Court concluded that the right to free legal service is an essential ingredient of 'reasonable fair and just procedure' for an accused person, and it must be held to be implicit in the guarantee of Article 21—'Protection of Life and Liberty', in the Constitution of India. This is the constitutional right of every accused person who is unable to engage a lawyer and secure legal services 'on account of reasons such as poverty, indigence or incommunicado situation'. The State is under a mandate to provide a lawyer to an accused person if the circumstances of a case and the needs of justice so require, provided of course that the accused person does not object to the provision of such a lawyer.[5]

This right to free legal service has been reiterated in many decisions of the court, including the case of *Suk Das* v. *Union Territory of Arunachal Pradesh*, where the court held that the right to free legal services was a fundamental right which is not conditional upon the accused applying for free legal assistance.[6] The Supreme Court has also ruled that the State cannot seek to avoid this constitutional obligation by pleading financial or administrative inability.[7]

In addition to its constitutional mandate, and the judgements of the Supreme Court, the Indian Parliament has passed the Legal Service Authorities Act 1987. The Preamble to the Act pledges to provide free and competent legal advice to those who cannot afford it. The Legal Services Authorities Act 1987, establishes both National and State authorities to administer the provision of legal aid.

Free legal aid is also provided for in the CrPC. Section 304 CrPC states that if an accused is unrepresented at trial before the Court of Session, the court should assign a lawyer to the accused. The legal advice provided should be independent and competent, and not from lawyers who are attached to a police station, or raw recruits.[8] Thus, judges have an obligation to explain to an unrepresented accused person the rules relating to the provision of free legal aid as soon as the accused is produced before them for the first time.[9]

---

[4] *Khatri (II)* v. *State of Bihar* AIR 1981 SCR 408; *Maneka Gandhi* v. *Union of India and Anr* (1978) 1 SCC 248; *Suk Das* v. *Union Territory of Arunachal Pradesh*, AIR 1986 SC 991 (holding that the right to free legal service was a fundamental right which is not conditional upon the accused applying for free legal assistance).

[5] *Hussainara Khatoon and Ors* v. *Home Secretary, State of Bihar, Patna*, AIR 1979 SC 1369.

[6] *Suk Das* v. *Union Territory of Arunachal Pradesh*, AIR 1986 SC 991.

[7] *Khatri (II)* v. *State of Bihar*, (1981) 1 SCC 627.

[8] *Ranchod Mathur Wasawa* v. *State of Gujarat*, AIR 1974 SC 1143.

[9] *Khatri(II)* v. *State of Bihar*, (1981) 1 SCC 627.

Box 8.1   *Khatri* v. *State of Bihar*
AIR 1981 SC 928

Facts: Several blind prisoners were not provided with legal representation, from the time of their initial appearance in front of a judicial magistrate, to the time when their remand orders were passed. The records of the judicial magistrates indicated that no legal representation was provided because the prisoners had not asked for it. The judicial magistrates did not ask them if they wanted legal representation at the expense of the State.

Held: The Supreme Court reaffirmed that the right to free legal representation attaches itself at the first appearance in front of a judicial magistrate, not just at trial. The first appearance in front of a magistrate is when the personal liberty of the accused is in jeopardy, and therefore, he is entitled to competent legal advice and representation.

Noting the lack of legal awareness in India, the Court stated that it would not be fair to expect a poor and illiterate person to ask for legal representation when he most likely does not know he has a right to free legal representation. Therefore, the Court held that magistrates and Sessions Judges must inform every accused that he is entitled to free legal services at the cost of the State.

The Supreme Court noted that despite its previous declaration of free legal services being a fundamental right guaranteed by the Constitution, most of the States had not actually provided free legal services. Thus the Court required every State to make provisions for the grant of free legal services to an accused who is unable to hire a lawyer because of poverty or indigence. As long as the accused is charged with an offence that could result in a conviction and imprisonment, he should be given free legal representation.

When an indigent person is arrested they have the right to be informed by the police of their right to legal representation[10] (see Chapter 4—'Rights When Arrested').

From the time the accused is taken into custody, he or she has the right to be given a reasonable opportunity to communicate with a legal advisor.[11] The police must inform the nearest Legal Aid Committee about the arrest of a person immediately after such arrest.[12] Police officers are permitted to be present during a legal consultation when an accused is in custody, but they should not be within hearing distance. It is the responsibility of the police

---

[10] *Khatri (II)* v. *State of Bihar*, (1981) 1 SCC 627; *Suk Das* v. *Union Territory of Arunchal Pradesh*, AIR 1986 SC 991.

[11] *Llewelyn Evens, Re*, AIR 1926 Bom 551, 552; 27 Cri LJ 1169; *Moti Bai* v. *State*, AIR 1954 Raj 241, 243; 55 Cri LJ 1591.

[12] *Sheela Barse* v. *State of Maharashtra*, JT 1988 (3) 15.

'to allow legal advisers of the accused to interview him'.[13] Furthermore, the Indian Evidence Act stipulates that all attorney-client correspondence should be treated as 'privileged.'[14]

However, there are exceptions to the right to free legal representation. This right should not be interpreted as an unconditional duty of the State to provide the accused with an advocate. The State is obligated to provide free legal aid only if the accused is unable to procure his or her own legal representation due to poverty or indigence. (See 'Eligibility for Free Legal Aid' below.) If the accused is not entitled to legal aid from the State, he or she must exercise his or her right to legal representation by making arrangements for a lawyer.

It should further be noted that this right may also be superceded by provisions of the specific Act that the accused was apprehended under. For example, under the National Security Act (NSA), the accused is granted legal representation in hearings before the Advisory Board only if the Government also has legal representation. If the Government does not have a lawyer at such a hearing, then the accused will not be entitled to one either.[15]

Finally, if this right to legal representation has been violated or infringed upon, a court of appeal may vitiate the criminal proceedings if the breach compromised the right to a fair trial.[16]

8.2 ELIGIBILITY FOR FREE LEGAL AID

In 1987, the Indian Parliament passed the Legal Service Authorities Act 1987 which established both National and State authorities to administer the provision of legal aid to people who are deemed eligible. The Legal Services Authorities Act provides the criteria that should be fulfilled by a person in order to be eligible for legal aid.

Section 12 of the Legal Services Authorities Act provides that 'every person who has to file or defend a case will be entitled to legal aid, if that person is:

(a) a member of a Scheduled Caste or Scheduled Tribe;

(b) a victim of trafficking in human beings or *begar*;

(c) a woman or a child;

(d) a mentally ill or otherwise disabled person;

(e) a person under circumstances of undeserved want such as being a victim of a mass disaster, ethnic violence, caste atrocity, flood, drought, earthquake or industrial disaster;

(f) an industrial workman;

---

[13] *Amolak Ram* v. *Emperor*, 32 Cri LJ 1022, 1023; AIR 1932 Lah 13; See also *Moti Bai* v. *State*, 1954 Cri LJ (Raj) 1591 (finding that the denial of a legal counsel interview violates Article 22(1) of the Indian Constitution and S. 303, CrPC).

[14] S. 126 Indian Evidence Act.

[15] *A. K. Roy* v. *Union of India*, AIR 1982 SC 710.

[16] *Muthukaruppa Servai* v. *Emperor*, AIR 1928 Mad 1234, 1235; 29 Cri LJ 1082.

(g) in custody, including custody in a protective home, in a juvenile home, or in a psychiatric hospital or psychiatric nursing home; or

(h) in receipt of annual income less than nine thousand rupees or such other higher amount as may be prescribed by the State Govt.; if the case is before a court other than the Supreme Court, and less than twelve thousand rupees or such other higher amount as may be prescribed by the Central Govt.; if the case is before the Supreme Court.'[17]

Despite the fact that the right to free legal aid has been declared a constitutional right, the Supreme Court has, rather inconsistently, made exceptions to this right. In the case of *M.H. Hoskot* v. *State of Maharashtra*, the court ruled that there may be cases involving offences against laws where social justice mandates that free legal service not be provided by the State.[18]

It should also be noted that eligibility for legal aid does not create a duty to accept that aid. The accused is under no obligation to accept any legal representation against his or her will.[19]

8.3 SECURING LEGAL AID

However, it is not enough to fall into one of the eligible categories. The accused must be able to secure legal aid. In order to secure legal aid, the appropriate Legal Services Authority must decide whether a valid case exists to either prosecute or defend. An accused individual should contact his/her local Legal Service Authority to determine whether he/she meets the exact eligibility requirements for free legal aid.

Each State and Union Territory of India has a Legal Services Authority. There is also a National Legal Services Authority. Among other programmes, the authorities provide legal services to people who satisfy the criteria set out above.[20]

The accused should be provided with free legal aid as soon as possible so that they may receive competent legal advice and representation throughout the proceedings. In practice, the first time he or she will be able to get access to legal aid is when they are initially brought in front of the magistrate.[21]

---

[17] Section 12, *Legal Services Authorities Act of 1987*; note that the original version of Section 12(h) of the *Legal Services Authorities Act 1987* set forth a maximum annual income of eighteen thousand rupees in order to be eligible for free legal aid for a case in the Supreme Court, and a maximum annual income of nine thousand rupees for eligibility in any other Court. However, upon recommendation of the Central Legal Services Authority, the annual income limit has been increased to fifty thousand rupees for cases in the Supreme Court and twenty five thousand rupees for cases up to the High Court in a number of States.

[18] *M.H. Hoskot* v. *State of Maharashtra*, AIR 1978 SC 1548; *Khatri (II)* v. *State of Bihar*, AIR 1981 SCR 408.

[19] *Maneka Gandhi* v. *Union of India*, (1978) 1 SCC 248; AIR 1978 SC 597.

[20] See Section 2. Eligibility for Free Legal Aid, *supra*.

[21] *Khatri (II)* v. *State of Bihar*, AIR 1981 SCR 408.

To receive legal aid from the Legal Services Authority, the accused will have to swear an affidavit stating his or her income. The accused is not required to provide any additional documentation. However, the authority in charge of granting legal aid may demand additional evidence if they have good reason to disbelieve the affidavit.[22]

After examining the eligibility criteria of an applicant, the Legal Services Authorities will provide the accused with counsel at State expense, pay the required Court Fee in the matter, and bear all incidental expenses in connection with the case.

The Supreme Court of India has held that the failure of an accused to be represented free of charge, if he or she desires, can invalidate a trial and result in the setting aside of a conviction and sentence.[23] Unfortunately, while this is the precedent set by the Supreme Court, it is not often followed in the lower courts.

8.4 APPEALS

The requirement of a fair trial under Article 21 of the Constitution, including the right to free legal representation, extends to the appeal procedure. In fact, it has been argued that the need for adequate legal representation for all accused persons is even greater in appeal cases, given the fact they are usually complex and legalistic, and the State is usually represented by well-qualified and experienced lawyers.[24]

However, although the Supreme Court has interpreted the right to free legal representation to extend to appeal, unfortunately there is no specific provision for this in the CrPC. Although the CrPC does provide for a right of appeal against conviction (see Chapter 7: 'Trials'), this right does not appear to include the right to free representation in appeal cases.

The Supreme Court has upheld the right to free legal aid in appeal becasue the right to appeal does not become meaningful unless and until the accused person is given able representation by a competent lawyer.[25] If this right to legal representation has been violated or infringed upon, an appeals court may vitiate the criminal proceedings if it finds that the breach amounted to a negation of a fair trial.[26]

8.5 CHOOSING AN ADVOCATE

Normally, only people who have been admitted as qualified advocates to their State Bar Council can practice law in India. However, non-advocates may be exempted from this

---

[22] Mathew, P.D., 'Free Legal Services to the Poor', Indian Social Institute, no. 65/96 1996, p. 24.

[23] *Suk Das* v. *Union Territory of Arunchal Pradesh,* AIR 1986 SC 991; *Moolchand* v. *State,* (1990) Cri LJ 682.

[24] *Hussainara Khatoon* v. *State of Bihar IV,* 1980 SCC 98 at 102.

[25] *M.H. Hoskot* v. *State of Maharashtra,* AIR 1978 SC 1548.

[26] *Muthukaruppa Servai* v. *Emperor,* AIR 1928 Mad 1234, 1235; 29 Cri LJ 1082 (holding that a case may be set a aside if there is evidence of unfairness on the part of the sub-magistrate); See *Suk Das* v. *Union Territory of Arunachal Pradesh* 1986 2 SCC 401; 1986 SCC (Cri) 166.

requirement if they apply for, and receive, prior permission from the Court in which they wish to appear.[27]

An Advocate's Duties to the Client

The professional conduct of advocates in India is governed by the Advocate Act 1961. Some important duties that advocates owe to their client include:

- An advocate is obliged to accept any case if they are paid a sum appropriate to their standing at the Bar. Only special circumstances may justify an advocate to refuse to accept a case.
- An advocate should not withdraw from commitments without sufficient cause, and without giving notice. If an advocate does withdraw from a case, he or she must refund the unearned portion of the fees he or she has received.
- An advocate must not accept a case where he or she may be a witness. If during the case it becomes clear that the advocate may be a witness, the advocate should retire so long as the client's best interest is not jeopardised.
- An advocate has a duty to defend the client's rights and interests fairly and honourably notwithstanding his or her personal opinion of the case or the client.
- An advocate should not jeopardise or take advantage of his or her client's confidence in any way, including in dealings with the client's money.[28]

Additionally, an advocate may not disclose any communication made during consultation without the client's express consent. All communications between a client and a lawyer are privileged and confidential unless they relate to the furtherance of some illegal purpose, or reveal that a crime has been committed since the commencement of the advocate's employment.[29]

For example, if the client admits to his lawyer that he has committed the crime he is charged with, the lawyer may not disclose this information to any third party, since defending a client known to be guilty is not a criminal offence. In contrast, if the client tells his lawyer about plans to commit forgery, that particular communication concerns the furtherance of an illegal act, and consequentially may be legally disclosed.[30]

If a lawyer violates any of his or her duties, whether the misconduct is professional or not, the appropriate State Bar Council may discipline and punish the advocate. The Council may reprimand him or her, suspend him or her from practice for such period as it deems fit, or remove the name of the advocate from the state roll of advocates.[31]

---

[27] S. 32 Advocates Act 1961.

[28] Rajesh Talwar, *How to Choose Your Lawyer*, Vision Books, New Delhi, 1998, pp. 82 6.

[29] S. 126 Indian Evidence Act.

[30] S. 126 Indian Evidence Act.

[31] Rajesh Talwar, *How to Choose Your Lawyer*, Vision Books, New Delhi, 1998, pp. 82–6.

8.6 COMPENSATION

A. An Introduction to Criminal Compensation

The purpose of criminal compensation is to compensate a victim of police brutality, or of a crime, for their suffering. It may also be awarded to the family and dependants of a victim in the case of murder. Compensation is not awarded to punish the perpetrator. The punishment of the perpetrator should be left to the relevant High Court that has jurisdiction.[32] The discussion below focuses only on compensation in criminal cases, not civil claims, as for compensation for negligence.

B. When a Person is a Victim of Police Brutality

Most illegal police brutality tends to take the form of illegal arrest, illegal detention, or the use of 'third degree' methods (i.e. torture) of an accused or witness while in custody. Neither international law nor Indian domestic law tolerates such abuses of human rights.

While India officially reserved its compliance with this Article 9(5) of the ICCPR, the Supreme Court of India has interpreted the Constitution as providing a right to compensation.[33] The courts are thus allowed to award monetary compensation for the violation of a fundamental right under Articles 32 and 226 of the Constitution.[34] However, the Supreme Court has recently held that compensation is not a blanket remedy available in all cases where a fundamental right has been violated with a view to safeguard against groundless cases and minor cases of custodial violence. Before ordering compensation, the courts will examine whether the violation of the right to life is 'patent and incontrovertible', shakes the conscience of the court and results in the death or disability of the arrested person.[35]

The courts have granted compensation to the victim or family of the victim in many circumstances. These include:

- Where the victim died in police custody;[36]
- Where the victim was unlawfully handcuffed;[37]
- Where the victim has been falsely arrested;[38]

---

[32] *DK Basu* v. *State of West Bengal* 1997, Cri LJ 743.

[33] *Rudul Sah* v. *State of Bihar*, AIR 1983 SC 1086.

[34] *Nilabati Behera alias Lalita Behera* v. *State of Orissa*, AIR 1993 SC 1960 (holding 'Award of compensation in a proceeding under Article 32 by this Court or by the High Court under Article 226 of the Constitution is a remedy available in public law, based on strict liability for contravention of fundamental rights to which the principle of sovereign immunity does not apply, even though it may be available as a defence in private law in an action based on tort.'

[35] *Sube Singh* v. *State of Haryana* Judgment dated 3 February 2006 at *http://judis.nic.in/supremecourt/qrydisp.asp?tfnm=27456.*

[36] *Nilabati Behera alias Lalita Behera* v. *State of* Orissa, AIR 1993 SC 1960; *DK Basu* v. *State of West Bengal,* (1997) Cri LJ 743.

[37] *State of Maharashtra* v. *Ravikant S. Patil,* (1991) 2 SCC 373.

[38] *Pramod Kumar Padhi* v. *Goleka,* 1986 Cri LJ 1634.

- Where the victim was fired upon and killed by police in a public place;[39]
- Where the victim was illegally detained and abused;[40]
- Where the victim was beaten by police;[41] and
- Where the victim was killed in prison.[42]

The amount of compensation awarded to victims depends on the circumstances of the case, and the court awarding the compensation. Having paid the awarded compensation, the State may recover the amount from the concerned police officer or officers personally.[43]

In addition to the higher courts, the NHRC is also empowered to grant compensation to the victims of police brutality under the Protection of Human Rights Act 1993.

Box 8.2   *Rudul Sah* v. *State of Bihar and Anr*
AIR 1983 SC 1086

Facts: Rudul Sah was acquitted by a Court of Sessions in Bihar on 3 June 1968, but was not released from jail until 16 October 1982, fourteen years after he was acquitted. Rudul Sah petitioned the Supreme Court for his release and for compensation for the illegal incarceration.

Held: The Supreme Court held that Rudul Sah's right to life and liberty under Article 21 of the Constitution of India had been violated by the State of Bihar. The Supreme Court stated 'the right to compensation is some palliative for the unlawful acts of instrumentalities which act in the name of public interest and which present for their protection the powers of the State as a shield ... Therefore, the *State* must repair the damage done by its officers to the petitioner's rights.' The Supreme Court awarded compensation of thirty-five thousand rupees.

Box 8.3   *State of Madhya Pradesh* v. *Shyamsunder Trivedi and Ors*
(1995) 4 SCC 262

Facts: In 1981 Nathu Banjara was being interrogated by the police as a murder suspect. The police, while questioning him, beat and tortured him with the intention of extracting a confession from him. As a result of the extensive injuries inflicted on Banjara from the beatings, he died in police custody. He remained in police custody until the time his dead body was removed from the police station.

contd

---

[39] *Peoples' Union of Democratic Rights* v. *State of Bihar*, AIR 1987 SC 355.

[40] *Rudul Sah* v. *State of Bihar and Anr* AIR 1983 SC 1086; *Arvinder Singh Bagga* v. *State of Uttar Pradesh and Ors*, J.T. (1994) 6 SC 478.

[41] *Saheli, a Women's Resources Centre* v. *Commissioner of Police Delhi*, AIR 1990 SC 513.

[42] *State of Madhya Pradesh* v. *Shyamsunder Trivedi*, (1995) 4 SCC 262.

[43] *Arvinder Singh Bagga* v. *State of Uttar Pradesh*, 1994 SCC Supl. (1) 500 JT 1993 Supl. 594.

> Held: The Supreme Court noted that it is difficult to prosecute police officers in these types of cases because there is usually no direct evidence, and police officers tend to cover up for one another. Therefore, courts must deal with such cases in a realistic manner and should not adopt an exaggerated adherence to the establishment of proof beyond every reasonable doubt. Accordingly, in this case, the police officers were sentenced to jail and ordered to pay a fine. The fines were used for compensation to the family of the deceased.

C. When A Person is a Victim of Someone Other than the Police

Where a person is the victim of a crime, he or she may be eligible to receive compensation under the CrPC or through a civil suit for damages.

A civil suit is a personal action to recover compensation from the perpetrator of the crime. However, efforts to recover damages from offenders are generally hopeless, because they involve very complicated and expensive legal proceedings, and are most often against indigent and poor offenders.[44]

The other option is compensation under the CrPC. This is only possible where the accused is convicted and sentenced by the court. The compensation is payable for any physical or pecuniary loss, and the court should have regard to a number of factors including the nature of the injury, the manner in which the injury was inflicted, and the capacity of the offender to pay.[45] It is the duty of the court to take into account these factors as well as the nature of the crime, the justness of the claim for compensation, and any other relevant circumstances.[46]

Where an offender is sentenced to pay a fine, the court may order that the paid fine be awarded to the victim of the crime as compensation.[47] In this case, the award of compensation must not exceed the amount of fine imposed; the fine can only be within the limits of that specified by the IPC. However, fines are very rarely imposed, and when they are, the amount is very small.

Alternatively, where a fine is not part of the sentence, the Court may order an accused person to pay, by way of compensation to the victim, such amount as may be specified by the

---

[44] Subhash Chandra Singh, 'Compensation and Restitution to the Victims of Crime: the Centuries Old Correctional Aim Modernised—Modernisation on the Basis of Public Responsibility Needed' 1992 Cri LJ 100.

[45] *Hari Kishan and Anr v. Sukhbir Singh and Ors,* AIR 1988 SC 2127.

[46] *Hari Kishan and Anr v. Sukhbir Singh and Ors,* AIR 1988 SC 2127.

[47] S. 357(1) CrPC: When a court imposes a sentence of which a fine does not form part, the Court may, when passing judgment, order the accused person to pay, by way of compensation, such amount as may be specified to the order of the person who has suffered any loss or injury by reason of the act for which the accused person has been so sentenced.

court.[48] When no fine is imposed, there are no limits on the amount of compensation that the court can award to the victim.

In Andhra Pradesh, S. 357(1) CrPC provides that where the offence is committed against a person who belongs to a Scheduled Caste or Tribe, as defined by Art. 366 of the Constitution, the court must order compensation out of the fine. In the same circumstances, the court must also order compensation be paid under S. 357(3) CrPC. However, the court must not do this where both the offender and victim belong to a Scheduled Caste or Tribe.

The states of Uttar Pradesh, Madhya Pradesh, Rajasthan, and West Bengal all have a similar provision. Karnataka and Bihar have a similar provision but without the S. 357(3) equivalent.

Although the Supreme Court has held that S. 357(3) should be used liberally, this is not yet the case.[49] This is despite the fact that the Court has also stated that in the case of murder, it is only fair that proper compensation should be awarded to provide for the dependants of the deceased.[50]

In addition, the problem of impoverished offenders persists to make this form of victim compensation ineffective.

In recent years, official criminal injuries compensation legislation has only been proposed.[51] This legislation would mean that the government would compensate the victims of certain crimes.

However, some other legislation provides for compensation. For example, The Scheduled Castes and the Scheduled Tribes (Prevention of Atrocities) Rules 1995, provide for compensation for victims of certain atrocities in accordance with a Schedule of compensation. It provides that victims should receive immediate relief including food, water, shelter, medical aid, and other essentials of life.[52]

In addition, the Code also provides that the magistrate's court can order a person to pay compensation to someone whom they have caused to be wrongfully arrested by the police.[53] If a person causes a police officer to arrest someone, and it appears to the magistrate that there were insufficient grounds for causing the arrest, then the magistrate can award the wrongfully arrested person compensation of up to one hundred rupees, to be paid by the person who caused the wrongful arrest. For S. 358 to apply, it must be shown that there is some proximate and direct connection between the complainant and the arrest.[54]

---

[48] S. 357(3) CrPC.

[49] *Hari Kishan and Anr* v. *Sukhbir Singh and Ors*, AIR 1988 SC 2127.

[50] *Guruswamy* v. *State of T.N.*, (1979) 3 SC 797; 1979 SCC (Cri) 879, 881.

[51] Supra n. 44.

[52] Rule 12(4), The Scheduled Castes and the Scheduled Tribes (Prevention of Atrocities) Rules 1995.

[53] S. 358 CrPC.

[54] *Mallapa* v. *Veerabasappa*, 1977 Cri LJ 1856, 1858 (Kant HC).

There are a few other situations where compensation may be awarded. One is where an innocent purchaser of stolen property is awarded compensation, to the amount of the property they innocently purchased, out of money found in the possession of the person convicted of theft or receiving stolen property.[55] Another is where a person is accused without reasonable cause before a magistrate of an offence and is acquitted or discharged. If the magistrate thinks there is no reasonable ground for the accusation then the magistrate can call upon the person who made the accusation to show cause why they should not pay compensation to the accused.[56] The magistrate can then order compensation to be paid to the accused person if it appears that there was no reasonable cause for the accusation.[57]

---

[55] S. 453 CrPC.
[56] S. 250 CrPC.
[57] S. 250(2) CrPC.

9 Recent Developments in the Criminal Justice System

This chapter updates the previous edition of the *Handbook of Human Rights and Criminal Justice in India* with some recent developments in the criminal justice system. It should therefore be read in conjunction with the relevant provisions described and explained in the foregoing chapters.

The last few years have witnessed an extensive debate centered on the reform of criminal justice administration in India. Recent efforts by the legislature, judiciary, bureaucracy, and civil society have sought to address some of the institutional problems that affect the delivery of criminal justice. These include, inter alia, amendments to the Criminal Procedure Code, judgments by high courts and the Supreme Court and reports by various committees and commissions. This chapter sets out some of those developments.

The chapter is divided into two parts, which discuss the 2008 amendments to the Criminal Procedure Code and a few landmark judgments respectively.

9.1 CODE OF CRIMINAL PROCEDURE (AMENDMENT) ACT, 2008

This part discusses the changes brought through the Code of Criminal Procedure (Amendment) Act, 2008 [hereinafter 'Amendment Act'], notified in the *Gazette of India Extraordinary* on 30 December 2009. Notably, the final notification excluded Section 5, Section 6, and sub-section (b) of Section 21 from coming into force with the rest of the Act. However, a new bill introduced in Parliament in March 2010—the Code of Criminal Procedure (Amendment) Bill, 2010—seeks to bring in some of the provisions envisaged in those sections of the 2008 Amendment Act with some modifications.

A. Definition of Victim

The Code of Criminal Procedure, 1973 (hereinafter 'CrPC') did not define the term 'victim' in the definitional clause under Section 2. The Supreme Court and high courts have interpreted the term 'victim' in various instances. The Amendment Act defines the term victim as 'a person who has suffered any loss or injury caused by reason of the act or omission for which the accused person has been charged.' The expression 'victim' also includes his or her guardian or legal heir.[1]

B. Representation by a Lawyer of Choice

A criminal act is considered as a wrong against the state and hence it is the duty of the state to institute the case on behalf of the victim. The CrPC provides for the appointment of a public prosecutor and assistant public prosecutor to represent the case of the victim on behalf of the state.[2] The Amendment Act adds a clause in Section 24 which states that that the court has the power to permit the victim to engage an advocate of his choice to assist the prosecution under sub-section (8) of the said section.[3]

C. Cases Tried by Women Judges

The Amendment Act adds a clause in Section 26 of the CrPC under which any offence under Section 376 and Sections 376A to 376D of the Indian Penal Code (45 of 1860), which relate to the offence of rape, shall be tried as far as practicable by a court presided over by a woman.[4] This has been done to deal with concerns that the legal system is not always as sympathetic to victims of rape as it ought to be.

D. Law Relating to Arrest

The Amendment Act sought to bring about considerable changes in laws relating to arrest in order to reduce the high incidence of arbitrary and unnecessary arrests. Despite this, due to pressure from a section of the legal profession, the amendments relating to arrest—Sections 5 and 6 of the Amendment Act, as mentioned above—were excluded from the Gazette of India notification, and thus are not in force. However, a discussion of their impact would be useful as they might be included in future amendments. Already, as noted above, the Code of Criminal Procedure (Amendment) Bill, 2010, introduced in Parliament in March 2010, seeks to address some of the objections to the 2008 Amendment Act.

The original Section 41 of the CrPC empowers the police to arrest without warrant any person in connection with the commission of any cognizable offence or against whom a reasonable complaint has been made. The section also empowers police to arrest a person on the basis of reasonable suspicion. These powers are limited and the Supreme Court, in *DK Basu* v. *State of West Bengal,* has laid down detailed guidelines regarding the procedure to

---

[1] Section 2, CrPC (Amendment) Act, 2008.

[2] Sections 24 and 25, CrPC.

[3] Section 3, CrPC (Amendment) Act, 2008.

[4] Section 4, CrPC (Amendment) Act, 2008.

be followed during and after arrest. These guidelines seek to ensure the protection of the rights of the accused.[5]

The 2008 Amendment Act sought to restrict the power of the police—as found in Section 41 CrPC—to arrest a person without warrant against whom reasonable complaint has been made, or credible information has been received, or a reasonable suspicion exists that he has committed a cognizable offence punishable with imprisonment for a term which may be less than seven years or which may extend to seven years.[6] Therefore, the Amendment Act, by amending Section 41(1)(b), seeks to ensure that the police cannot arrest merely on the basis of reasonable complaint. The police, if they wish to make an arrest in such cases, must be satisfied that such an arrest is necessary:

1. to prevent such person from committing any further offence; or
2. for proper investigation of the offence; or
3. to prevent such person from causing the evidence of the offence to disappear or tampering with such evidence in any manner; or
4. to prevent such person from influencing witnesses of the case.

It must be pointed out that in all such cases, the police officer is obliged to record, in writing, that the conditions mentioned above exist and make necessary the arrest of the accused in such a case.

The 2010 Amendment Bill now seeks to insert a proviso at the end of Section 41(1)(b) as sought to be amended by the 2008 Amendment Act. The Bill seeks to provide that in all cases where the arrest of a person is not required, the police officer shall records reasons in writing for not making the arrest.[7]

The 2008 Amendment Act further inserted new Sections 41A, 41B, 41C, and 41D.[8] Section 41A states that the police may issue a notice to appear if the arrest of the person is not required under the provisions of sub-section 1 of Section 41.[9] The new 2010 Amendment Bill amends this to require the police to issue such a notice.[10]

Section 41A inserted by the Amendment Act also provided that where such a person fails to comply with the notice, the police officer may arrest him subject to the orders passed by a competent court.[11] The new 2010 Amendment Bill additionally makes the arrest applicable when the person refuses to identify himself.[12]

---

[5] See Appendix 2.

[6] Section 5, CrPC (Amendment) Act, 2008.

[7] Section 2, Criminal Procedure (Amendment) Bill, 2010.

[8] Section 6, CrPC (Amendment) Act, 2008.

[9] Ibid.

[10] Section 2, Criminal Procedure (Amendment) Bill, 2010

[11] Section 6, CrPC (Amendment) Act, 2008.

[12] Section 3, Criminal Procedure (Amendment) Bill, 2010

Section 41B of the Amendment Act lays down the requirements to be followed by the police officer while making arrest:

1. Every police officer while making an arrest shall bear an accurate, visible and clear identification of his name, which will facilitate easy identification.
2. At the time of the arrest, the police are required to prepare a memorandum of arrest, which shall be attested by at least one respectable member of the locality where the arrest is made and must be countersigned by the person arrested.
3. It also makes mandatory for the police officer to inform the person arrested that he has a right to have a relative or a friend, named by him, to be informed of his arrest unless a member of his family attests the memorandum.

Section 41C as inserted by the Amendment Act provides for:

1. The establishment of control rooms in every district and at state level, which shall display the names and addresses of the persons arrested and the name and designation of the police officer who made the arrests on the notice board.
2. The establishment of a database about the persons arrested and the nature of the offence with which they are charged for the information of general public.

Section 41D gives the statutory right that when any person is arrested and interrogated by the police, he shall be entitled to meet an advocate of his choice during interrogation, though not throughout interrogation.

Further, the amendment has added a new proviso in Section 46 of the CrPC, which provides that where a woman is to be arrested; her submission to custody on an oral intimation of arrest shall be presumed unless the circumstances indicate to the contrary. The police officer shall not touch the person of the woman for making her arrest unless the police officer is a female.[13] This amendment has been introduced in the Code as until now, the law required that a person to be arrested is considered arrested only after a physical act of confining or touching the person, which is a formal requirement that may be found offensive by many women, if they are arrested by a male police officer.

E. Medical Examination of an Arrested Person

The amendment substitutes the provisions of Section 54 with a new provision for the medical examination of an arrested person.[14]

1. Sub-section (1) makes it mandatory to conduct a medical examination of the arrested person by a medical officer in the service of central or state governments and in case the medical officer is not available, by a registered medical practitioner soon after the arrest is made.

---

[13] Section 7, CrPC (Amendment) Act, 2008.
[14] Section 8, CrPC (Amendment) Act, 2008.

2. If the arrested person is a female, the medical examination shall be made only by or under the supervision of a female medical officer, and in case the female medical officer is not available, by a female registered medical officer.

3. Sub-section (2) requires the medical officer to prepare the record of such examination, mentioning therein any injuries or marks of violence upon the person arrested, and the approximate time when such injuries or marks may have been inflicted. The medical officer shall furnish a copy of the report of such examination to the arrested person.

The new amendment also inserted a new Section 55A, which says that it shall be the duty of the person having the custody of an accused to take reasonable care of the health and safety of the accused.[15] As such, police officers who have persons under their custody are to be held directly responsible for the welfare of persons in their custody.

F. Recording of Statement of a Rape Victim

The amendment adds a proviso in Sub-section (1) of Section 157 of the principal Act. It stipulates that in relation to an offence of rape, the recording of statement of the victim shall be conducted at the residence of the victim or in the place of her choice. It should be done as far as practicable by a woman police officer in the presence of her parents or guardian or near relatives or a social worker of the locality.[16]

G. Audio/Video Electronic Means to Record the Statements

A proviso is added in Sub-section (3) of Section 161, which provides that a statement made under this sub-section may also be recorded by audio-video electronic means.[17]

Sub-section (1) of Section 164 of the principal legislation gives the power to a metropolitan magistrate or judicial magistrate to record confessions or statements in the course of an investigation. The amendment provides that any confession or statement made under this sub-section may also be recorded by audio-video electronic means in the presence of the advocate of the person accused of an offence. However, no confession may be made before a police officer who has been conferred magisterial powers under any law for the time being in force.[18] Section 275 deals with the recording of statements in warrant-cases by the magistrate.

H. Completion of Trial for Offences under Sections 376 to 376D of IPC

Section 309 of the Code of Criminal Procedure gives the power to the court to adjourn the proceeding for a future date. The amendment has added a new proviso in sub-section (1) of

[15] Section 9, CrPC (Amendment) Act, 2008.
[16] Section 11, CrPC (Amendment) Act, 2008.
[17] Section 12, CrPC (Amendment) Act, 2008.
[18] Section 13, CrPC (Amendment) Act, 2008.

Section 309 of the code. It provides that when the inquiry or trial relates to an offence under Sections 376 to 376D of the Indian Penal Code, the inquiry or trial shall, as far as possible, be completed within a period of two months from the date of commencement of the examination of witnesses.[19]

I. Rules relating to Adjournment of Cases

A proviso is inserted in Sub-section (2) of Section 309, which provides that no adjournment shall be granted at the request of a party, except where the circumstances are beyond the control of that party. The fact that the pleader of a party is engaged in another court shall not be a ground for adjournment and where a witness is present in court but a party or his pleader is not present or the party or his pleader though present in court, is not ready to examine or cross-examine the witness, the court may, if thinks fit, record the statement of the witness and pass such orders as it thinks fit dispensing with the examination-in-chief or cross-examination of the witness, as the case may be.[20]

J. Compoundable Offences

Section 320 of the CrPC deals with the compounding of offences. It lays down the list of offences, which can be compounded, and the party by whom the offences may be compounded.[21]

Following the amendment, the charts in sub-sections (1) and (2) of the original Act are replaced with the ones below.

New chart in sub-section (1):

Offence	Section of the Indian Penal Code applicable	Person by whom offence may be compounded
1	*2*	*3*
Uttering words, etc., with deliberate intent to wound the religious feelings of any person.	298	The person whose religious feelings are intended to be wounded.
Voluntarily causing hurt.	323	The person to whom the hurt is caused.
Voluntarily causing hurt on provocation.	334	As above
Voluntarily causing grievous hurt on grave and sudden provocation.	335	As above

contd

---

[19] Section 21, CrPC (Amendment) Act, 2008.

[20] Ibid.

[21] S. 23, CrPC (Amendment) Act, 2008.

Offence	Section of the Indian Penal Code applicable	Person by whom offence may be compounded
1	*2*	*3*
Wrongfully restraining or confining any person.	341, 342	The person restrained or confined.
Wrongfully confining a person for three days or more	343	The person confined.
Wrongfully confining a person for ten days or more.	344	As above
Wrongfully confining a person in secret.	346	As above
Assault or use of criminal force.	352, 355, 358	The person assaulted or to whom criminal force is used.
Theft.	379	The owner of the property stolen.
Dishonest misappropriation of property.	403	The owner of the property misappropriated.
Criminal breach of trust by a carrier, wharfinger, etc.	407	As above
Dishonestly receiving stolen property knowing it to be stolen.	411	The owner of the property stolen.
Assisting in the concealment or disposal of stolen property, knowing it to be stolen.	414	As above
Cheating.	417	The person cheated.
Cheating by personation.	419	As above
Fraudulent removal or concealment of property, etc., to prevent distribution among creditors.	421	The creditors who are affected thereby.
Fraudulently preventing from being made available for his creditors a debt or demand due to the offender.	422	As above
Fraudulent execution of deed of transfer containing false statement of consideration.	423	The person affected thereby.
Fraudulent removal or concealment of property.	424	As above

contd

Offence	Section of the Indian Penal Code applicable	Person by whom offence may be compounded
1	2	3
Mischief, when the only loss or damage caused is loss or damage to a private person.	426, 427	The person to whom the loss or damage is caused.
Mischief by killing or maiming animal.	428	The owner of the animal.
Mischief by killing or maiming cattle, etc.	429	The owner of the cattle or animal.
Mischief by injury to works of irrigation by wrongfully diverting water when the only loss or damage caused is loss or damage to private person.	430	The person to whom the loss or damage is caused.
Criminal trespass.	447	The person in possession of the property trespassed upon.
House-trespass.	448	As above
House-trespass to commit an offence (other than theft) punishable with imprisonment.	451	The person in possession of the house trespassed upon.
Using a false trade or property mark.	482	The person to whom loss or injury is caused by such use.
Counterfeiting a trade or property mark used by another.	483	The person to whom loss or injury is caused by such use.
Knowingly selling, or exposing or possessing for sale or for manufacturing purpose, goods marked with a counterfeit property mark.	486	As above
Criminal breach of contract of service.	491	The person with whom the offender has contracted.
Adultery.	497	The husband of the woman.
Enticing or taking away or detaining with criminal intent a married woman.	498	The husband of the woman and the woman

contd .

Offence	Section of the Indian Penal Code applicable	Person by whom offence may be compounded
1	2	3
Defamation, except such cases as are specified against section 500 of the Indian Penal Code (45 of 1860) in column 1 of the Table under sub-section (2).	500	The person defamed.
Printing or engraving matter, knowing it to be defamatory.	501	As above
Sale of printed or engraved substance containing defamatory matter, knowing it to contain such matter.	502	As above
Insult intended to provoke a breach of the peace.	504	The person insulted.
Criminal intimidation.	506	The person intimidated.
Inducing person to believe himself an object of divine displeasure.	508	The person induced.

New chart in sub-section (2):

Offence	Section of the Indian Penal Code applicable	Person by whom offence may be compounded
1	2	3
Causing miscarriage.	312	The woman to whom miscarriage is caused.
Voluntarily causing grievous hurt.	325	The person to whom hurt is caused.
Causing hurt by doing an act so rashly and negligently as to endanger human life or the personal safety of others.	337	As above
Causing grievous hurt by doing an act so rashly and negligently as to endanger human life or the personal safety of others.	338	As above

contd

Offence	Section of the Indian Penal Code applicable	Person by whom offence may be compounded
1	2	3
Assault or criminal force in attempting wrongfully to confine a person.	357	The person assaulted or to whom the force was used.
Theft, by clerk or servant of property in possession of master.	381	The owner of the property stolen.
Criminal breach of trust	406	The owner of property in respect of which breach of trust has been committed.
Criminal breach of trust by a clerk or servant.	408	The owner of the property in respect of which the breach of trust has been committed.
Cheating a person whose interest the offender was bound, either by law or by legal contract, to protect.	418	The person cheated.
Cheating and dishonestly inducing delivery of property or the makings alteration or destruction of a valuable security	420	The person cheated.
Marrying again during the life-time of a husband or wife.	494	The husband or wife of the person so marrying.
Defamation against the President or the Vice-President or the Governor of a State or the Administrator of a Union territory or a Minister in respect of his public functions when instituted upon a complaint made by the Public Prosecutor.	500	The person defamed.
Uttering words or sounds or making gestures or exhibiting any object intending to insult the modesty of a woman or intruding upon the privacy of a woman.	509	The woman whom it was intended to insult or whose privacy was intruded upon.

Sub-section (3) of this section is also substituted by a new provision which provides that when an offence is compoundable under this section, the abetment of such offence, or the attempt to commit such an offence, or where the accused is liable under Sections 34 or 149 of the Indian Penal Code, may be compounded in a like manner.[22]

K. In Camera Trials

Sub-section (2) of Section 327 provides the circumstances (mostly sexual offences) in which the trial shall be conducted 'in camera'. The new amendment added a proviso to this sub-section, which provides that an 'in camera' trial shall be conducted, as far as practicable, by a woman judge or magistrate.[23] A proviso is also added to sub-section (3) which states that the ban on printing or publication of trial proceedings in relation to an offence of rape may be lifted, subject to maintaining confidentiality of the name and address of the parties.[24]

L. Criminal Proceedings against Persons of Unsound Mind

Section 328 of the Code of Civil Procedure lays down the procedures to be followed by the court in cases where accused suffers from mental retardation or is of unsound mind. The amendment has inserted a new sub-section (1A), which states that if the civil surgeon finds the accused to be of unsound mind, he shall refer such person to a psychiatrist or clinical psychologist for care, treatment and prognosis of the condition.[25] The psychiatrist or clinical psychologist shall inform the Magistrate whether the accused is suffering from unsoundness of mind or mental retardation. If the accused is aggrieved by the information given by the psychiatric or clinical psychologist he may pursue an appeal before the medical board. This board shall consist of the head of psychiatry unit in the nearest government hospital and a faculty member in psychiatry from the nearest medical college.[26]

The amendment substituted Sub-section (3) with a new provision, which provides for the discharge of the accused after the satisfaction of the magistrate that on account of unsoundness of mind, he is incapable of entering defence and if no prima facie case is made out against the accused. If the magistrate finds that a prima facie case is made out against the accused, he shall postpone the proceeding for such period as in the opinion of the psychiatrist or clinical psychologist is required for the treatment of the accused, and order the accused to be dealt with as provided under Section 330. If such Magistrate is informed that the person referred to in Sub-section 1(A) is a person with mental retardation, the Magistrate shall further determine whether the mental retardation renders the accused incapable of entering

---

[22] Ibid.

[23] Section 24, CrPC (Amendment) Act, 2008.

[24] Ibid.

[25] Section 25, CrPC (Amendment) Act, 2008.

[26] Ibid.

defence, and if the accused is found so incapable, the Magistrate shall order closure of the inquiry and deal with the accused in the manner provided under Section 330.[27]

The amendment also substitutes Section 330 with a new provision, which gives the power to the magistrate to release the person on bail if he is incapable of entering defence by reason of unsoundness of mind under Section 328 or Section 329.[28]

M. Victim Compensation Scheme

The amendment has inserted a new Section 357A, which provides a mechanism for providing compensation to the victim. Every state government in consultation with the central government shall prepare a scheme for providing compensation to victim or his dependents who have suffered loss as a result of the crime and who require rehabilitation. The District Legal Service Authority or the State Legal Service Authority shall decide the quantum of compensation following the recommendations made by the court.[29]

N. Right to Appeal by the Victim

The amendment to Section 372 provides that the victim shall have the right to appeal against any order passed by the court acquitting the accused or convicting for a lesser offence or imposing inadequate compensation.[30]

9.2 LANDMARK JUDGMENTS

This section analyses some of the landmark judgments in criminal justice over the last few years. The facts of the cases are discussed in brief and the ratio decidendi is provided.

A. *Naz Foundation* v. *Government of NCT of Delhi*[31]

The *Naz Foundation* case, decided in July 2009, marks a pivotal moment in Indian legal history in the areas of both criminal and constitutional law. In this case, the Delhi High Court ruled that Section 377[32] (prohibiting same-sex intercourse) of the Indian Penal Code

---

[27] Ibid.

[28] Section 27, CrPC (Amendment) Act, 2008.

[29] Section 28, CrPC (Amendment) Act, 2008.

[30] Section 29, CrPC (Amendment) Act, 2008.

[31] WP(C) No.7455/2001.

[32] Section 377. Unnatural offences: Whoever voluntarily has carnal intercourse against the order of nature with any man, woman, or animal, shall be punished with imprisonment for life, or with imprisonment of either description for term which may extend to ten years, and shall also be liable to fine.

Explanation: Penetration is sufficient to constitute the carnal intercourse necessary to the offence described in this section.

violated the constitutional right to privacy (read into the right to life and liberty contained in Article 21). This has the practical effect of decriminalizing same-sex intercourse in India.

The Naz Foundation filed a public interest litigation challenging Section 377 in the Delhi High Court in September 2001. The applicant argued that Section 377 was in breach of Articles 14, 15, 19, and 21 of the Constitution.[33] The Court accepted the submission that Section 377 was violative of Articles 21, 14, and 15 of the Constitution.

The court was not convinced by the submissions of the Union of India that Section 377 should be maintained to stem the spread of HIV/AIDS, or on the grounds of public morality.[34] The court referred at length to similar decisions in other jurisdictions, and scientific findings with regards to the nature of homosexuality in coming to its decision.[35]

While the decision reflects a significant progression for homosexual rights in India, the decision is on appeal in the Supreme Court. Further, it remains only a persuasive authority in the other states of India, and the decision to follow or ignore its findings rests with the high court of each state.

B. *Manish Jalan* v. *State of Karnataka*[36]

The Appellant was convicted for rash and negligent driving and for causing death by rash or negligent driving, not amounting to culpable homicide. The trial court and the high court sentenced him to a term of imprisonment and imposed a fine. The appellant challenged the quantum of sentence before the Supreme Court. The counsel on behalf of appellant submitted that the mother of the victim did not hold any grievances against the appellant, as she believed that the death of her son was an act of God. He also submitted that the defendant be ordered to pay reasonable compensation as determined by the Court.[37]

The Supreme Court elaborately discussed the scope of Section 357 of the CrPC which enables the Court to direct payment of compensation to the dependents of the victim. The Court after examining the scope and purpose of imposing a fine found that if the Court is convinced that compensation should be paid, then quantum of compensation is to be determined by taking into consideration the nature of the crime, the injury suffered, and the capacity of the convict to pay compensation.

In this case, the Court took a lenient view and reduced the sentence of imprisonment. It further directed the appellant to pay an amount of Rs 100,000 to the mother of the deceased by way of compensation.[38]

---

[33] WP(C) No.7455/2001, 1.

[34] WP(C) No.7455/2001, 73.

[35] WP(C) No.7455/2001, 61–73. Notably the court cited the court in *Lawrence* v. *Texas*, 539, U.S. 558 (2003), the seminal decision decriminalizing sodomy in the United States.

[36] AIR 2008 SC 3074.

[37] AIR 2008 SC 3074, 3078–9.

[38] AIR 2008 SC 3074, 3088.

C. *Som Mittal* v. *Govt. of Karnataka*[39]

The Government of Karnataka lodged a complaint under Section 200 of the CrPC against the appellant in the court of the Metropolitan Magistrate for taking cognizance of an offence punishable under Section 30(3) of the Karnataka Shops & Commercial Establishments Act, (1961). The Magistrate ruled in favour of the applicant.[40]

The Appellant then filed a petition under Section 482 of the CrPC for setting aside the order of the Magistrate and for quashing the complaint. The High Court rejected the plea for quashing the complaint, but altered the offence in respect of which cognizance was taken.[41]

The Appellant further appealed the decision to the Supreme Court. A Bench consisting of Justices H.K. Sema and Markandey Katju heard the appeal. Justice Sema dismissed the appeal, observing that the court was not expressing any opinion on the merits of the case and that the Magistrate shall decide the merit of the complaint at the time of framing of the charge, uninfluenced by any observations made by this court or the high court. In the course of his judgment, Justice Sema criticised the interference by the high court through exercise of its powers under Section 482 of the Code in a routine manner. The judge commented that it has been consistently held that the power under Section 482 must be exercised sparingly, with circumspection, and in the rarest of rare cases.[42]

In his concurring judgment, Justice Katju agreed that the appeal should be dismissed, without expressing any opinion on merits. He stated that he was rendering a separate opinion as he was not in agreement with the view expressed by Justice Sema that the power under Section 482, CrPC should be used only in the 'rarest of rare cases', though he agreed with the observation that the said power should be used sparingly. He was of the view that the words 'rarest of rare cases' are used only with reference to the death penalty for an offence under Section 302 of the Indian Penal Code (See *Bachan Singh* v. *State of Punjab*[43]) and the use of that phrase was inappropriate while referring to the scope of exercise of power under Section 482.[44] Paras 1 to 16 of his judgment related to the criminal appeal.

Because of the difference of opinion on this legal issue, the appeal was directed to be placed before the Chief Justice of India for appropriate orders, even though both judges had concurred that the appeal should be dismissed. The matter was placed before a Bench of three judges of the Supreme Court. The main issue before the Court was whether the power under Section 482 CrPC should be exercised 'sparingly' or 'sparingly with circumspection and in the rarest of rare cases'.[45]

---

[39] AIR 2008 SC 1528.

[40] AIR 2008 SC 1528, [1].

[41] AIR 2008 SC 1528, [1].

[42] AIR 2008 SC 1528, [2].

[43] AIR 1980 SC 898.

[44] AIR 2008 SC 1528, [3].

[45] AIR 2008 SC 1528, [6].

The Court, after discussing a number of cases, observed that when the words 'rarest of rare cases' are used after the words 'sparingly and with circumspection' while describing the scope of Section 482, those words merely emphasise and reiterate what is intended to be conveyed by the words 'sparingly and with circumspection'. They mean that the power under Section 482 to quash proceedings should not be used mechanically or routinely, but with care and caution, only when a clear case for quashing is made out and failure to interfere would lead to a miscarriage of justice. The expression 'rarest of rare cases' is not used in the sense in which it is used with reference to punishment for offences under Section 302 IPC, but to emphasize that the power under Section 482 CrPC to quash the FIR or criminal proceedings should be used sparingly and with circumspection.[46]

D. *Savitri Agarwal* v. *State of Maharashtra*[47]

The Supreme Court examined the scope of Section 438, CrPC in this case and warned the trial and high courts against imposing unnecessary conditions while granting anticipatory bail. The two-judge Bench of the Supreme Court observed this while hearing the petition filed against the order of the High Court of Bombay, Nagpur Bench, to withdraw the protection given by the sessions judge under Section 438 of the CrPC. The bench reiterated the earlier view expressed by the constitutional bench in *Gurbaksh Singh Sibbia* v. *State of Punjab*,[48] where the Court observed that Section 438 gives wide discretion to the High Courts and the Supreme Court to grant anticipatory bail. It would be difficult to enumerate the conditions under which anticipatory bail should or should not be granted.[49] The discretionary power under this section depends upon the facts and circumstances of each case. However, the court laid down several guidelines to keep in mind dealing with an application of granting anticipatory bail:[50]

1. Although the power to order anticipatory bail is of an extraordinary character, it need not be exercised only in extraordinary cases;

2. Before the power is exercised, the court must be convinced that the applicant has reason to believe that he or she is likely to be arrested for a non-bailable offence. Mere 'fear is insufficient;'

3. The conditions for granting bail under Section 437(1) of the CrPC do not apply to a grant of anticipatory bail;

4. No blanket order of bail should be granted, and the court must take care to specify the offence or offences in respect of which the order will be effective;

---

[46] AIR 2008 SC 1528, [7]–[9].

[47] Criminal Appeal Nos. 1178–9, 2009.

[48] 1980 SCR (3) 383.

[49] Criminal Appeal Nos. 1178–9, 2009, [17].

[50] Criminal Appeal Nos. 1178–9, 2009, [17].

5. The filing of a First Information Report is not a condition precedent to a grant of anticipatory bail;

6. Section 438 cannot be used to grant bail after the arrest of the accused;

7. An interim bail order can be passed under Section 438 without notice to the public prosecutor; and

8. The court may limit the operation of the order to a short period after the filing of the First Information Report, if there are good reasons for doing so.

The court observed that the power conferred by Section 438 is an extraordinary character and hence the power to grant anticipatory bail should be exercised with due care and circumspection. According to Justice D.K. Jain, 'Very cogent and overwhelming circumstances are necessary for an order directing the cancellation of bail already granted, which, in our opinion, were missing in the instant case.'[51]

The Court allowed the appeal holding that the high court had committed a serious error in reversing the order passed by the trial court granting anticipatory bail to the petitioner and others.[52]

E. *Sarabjit Singh* v. *State of Punjab*[53]

This case deals with the interpretation and application of Section 319 of the CrPC which gives the power to the court to proceed against a person, other than the accused, appearing to be guilty of an offence in the course of trial.[54]

Section 319 provides that this must only occur where extraordinary circumstances are put before the court.[55] The nature of the evidence should be such that would make out grounds for exercise of extraordinary power before an additional accused can be summoned for trial.[56]

In this case, the court observed that an order under Section 319 of the CrPC should not be passed simply because an informant or one of the witnesses seeks to implicate other person(s).[57] The court must be satisfied that the entire materials on record would be sufficient, if left unrebutted, to convict the accused.[58]

---

[51] Criminal Appeal Nos. 1178–9, 2009, [21].

[52] Criminal Appeal Nos. 1178–9, 2009, [20]–[21].

[53] Criminal Appeal Nos. 998, 2009.

[54] Criminal Appeal Nos. 998, 2009, [12].

[55] Criminal Appeal Nos. 998, 2009, [16].

[56] Ibid.

[57] Criminal Appeal Nos. 998, 2009, [17].

[58] Criminal Appeal Nos. 998, 2009, [18].

F. *Santosh Kumar Satishbhushan Bariyar* v. *State of Maharashtra*[59]

This case is a landmark case on the death penalty in India. The case deals with the following two important legal principles:[60]

1. Power of the Sessions Court to grant pardon under the provision of Section 306 of the CrPC Code; and
2. Interpretation of the "rarest of rare" doctrine in awarding the death sentence.

Brief Facts of the Case

The appellant Santosh Kumar Bariyar along with three others had kidnapped one Kartik Raj on 7 August 2001. The victim was killed and his body parts, including his head, hands and legs, were severed and disposed of at different locations. The trial court awarded the death sentence to Bariyar and life imprisonment to the other two accused. The conviction was upheld by the high court on appeal. One of the accused had become an approver in this case. The sessions court judge granted him pardon under Section 307, CrPC.[61]

Power to Grant Pardon

Sections 306 and 307 of the CrPC empower the sessions judge to order the pardon of an accused where that accused tenders a full and true disclosure of the whole of the circumstances within his knowledge relating to the offence.

In this case, the Supreme Court, among other things, examined the timing and degree of discretion available to a sessions judge to grant pardon under Section 307 of the CrPC.[62] The Court concluded that 'if it is to be held that that in each and every case pardon can only be granted at the initial stage, the power conferred to the Sessions Judge grant under Section 307 of the CrPC for all intent purport shall become otiose.[63] Hence the Court reaffirmed the wide discretion of the Sessions Judge to grant pardon under Section 307 of the CrPC.

Interpretation of the 'Rarest of Rare' Doctrine

The court found that the application of the 'rarest of rare' doctrine is to be determined according to the facts and circumstances of the case and there are no hard and fast rules for determining when the doctrine should apply.[64] The sentencing procedure to award the death

---

[59] 2009 (7) SCALE 341.

[60] 2009 (7) SCALE 341, 353.

[61] Section 306 empowers the Chief Judicial Magistrate or a Metropolitan Magistrate or a Magistrate of the First Class inquiring into or trying the offence to tender a pardon to such person on condition of his making a full and true disclosure of the whole of the circumstances within his knowledge relating to the offence.

[62] 2009 (7) SCALE 341, 353

[63] 2009 (7) SCALE 341, 362

penalty should read with Articles 14 and 21 of the Indian Constitution.[65] While upholding the law decided in the *Bachan Singh Case*[66], Justice S.B. Sinha commented that the 'rarest of rare' doctrine explicitly proposes that life imprisonment is the rule and that the death penalty is the exception. Hence, the 'rarest of rare' doctrine places an extraordinary burden on the court to carry out an objective assessment of facts to justify the use of capital punishment in a given case.[67] The court is duty bound to equally consider aggravating or mitigating circumstances before arriving at a decision.[68]

This means that for awarding the death penalty, the court will have to provide clear evidence as to why the convict is not fit for any kind of reformatory and rehabilitation scheme.[69] The evidence must not only relate to the crime, but also the criminal, including his or her socio-economic background.[70]

Outcome

The court found that there were sufficient mitigating factors to place the appellant's crime outside the 'rarest of rare' case that justifies capital punishment. The court accordingly reduced this sentence to rigorous life imprisonment. Other grounds of appeal, including the submission that the sessions judge unlawfully pardoned an approver, were dismissed.[71]

---

[64] 2009 (7) SCALE 341, 368

[65] Ibid.

[66] *Bachan Singh* v. *State of Punjab*, (1983) 3 SCC 470.

[67] 2009 (7) SCALE 341, 371

[68] 2009 (7) SCALE 341, 372

[69] 2009 (7) SCALE 341, 375–6.

[70] 2009 (7) SCALE 341, 369.

[71] 2009 (7) SCALE 341, 438–9.

Appendix 1

Directions of the Supreme Court in *Prakash Singh* v. *Union of India*[1]

(W)e issue the following directions to the Central Government, State Governments, and Union Territories for compliance till framing of the appropriate legislations:

State Security Commission

(1) The State Governments are directed to constitute a State Security Commission in every State to ensure that the State Government does not exercise unwarranted influence or pressure on the State police and for laying down the broad policy guidelines so that the State police always acts according to the laws of the land and the Constitution of the country. This watchdog body shall be headed by the Chief Minister or Home Minister as Chairman and have the DGP of the State as its ex-officio Secretary. The other members of the Commission shall be chosen in such a manner that it is able to function independent of Government control. For this purpose, the State may choose any of the models recommended by the National Human Rights Commission, the Ribeiro Committee or the Sorabjee Committee, which are as under:

NHRC	*Ribeiro Committee*	*Sorabjee Committee*
1. Chief Minister/HM as Chairman	1. Minister i/c Police as Chairman	1. Minister i/c Police (ex-officio Chairperson)

contd

[1] Judgment dated 22 September 2006 *http://judis.nic.in/supremecourt/qrydisp.asp?tfnm=28072*, JT (2006) 12 SC225, (2006) 8SCC 1.

NHRC	Ribeiro Committee	Sorabjee Committee
2. Lok Ayukta or, in his absence, a retired Judge of High Court to be nominated by Chief Justice or a Member of State Human Rights Commission.	2. Leader of Opposition.	2. Leader of Opposition.
3. A sitting or retired Judge nominated by Chief Justice of High Court.	3. Judge, sitting or retired, nominated by Chief Justice of High Court.	3. Chief Secretary
4. Chief Secretary	4. Chief Secretary	4. DGP (ex-officio Secretary)
5. Leader of Opposition in Lower House.	5. Three non-political citizens of proven merit and integrity.	5. Five independent Members.
6. DGP as ex-officio Secretary.	6. DG Police as Secretary.	

The recommendations of this Commission shall be binding on the State Government. The functions of the State Security Commission would include laying down the broad policies and giving directions for the performance of the preventive tasks and service oriented functions of the police, evaluation of the performance of the State police and preparing a report thereon for being placed before the State legislature.

Selection and Minimum Tenure of DGP

(2) The Director General of Police of the State shall be selected by the State Government from amongst the three senior-most officers of the Department who have been empanelled for promotion to that rank by the Union Public Service Commission on the basis of their length of service, very good record and range of experience for heading the police force. And, once he has been selected for the job, he should have a minimum tenure of at least two years irrespective of his date of superannuation. The DGP may, however, be relieved of his responsibilities by the State Government acting in consultation with the State Security Commission consequent upon any action taken against him under the All India Services (Discipline and Appeal) Rules or following his conviction in a court of law in a criminal offence or in a case of corruption, or if he is otherwise incapacitated from discharging his duties.

Minimum Tenure of I.G. of Police and other Officers

(3) Police Officers on operational duties in the field like the Inspector General of Police in-charge Zone, Deputy Inspector General of Police in-charge Range, Superintendent of Police

in-charge district and Station House Officer in-charge of a Police Station shall also have a prescribed minimum tenure of two years unless it is found necessary to remove them prematurely following disciplinary proceedings against them or their conviction in a criminal offence or in a case of corruption or if the incumbent is otherwise incapacitated from discharging his responsibilities. This would be subject to promotion and retirement of the officer.

Separation of Investigation

(4) The investigating police shall be separated from the law and order police to ensure speedier investigation, better expertise and improved rapport with the people. It must, however, be ensured that there is full coordination between the two wings. The separation, to start with, may be effected in towns/urban areas which have a population of ten lakhs or more, and gradually extended to smaller towns/urban areas also.

Police Establishment Board

(5) There shall be a Police Establishment Board in each State which shall decide all transfers, postings, promotions and other service related matters of officers of and below the rank of Deputy Superintendent of Police. The Establishment Board shall be a departmental body comprising the Director General of Police and four other senior officers of the Department. The State Government may interfere with decision of the Board in exceptional cases only after recording its reasons for doing so. The Board shall also be authorized to make appropriate recommendations to the State Government regarding the posting and transfers of officers of and above the rank of Superintendent of Police, and the Government is expected to give due weight to these recommendations and shall normally accept it. It shall also function as a forum of appeal for disposing of representations from officers of the rank of Superintendent of Police and above regarding their promotion/transfer/disciplinary proceedings or their being subjected to illegal or irregular orders and generally reviewing the functioning of the police in the State.

Police Complaints Authority

(6) There shall be a Police Complaints Authority at the district level to look into complaints against police officers of and up to the rank of Deputy Superintendent of Police. Similarly, there should be another Police Complaints Authority at the State level to look into complaints against officers of the rank of Superintendent of Police and above. The district level Authority may be headed by a retired District Judge while the State level Authority may be headed by a retired Judge of the High Court/Supreme Court. The head of the State level Complaints Authority shall be chosen by the State Government out of a panel of names proposed by the Chief Justice; the head of the district level Complaints Authority may also be chosen out of a panel of names proposed by the Chief Justice or a Judge of the High Court nominated by him. These Authorities may be assisted by three to five members depending upon the volume

of complaints in different States/districts, and they shall be selected by the State Government from a panel prepared by the State Human Rights Commission/Lok Ayukta/State Public Service Commission. The panel may include members from amongst retired civil servants, police officers or officers from any other department, or from the civil society. They would work whole time for the Authority and would have to be suitably remunerated for the services rendered by them. The Authority may also need the services of regular staff to conduct field inquiries. For this purpose, they may utilize the services of retired investigators from the CID, Intelligence, Vigilance or any other organization. The State level Complaints Authority would take cognizance of only allegations of serious misconduct by the police personnel, which would include incidents involving death, grievous hurt or rape in police custody. The district level Complaints Authority would, apart from above cases, may also inquire into allegations of extortion, land/house grabbing or any incident involving serious abuse of authority. The recommendations of the Complaints Authority, both at the district and State levels, for any action, departmental or criminal, against a delinquent police officer shall be binding on the concerned authority.

National Security Commission

(7) The Central Government shall also set up a National Security Commission at the Union level to prepare a panel for being placed before the appropriate Appointing Authority, for selection and placement of Chiefs of the Central Police Organisations CPO), who should also be given a minimum tenure of two years. The Commission would also review from time to time measures to upgrade the effectiveness of these forces, improve the service conditions of its personnel, ensure that there is proper coordination between them and that the forces are generally utilized for the purposes they were raised and make recommendations in that behalf. The National Security Commission could be headed by the Union Home Minister and comprise heads of the CPOs and a couple of security experts as members with the Union Home Secretary as its Secretary.

Appendix 2

Guidelines Laid Down by the Supreme Court in *D.K.Basu* v. *State of West Bengal*[1] to be followed in Cases of Arrest and Detention

1. The police personnel carrying out the arrest and handling the interrogation of the arrestee should bear accurate, visible and clear identification and name tags with their designations. The particulars of all such police personnel who handle interrogation of the arrestee must be recorded in a register.

2. That the police officer carrying out the arrest of the arrestee shall prepare a memo of arrest at the time of arrest and such memo shall be attested by at least one witness, who may either be a member of the family of the arrestee or a respectable person of the locality from where the arrest is made. It shall also be countersigned by the arrestee and shall contain the time and date of arrest.

3. A person who has been arrested or detained and is being held in custody in a police station or interrogation centre or other lock-up, shall be entitled to have one friend or relative or other person known to him or having interest in his welfare being informed, as soon as practicable, that he has been arrested and is being detained at the particular place, unless the attesting witness of the memo of arrest is himself such a friend or a relative of the arrestee.

4. The time, place of arrest and venue of custody of an arrestee must be notified by the police where the next friend or relative of the arrestee lives outside the district or town

---

[1] (1997) 1 SCC 416 *http://judis.nic.in/supremecourt/qrydisp.asp?tfnm=14580.*

through the Legal Aid Organisation in the District and the police station of the area concerned telegraphically within a period of 8 to 12 hours after the arrest.

5. The person arrested must be made aware of this right to have someone informed of his arrest or detention as soon as he is put under arrest or is detained.

6. An entry must be made in the diary at the place of detention regarding the arrest of the person which shall also disclose the name of the next friend of the person who has been informed of the arrest and the names and particulars of the police officials in whose custody the arrestee is.

7. The arrestee should, where he so requests, be also examined at the time of his arrest and major and minor injuries, if any present on his/her body, must be recorded at that time. The 'Inspection Memo' must be signed both by the arrestee and the police officer effecting the arrest and a copy provided to the arrestee and the police officer effecting the arrest and its copy provided to the arrestee.

8. The arrestee should be subjected to medical examination by a trained doctor every 48 hours during his detention in custody, by a doctor on the panel of approved doctors appointed by Director, Health Services of the State or Union Territory concerned. Director, Health Services should prepare such a panel for all tehsils and districts as well.

9. Copies of all the documents including the memo of arrest, referred to above, should be sent to the Illeka Magistrate for his record.

10. The arrestee may be permitted to meet his lawyer during interrogation, though not throughout the interrogation.

11. A police control room could be provided at all district and State headquarters, where information regarding the arrest and the place of custody of the arrestee shall be communicated by the officer causing the arrest, within 12 hours of effecting the arrest and at the police control room it should be displayed on a conspicuous notice board.

Appendix 3

The First Schedule[*]
Classification of Offences

Explanatory Note—

(1) In regard to offences under the Indian Penal Code, the entries in the second and third columns against a section the number of which is given in the first column are not intended as the definition of, and the punishment prescribed for, the offence in the Indian Penal Code, but merely as indication of the substance of the section.

(2) In this Schedule, (i) the expression 'Magistrate of the first class' and 'Any Magistrate' include Metropolitan Magistrates but not Executive Magistrates; (ii) the word 'cognizable' stands for 'a police officer may arrest without warrant'; and (iii) the word 'non-cognizable' stands for 'a police officer shall not arrest without warrant'.

I. OFFENCES UNDER THE INDIAN PENAL CODE
CHAPTER V—ABETMENT

Section	Offence	Punishment	Cognizable or non-cognizable	Bailable or non-bailable	By what court triable
109	Abetment of any offence, if the act abetted is committed in consequence, and where no express provision is made for its punishment.	Same as for offence abetted	According as offence abetted is cognizable or non-cognizable.	According as offence abetted is bailable or non-bailable.	Court by which offence abetted is triable.
110	Abetment of any offence, if the person abetted does the act with a different intention from that of the abettor.	Same as for offence abetted	According as offence abetted is cognizable or non-cognizable.	According as offence abetted is bailable or non-bailable.	Court by which offence abetted is triable.

contd

* of the Code of Criminal Procedure, 1973.

Section	Offence	Punishment	Cognizable or non-cognizable	Bailable or non-bailable	By what court triable
111	Abetment of any offence, when one act is abetted and a different act is done; subject to the proviso.	Same as for offence intended to be abetted.	According as offence abetted is cognizable or non-cognizable.	According as offence abetted is bailable or non-bailable.	Court by which offence abetted is triable.
113	Abetment of any offence, when an effect is caused by the act abetted different from that intended by the abettor.	Same as for offence committed	According as offence abetted is cognizable or non-cognizable.	According as offence abetted is bailable or non-bailable.	Court by which offence abetted is triable.
114	Abetment of any offence, if abetor is present when offence is committed.	Same as for offence committed	According as offence abetted is cognizable or non-cognizable.	According as offence abetted is bailable or non-bailable.	Court by which offence abetted is triable.
115	Abetment of an offence, punishable with death or imprisonment for life, if the offence be not committed in consequence of the abetment.	Imprisonment for 7 years and fine.	According as offence abetted is cognizable or non-cognizable.	Non-bailable	Court by which offence abetted is triable.
	If an act which causes harm be done in consequence of the abetment.	Imprisonment for 14 years and fine.	According as offence abetted is cognizable or non-cognizable.	Non-bailable	Court by which offence abetted is triable.
116	Abetment of an offence, punishable with imprisonment, if the offence be not committed in consequence of the abetment.	Imprisonment extending to a quarter part of the longest term provided for the offence or fine, or both.	According as offence abetted is cognizable or non-cognizable.	According as offence abetted is bailable or non-bailable.	Court by which offence abetted is triable.

150

contd

	If the abettor or the person abetted be a public servant whose duty it is to prevent the offence.	Imprisonment extending to half of the longest term provided for the offence or fine, or both.	According as offence abetted is cognizable or non-cognizable.	According as offence abetted is bailable or non-bailable.	Court by which offence abetted is triable.
117	Abetting the commission of an offence by the public or by more than ten persons.	Imprisonment for 3 years, or fine, or both.	According as offence abetted is cognizable or non-cognizable.	According as offence abetted is bailable or non-bailable.	Court by which offence abetted is triable.
118	Concealing a design to commit an offence punishable with death or imprisonment for life, if the offence be committed.	Imprisonment for 7 years, or fine, or both.	According as offence abetted is cognizable or non-cognizable.	Non-bailable	Court by which offence abetted is triable.
	If the offence be not committed.	Imprisonment for 3 years, or fine, or both.	According as offence abetted is cognizable or non-cognizable.	Bailable	Court by which offence abetted is triable.
119	A public servant concealing a design to commit an offence which it is his duty to prevent, if the offence be committed.	Imprisonment extending to half of the longest term provided for the offence or fine, or both.	According as offence abetted is cognizable or non-cognizable.	According as offence abetted is bailable or non-bailable.	Court by which offence abetted is triable.
	If the offence be punishable with death or imprisonment for life.	Imprisonment for 10 years	According as offence abetted is cognizable or non-cognizable.	Non-bailable	Court by which offence abetted is triable.
	If the offence be not committed.	Imprisonment extending to a quarter part of the longest term provided for the offence or fine, or both.	According as offence abetted is cognizable or non-cognizable.	Bailable	Court by which offence abetted is triable.

Section	Offence	Punishment	Cognizable or non-cognizable	Bailable or non-bailable	By what court triable
120	Concealing a design to commit an offence punishable with imprisonment, if offence be committed	Imprisonment extending to a quarter part of the longest term provided for the offence or fine, or both.	According as offence abetted is cognizable or non-cognizable.	According as offence abetted is bailable or non-bailable.	Court by which offence abetted is triable.
	If offence be not committed	Imprisonment extending to one-eighth part of the longest term provided for the Offence or fine, or both.	According as offence abetted is cognizable or non-cognizable.	Bailable	Court by which offence abetted is triable.
CHAPTER V A—CRIMINAL CONSPIRACY					
120B	Criminal conspiracy to commit an offence punishable with death, imprisonment for life or rigorous imprisonment for a term of two years or upwards.	Same as for abetment of offence which is the object of the conspiracy.	According as the offence which is the object of conspiracy is cognizable or non-cognizable.	According as offence which is the object of conspiracy is bailable or non-bailable.	Court by which abetment of the offence which is the object of conspiracy is triable.
	Any other criminal conspiracy.	Imprisonment for 6 months, or fine, or both.	Non-cognizable	Bailable	Magistrate of the first class.
CHAPTER VI—OFFENCES AGAINST THE STATE					
121	Waging or attempting to wage war or abetting the waging of war, against the Government of India.	Death, or imprisonment for life and fine.	Cognizable	Non-bailable	Court of Session.

contd

Section	Offence	Punishment			Court
121A	Conspiring to commit certain offences against the State.	Imprisonment for life, or imprisonment for 10 years and fine.	Cognizable	Non-bailable	Court of Session.
122	Collecting arms, etc., with the intention of waging war against the Government of India.	Imprisonment for life, or imprisonment for 10 years and fine.	Cognizable	Non-bailable	Court of Session.
123	Concealing with intent to facilitate a design to wage war.	Imprisonment for 10 years and fine.	Cognizable	Non-bailable	Court of Session.
124	Assaulting President, Governor, etc., with intent to compel or restrain the exercise of any lawful power.	Imprisonment for 7 years and fine.	Cognizable	Non-bailable	Court of Session.
124A	Sedition	Imprisonment for life and fine, or imprisonment for 3 years and fine, or fine.	Cognizable	Non-bailable	Court of Session.
125	Waging war against any Asiatic power in alliance or at peace with the Government of India, or abetting the waging of such war.	Imprisonment for life and fine, or imprisonment for 7 years and fine, or fine.	Cognizable	Non-bailable	Court of Session.
126	Committing depredation on the territories of any power in alliance or at peace with the Government of India.	Imprisonment for 7 years and fine, and forfeiture of certain property.	Cognizable	Non-bailable	Court of Session.
127	Receiving property taken by war or depredation mentioned in sections 125 and 126.	Imprisonment for 7 years and fine, and forfeiture of certain property.	Cognizable	Non-bailable	Court of Session.

153

Section	Offence	Punishment	Cognizable or non-cognizable	Bailable or non-bailable	By what court triable
128	Public servant voluntarily allowing prisoner of State or war in his custody to escape.	Imprisonment for life, or imprisonment for 10 years and fine.	Cognizable	Non-bailable	Court of Session.
129	Public servant negligently suffering prisoner of State or war in his custody to escape.	Simple imprisonment for 3 years and fine.	Cognizable	Bailable	Magistrate of the first class.
130	Aiding escape of, rescuing or harbouring, such prisoner, or offering any resistance to the recapture of such prisoner.	Imprisonment for life, or imprisonment for 10 years and fine.	Cognizable	Non-bailable	Court of Session.

CHAPTER VII—OFFENCES RELATING TO THE ARMY, NAVY, AND AIR FORCE

Section	Offence	Punishment	Cognizable or non-cognizable	Bailable or non-bailable	By what court triable
131	Abetting mutiny, or attempting to seduce an officer, soldier, sailor or airman from his allegiance or duty.	Imprisonment for life, or imprisonment for 10 years and fine.	Cognizable	Non-bailable	Court of Session.
132	Abetment of mutiny, if mutiny is committed in consequence thereof.	Death, or imprisonment for life, or imprisonment for 10 years and fine.	Cognizable	Non-bailable	Court of Session.
133	Abetment of an assault by an officer, soldier, sailor or airman on his superior officer, when in the execution of his office.	Imprisonment for 3 years and fine.	Cognizable	Non-bailable	Magistrate of the first class.
134	Abetment of such assault, if the assault is committed.	Imprisonment for 7 years and fine.	Cognizable	Non-bailable	Magistrate of the first class.

135	Abetment of the desertion of an officer, soldier, sailor or airman.	Imprisonment for 2 years, or fine, or both.	Cognizable	Bailable	Any Magistrate.
136	Harbouring such an officer, soldier, sailor or airman who has deserted.	Imprisonment for 2 years, or fine, or both.	Cognizable	Bailable	Any Magistrate.
137	Deserter concealed on board merchant vessel, through negligence of master or person in charge thereof.	Fine of 500 rupees	Non-cognizable	Bailable	Any Magistrate.
138	Abetment of act of insubordination by an officer, soldier, sailor or airman, if the offence be committed in consequence.	Imprisonment for 6 months, or fine, or both.	Cognizable	Bailable	Any Magistrate.
140	Wearing the dress or carrying any token used by a soldier, sailor or airman with intent that it may be believed that he is such a soldier, sailor or airman.	Imprisonment for 3 months, or fine of 500 rupees, or both.	Cognizable	Bailable	Any Magistrate.

CHAPTER VIII—OFFENCES AGAINST THE PUBLIC TRANQUILITY

143	Being member of an unlawful assembly.	Imprisonment for 6 months, or fine, or both.	Cognizable	Bailable	Any Magistrate.
144	Joining an unlawful assembly armed with any deadly weapon.	Imprisonment for 2 years, or fine, or both.	Cognizable	Bailable	Any Magistrate.
145	Joining or continuing in an unlawful assembly, knowing that it has been committed to disperse.	Imprisonment for 2 years, or fine, or both.	Cognizable	Bailable	Any Magistrate.
147	Rioting	Imprisonment for 2 years, or fine, or both.	Cognizable	Bailable	Any Magistrate.

contd

Section	Offence	Punishment	Cognizable or non-cognizable	Bailable or non-bailable	By what court triable
148	Rioting armed with a deadly weapon.	Imprisonment for 3 years, or fine, or both.	Cognizable	Bailable	Magistrate of the first class.
149	If an offence be committed by any member of an unlawful assembly, every other member of such assembly shall be guilty of the offence.	The same as for the offence	According as offence is cognizable or non-cognizable.	According as offence is bailable or non-bailable.	The Court by which the offence is triable.
150	Hiring, engaging or employing persons to take part in an unlawful assembly.	The same as for a member of such assembly, and for any offence committed by any member of such assembly.	Cognizable	According as offence is bailable or non-bailable.	The Court by which the offence is triable.
151	Knowingly joining or continuing in any assembly of five or more persons after it has been commanded to disperse.	Imprisonment for 6 months, or fine, or both.	Cognizable	Bailable	Any Magistrate.
152	Assaulting or obstructing public servant when suppressing riot, etc.	Imprisonment for 3 years, or fine, or both.	Cognizable	Bailable	Magistrate of the first class.
153	Wantonly giving provocation with intent to cause riot, if rioting be committed.	Imprisonment for 1 year, or fine, or both.	Cognizable	Bailable	Any Magistrate.
	If not committed	Imprisonment for 6 months, or fine, or both.	Cognizable	Bailable	Magistrate of the first class.
153A	Promoting enmity between classes.	Imprisonment for 3 years, or fine, or both.	Cognizable	Non-bailable	Magistrate of the first class.

156

	Offence	Punishment	Cognizable or non-cognizable	Bailable or non-bailable	By what Court triable
	Promoting enmity between classes in place of worship, etc.	Imprisonment for 5 years, or fine, or both.	Cognizable	Non-bailable	Magistrate of the first class.
153B	Imputations, assertions prejudicial to national integration.	Imprisonment for 3 years, or fine, or both.	Cognizable	Non-bailable	Magistrate of the first class.
	If committed in a place of public worship, etc.	Imprisonment for 5 years, or fine, or both.	Cognizable	Non-bailable	Magistrate of the first class.
154	Owner or occupier of land not giving information of riot, etc.	Fine of 1,000 rupees.	Non-cognizable	Bailable	Any Magistrate.
155	Person for whose benefit or on whose behalf a riot takes place not using all lawful means to prevent it.	Fine	Non-cognizable	Bailable	Any Magistrate.
156	Agent of owner or occupier for whose benefit a riot is committed not using all lawful means to prevent it.	Fine	Non-cognizable	Bailable	Any Magistrate.
157	Harbouring persons hired for an unlawful assembly.	Imprisonment for 6 months, or fine, or both.	Cognizable	Bailable	Any Magistrate.
158	Being hired to take part in an unlawful assembly or riot.	Imprisonment for 6 months, or fine, or both.	Cognizable	Bailable	Any Magistrate.
	Or to go armed	Imprisonment for 2 years, or fine, or both.	Cognizable	Bailable	Any Magistrate.
160	Committing affray	Imprisonment for one month, or fine of 100 rupees, or both.	Cognizable	Bailable	Any Magistrate.

contd

CHAPTER IX—OFFENCES BY OR RELATING TO PUBLIC SERVANTS

Section	Offence	Punishment	Cognizable or non-cognizable	Bailable or non-bailable	By what court triable
*161	Being or excepting to be a public servant, and taking a gratification other than legal remuneration in respect of an official act.	Imprisonment for 3 years, or fine, or both.	Cognizable	Non-bailable	Magistrate of the first class.
*162	Taking a gratification in order, by corrupt or illegal means, to influence a public servant.	Imprisonment for 3 years, or fine, or both.	Cognizable	Non-bailable	Magistrate of the first class.
*163	Taking a gratification for the exercise of personal influence with a public servant.	Simple imprisonment for 1 year or fine, or both.	Cognizable	Non-bailable	Magistrate of the first class.
*164	Abetment by public servant of the offences defined in the last two preceding clauses with reference to himself.	Imprisonment for 3 years, or fine, or both.	Cognizable	Non-bailable	Magistrate of the first class.
*165	Public servant obtaining any valuable thing, without consideration, from a person concerned in any proceeding or business transacted by such public servant.	Imprisonment for 3 years, or fine, or both.	Cognizable	Non-bailable	Magistrate of the first class.
*165A	Punishment for abetment of offences punishable under section 161 or section 165.	Imprisonment for 3 years, or fine, or both.	Cognizable	Non-bailable	Magistrate of the first class.
166	Public servant disobeying a direction of the law with intent to cause injury to any person.	Simple imprisonment for 1 year or fine, or both.	Non-cognizable	Bailable	Magistrate of the first class.

* Sections 161 to 165A of the Indian Penal Code (45 of 1860) repealed by the Prevention of Corruption Act, 1988 (49 of 1988), sec. 31 (w.e.f. 9-9-1988).

contd

167	Public servant framing an incorrect document with intent to cause injury.	Imprisonment for 3 years, or fine, or both.	Cognizable	Bailable	Magistrate of the first class.
168	Public servant unlawfully engaging in trade.	Simple imprisonment for 1 year or fine, or both.	Non-cognizable	Bailable	Magistrate of the first class.
169	Public servant unlawfully buying or bidding for property.	Simple imprisonment for 2 years, or fine, or both, and confiscation of property, if purchased.	Non-cognizable	Bailable	Magistrate of the first class.
170	Personating a Public servant.	Imprisonment for 2 years, or fine, or both.	Cognizable	Non-bailable	Any Magistrate.
171	Wearing garb or carrying token used by public servant with fraudulent intent.	Imprisonment for 3 months, or fine up to 200 rupees, or both.	Cognizable	Bailable	Any Magistrate.

CHAPTER IX-A—OFFENCES RELATING TO ELECTIONS

171E	Bribery	Imprisonment for 1 years, or fine, or both, or if treating only, fine only.	Non-cognizable	Bailable	Magistrate of the first class.
171F	Undue influence at an election	Imprisonment for one year, or fine, or both.	Non-cognizable	Bailable	Magistrate of the first class.
	Personating at an election	Imprisonment for one year, or fine, or both.	Cognizable	Bailable	Magistrate of the first class.

Section	Offence	Punishment	Cognizable or non-cognizable	Bailable or non-bailable	By what court triable
171G	False statement in connection with an election.	Fine	Non-cognizable	Bailable	Magistrate of the first class.
171H	Illegal payments in connection with elections.	Fine of 500 rupees	Non-cognizable	Bailable	Magistrate of the first class.
171I	Failure to keep election accounts.	Fine of 500 rupees	Non-cognizable	Bailable	Magistrate of the first class.

CHAPTER X—CONTEMPTS OF THE LAWFUL AUTHORITY OF PUBLIC SERVANTS

Section	Offence	Punishment	Cognizable or non-cognizable	Bailable or non-bailable	By what court triable
172	Absconding to avoid service of summons of other proceeding from a public servant.	Simple imprisonment for 1 month, or fine of 500 rupees, or both.	Non-cognizable	Bailable	Any Magistrate.
	If summons or notice require attendance in person, etc., in a Court of Justice.	Simple imprisonment for 6 months, or fine of 1,000 rupees, or both.	Non-cognizable	Bailable	Any Magistrate.
173	Preventing the service of the affixing of any summons of notice, or the removal of it when it has been affixed, or preventing a proclamation.	Simple imprisonment for 1 months, or fine of 500 rupees, or both.	Non-cognizable	Bailable	Any Magistrate.
	If summons, etc., require attendance in person, etc., in a Court of Justice.	Simple imprisonment for 6 months or fine of 1,000 rupees, or both.	Non-cognizable	Bailable	Any Magistrate.
174	Not obeying a legal order to attend at a certain place in person or by agent, or departing therefrom without authority.	Simple imprisonment for 1 month or fine of 500 rupees, or both.	Non-cognizable	Bailable	Any Magistrate.

Section	Offence	Punishment	Cognizable or Non-cognizable	Bailable or Non-bailable	By what Court triable
	If the order requires personal attendance, etc., in a Court of Justice.	Simple imprisonment for 6 months, or fine or 1,000 rupees, or both.	Non-cognizable	Bailable	Any Magistrate.
175	Intentionally omitting to produce a document to a public servant by a person legally bound to produce or deliver such document.	Simple imprisonment for 1 month or fine of 500 rupees, or both.	Non-cognizable	Bailable	The court in which the offence is committed, subject to the provisions of Chapter XXVI; or, if not committed in a Court, any Magistrate.
	If the document is required to be produced in or delivered to a Court of Justice.	Simple imprisonment for 6 months, or fine or 1,000 rupees, or both.	Non-cognizable	Bailable	The court in which the offence is committed, subject to the provisions of Chapter XXVI; or, if not committed in a Court, any Magistrate.
176	Intentionally omitting to give notice or information to a public servant by a person legally bound to give such notice or information.	Simple imprisonment for 1 month or fine of 500 rupees, or both.	Non-cognizable	Bailable	Any Magistrate.
	If the notice or information required respects the commission of an offence, etc.	Simple imprisonment for 6 months, or fine or 1,000 rupees, or both.	Non-cognizable	Bailable	Any Magistrate.

contd

161

Section	Offence	Punishment	Cognizable or non-cognizable	Bailable or non-bailable	By what court triable
	If the notice or information is required by an order passed under sub-section (1) of section 356 of this Code.	Simple imprisonment for 6 months, or fine or 1,000 rupees, or both.	Non-cognizable	Bailable	Any Magistrate.
177	Knowingly furnishing false information to a public servant.	Simple imprisonment for 6 months, or fine or 1,000 rupees, or both.	Non-cognizable	Bailable	Any Magistrate.
	If the information required respects the commission of an offence, etc.	Imprisonment for 2 years, or fine, or both.	Non-cognizable	Bailable	Any Magistrate.
178	Refusing oath when duly required to take oath by a public servant.	Simple imprisonment for 6 months, or fine or 1,000 rupees, or both.	Non-cognizable	Bailable	The court in which the offence is committed, subject to the provisions of Chapter XXVI; or, if not committed in a Court, any Magistrate.
179	Being legally bound to state truth and refusing to answer questions.	Simple imprisonment for 6 months, or fine or 1,000 rupees, or both.	Non-cognizable	Bailable	The court in which the offence is committed, subject to the provisions of Chapter XXVI; or, if not committed in a Court, any Magistrate.

contd

	Offence	Punishment	Cognizable or non-cognizable	Bailable or non-bailable	By what court triable
180	Refusing to sign a statement made to a public servant when legally required to do so.	Simple imprisonment for 3 months, or fine of 500 rupees, or both.	Non-cognizable	Bailable	The court in which the offence is committed, subject to the provisions of Chapter XXVI; or, if not committed in a Court, any Magistrate.
181	Knowingly stating to a public servant on oath as true that which is false.	Imprisonment for 3 years and fine.	Non-cognizable	Bailable	Magistrate of the first class.
182	Giving false information to a public servant in order to cause him to use his lawful power to the injury or annoyance of any person.	Imprisonment for 6 months, or fine or 1,000 rupees, or both.	Non-cognizable	Bailable	Any Magistrate.
183	Resistance to the taking of property by the lawful authority of a public servant.	Imprisonment for 6 months, or fine or 1,000 rupees, or both.	Non-cognizable	Bailable	Any Magistrate.
184	Obstructing of property offered for sale by authority of a public servant.	Imprisonment for 1 month, or fine of 500 rupees, or both.	Non-cognizable	Bailable	Any Magistrate.
185	Bidding, by a person under a legal incapacity to purchase it, for property at a lawfully authorized sale, or bidding without intending to perform the obligations incurred there by.	Imprisonment for 1 month, or fine of 200 rupees, or both.	Non-cognizable	Bailable	Any Magistrate.
186	Obstructing public servant in discharge of his public functions.	Imprisonment for 3 months, or fine of 500 rupees, or both.	Non-cognizable	Bailable	Any Magistrate.

Section	Offence	Punishment	Cognizable or non-cognizable	Bailable or non-bailable	By what court triable
187	Omission to assist public servant when bound by law to give such assistance.	Simple imprisonment for 1 month, or fine of 200 rupees, or both.	Non-cognizable	Bailable	Any Magistrate.
	Wilfully neglecting to aid a public servant who demands aid in the execution of process, the prevention of offences, etc.	Simple imprisonment for 6 month, or fine of 500 rupees, or both.	Non-cognizable	Bailable	Any Magistrate.
188	Disobedience to an order lawfullypromulgated by a public servant, if such disobedience causes obstruction, annoyance or injury to persons lawfully employed.	Simple imprisonment for 1 month, or fine of 200 rupees, or both.	Cognizable	Bailable	Any Magistrate.
	If such disobedience causes danger to human life, health or safety, etc.	Imprisonment for 6 month, or fine of 1000 rupees, or both.	Cognizable	Bailable	Any Magistrate.
189	Threatening a public servant with injury to him or one in whom he is interested, to induce him to do or forbear to do any official act.	Imprisonment for 2 years, or fine, or both.	Non-cognizable	Bailable	Any Magistrate.
190	Threatening any person to induce him to refrain from making a legal application for protection from injury.	Imprisonment for 1 year, or fine, or both.	Non-cognizable	Bailable	Any Magistrate.
CHAPTER XI—FALSE EVIDENCE AND OFFENCES AGAINST PUBLIC JUSTICE					
193	Giving or fabricating false evidence in a judicial proceeding.	Imprisonment for 7 years and fine.	Non-cognizable	Bailable	Magistrate of the first class.
	Giving or fabricating false evidence in any other case.	Imprisonment for 3 years and fine.	Non-cognizable	Bailable	Any Magistrate.

contd

194	Giving or fabricating false evidence with intent to cause any person to be convicted of a capital offence.	Imprisonment for life, or rigorous imprisonment for 10 years and fine.	Non-cognizable	Non-bailable	Court of Session.
	If innocent person be thereby convicted and executed.	Death, or as above.	Non-cognizable	Non-bailable	Court of Session.
195	Giving or fabricating false evidence with intent to procure conviction of an offence punishable with imprisonment for life or with imprisonment for 7 years or upwards.	The same as for the offences.	Non-cognizable	Non-bailable	Court of Session.
195A	Threatening any person to give false evidence.	Imprisonment for 7 years, or fine or both.	Cognizable	Non-bailable	Court by which offence of giving false evidence is triable.
	If innocent person is convicted and sentenced in consequence of false evidence with death, or imprisonment for more than seven years.	The same as for the offence	Ditto	Ditto	Ditto
196	Using in a judicial proceeding evidence known to be false or fabricated.	The same as for giving or fabricating false evidence.	Non-cognizable	According as offence of giving such evidence is bailable or non-bailable.	Court by which offence of giving or fabricating false evidence is triable.
197.	Knowingly issuing or signing a false certificate relating to any fact of which such certificate is by law admissible in evidence.	The same as for giving or fabricating false evidence.	Non-cognizable	Bailable	Court by which offence of giving false evidence is triable.
198	Using as a true certificate one known to be false in a material point.	The same as for giving or fabricating false evidence.	Non-cognizable	Bailable	Court by which offence of giving false evidence is triable.

Section	Offence	Punishment	Cognizable or non-cognizable	Bailable or non-bailable	By what court triable
199	False statement made in any declaration which is by law receivable as evidence.	The same as for giving or fabricating false evidence.	Non-cognizable	Bailable	Court by which offence of giving false evidence is triable.
200	Using as true any such declaration known to be false.	The same as for giving or fabricating false evidence.	Non-cognizable	Bailable	Court by which offence of giving false evidence is triable.
201	Causing disappearance of evidence of an offence committed, giving false information touching it to screen the offender, if a capital offence.	Imprisonment for 7 years and fine.	According as the offence in relation to which disappearance of evidence is caused is cognizable or non-cognizable.	Bailable	Court of Session.
	If punishable with imprisonment for life or imprisonment for 10 years.	Imprisonment for 3 years and fine.	Non-cognizable	Bailable	Magistrate of the first class.
	If punishable with less than 10 years' imprisonment.	Imprisonment for a quarter of the longest term provided for the offence, or fine, or both.	Non-cognizable	Bailable	Court by which the offence is triable.
202	Intentional omission to give information of an offence by a person legally bound to inform.	Imprisonment for 6 months, or fine, or both.	Non-cognizable	Bailable	Any Magistrate.
203	Giving false information respecting an offence committed.	Imprisonment for 2 years, or fine, or both.	Non-cognizable	Bailable	Any Magistrate.
204	Secreting or destroying any document to prevent its production as evidence.	Imprisonment for 2 years, or fine, or both.	Non-cognizable	Bailable	Magistrate of the first class.

166

205	False personation for the purpose of any act or proceeding in a suit or criminal prosecution, or for becoming bail or security.	Imprisonment for 3 years, or fine, or both.	Non-cognizable	Bailable	Magistrate of the first class.
206	Fraudulent removal or concealment, etc., of property to prevent its seizure as a forfeiture, or in satisfaction, of a fine under sentence, or in execution of a decree.	Imprisonment for 2 years, or fine, or both.	Non-cognizable	Bailable	Any Magistrate.
207	Claiming property without right, or practising deception touching any right to it, to prevent its being taken as a forfeiture, or in satisfaction of a fine under sentence, or in execution of a decree.	Imprisonment for 2 years, or fine, or both.	Non-cognizable	Bailable	Any Magistrate.

CHAPTER XI—FALSE EVIDENCE AND OFFENCES AGAINST PUBLIC JUSTICE

208	Fraudulently suffering a decree or to pass for a sum not due, or suffering decree to be executed after it has been satisfied.	Imprisonment for 2 years, or fine, or both.	Non-cognizable	Bailable	Magistrate of the first class.
209	False claim in a Court of Justice.	Imprisonment for 2 years, or fine, or both.	Non-cognizable	Bailable	Magistrate of the first class.
210	Fraudulently obtaining a decree for a sum not due, or causing a decree to be executed after it has been satisfied.	Imprisonment for 2 years, or fine, or both.	Non-cognizable	Bailable	Magistrate of the first class.
211	False charge of offence made with intent to injure.	Imprisonment for 2 years, or fine, or both.	Non-cognizable	Bailable	Magistrate of the first class.
	If offence charged be punishable with imprisonment for 7 years or upwards.	Imprisonment for 7 years and fine.	Non-cognizable	Bailable	Magistrate of the first class.
	If offence charged be capital or punishable with imprisonment for life.	Imprisonment for 7 years and fine.	Non-cognizable	Bailable	Court of Session.

contd

Section	Offence	Punishment	Cognizable or non-cognizable	Bailable or non-bailable	By what court triable
212	Harbouring an offender, if the offence be capital.	Imprisonment for 5 years and fine.	Cognizable	Bailable	Magistrate of the first class.
	If punishable with imprisonment for life or with imprisonment for 10 years.	Imprisonment for 5 years and fine.	Cognizable	Bailable	Magistrate of the first class.
	If punishable with imprisonment for 1 year and not for 10 years.	Imprisonment for a quarter of the longest term, and of the description, provided for the offence, or fine, or both.	Cognizable	Bailable	Magistrate of the first class.
213	Taking gift, etc., to screen an offender from punishment if the offence be capital.	Imprisonment for 7 years and fine.	Cognizable	Bailable	Magistrate of the first class.
	If punishable with imprisonment for life or with imprisonment for 10 years.	Imprisonment for 3 years and fine.	Cognizable	Bailable	Magistrate of the first class.
	If punishable with imprisonment for less than 10 years	Imprisonment for a quarter of the longest term, and of the description, provided for the offence, or fine, or both.	Cognizable	Bailable	Magistrate of the first class.
214	Offering gift or restoration of property in consideration of screening offender if the offence be capital.	Imprisonment for 7 years and fine	Non-cognizable	Bailable	Magistrate of the first class.
	If punishable with imprisonment for life or with imprisonment for 10 years.	Imprisonment for 3 years and fine.	Non-cognizable	Bailable	Magistrate of the first class.

contd

	If punishable with imprisonment for less than 10 years	Imprisonment for a quarter of the longest term, and of the description, provided for the offence, or fine, or both.	Non-cognizable	Bailable	Magistrate of the first class.
215	Taking gift to help to recover moveable property of which a person has been deprived by an offence without causing apprehension of offender.	Imprisonment for 2 years, or fine, or both.	Cognizable	Bailable	Magistrate of the first class.
216	Harbouring an offender who has escaped from custody, or whose apprehension has been ordered, if the offence be capital.	Imprisonment for 7 years and fine	Cognizable	Bailable	Magistrate of the first class.
	If punishable with imprisonment for life or with imprisonment for 10 years.	Imprisonment for 3 years with or without fine.	Cognizable	Bailable	Magistrate of the first class.
	If punishable with imprisonment for 1 year and not for 10 years.	Imprisonment for a quarter of the longest term, and of the description, provided for the offence, or fine, or both.	Cognizable	Bailable	Magistrate of the first class.

CHAPTER XI—FALSE EVIDENCE AND OFFENCES AGAINST PUBLIC JUSTICE

216A	Harbouring robbers or dacoits	Rigorous imprisonment for 7 years and fine.	Cognizable	Bailable	Magistrate of the first class.
217	Public servant disobeying a direction of law with intent to save person from punishment, or property from forfeiture.	Imprisonment for 2 years, or fine, or both.	Non-cognizable	Bailable	Any Magistrate.

Section	Offence	Punishment	Cognizable or non-cognizable	Bailable or non-bailable	By what court triable
218	Public servant framing an incorrect record or writing with intent to save person from punishment, or property from forfeiture.	Imprisonment for 3 years, or fine, or both.	Cognizable	Bailable	Magistrate of the first class.
219	Public servant in a judicial proceeding corruptly making and pronouncing an order, report, verdict, or decision which he knows to be contrary to law.	Imprisonment for 7 years, or fine, or both.	Non-cognizable	Bailable	Magistrate of the first class.
220	Commitment for trial or confinement by a person having authority, who knows that he is acting contrary to law.	Imprisonment for 7 years, or fine, or both.	Non-cognizable	Bailable	Magistrate of the first class.
221	Intentional omission to apprehend on the part of a public servant bound by law to apprehend an offender, if the offence be capital.	Imprisonment for 7 years, with or without fine.	According as the offence in relation to which such omission has been made is cognizable or non-cognizable.	Bailable	Magistrate of the first class.
	If punishable with imprisonment for life or imprisonment for 10 years.	Imprisonment for 3 years, with or without fine.	Cognizable	Bailable	Magistrate of the first class.
	If punishable with imprisonment for less than 10 years.	Imprisonment for 2 years, with or without fine.	Cognizable	Bailable	Magistrate of the first class.
222	Intentional omission to apprehend on the part of a public servant bound by law to apprehend person under sentence of a Court of Justice if under sentence of death.	Imprisonment for life, or imprisonment for 14 years, with or without fine.	Cognizable	Non-bailable	Court of Session.
	If under sentence of imprisonment 10 years, or upwards.	Imprisonment for 7 years, with or without fine.	Cognizable	Non-bailable	Magistrate of the first class.

	If under sentence of imprisonment for less than 10 years or lawfully committed to custody.	Imprisonment for 3 years, or fine, or both.	Cognizable	Bailable	Magistrate of the first class.
223	Escape from confinement negligently suffered by a public servant.	Simple imprisonment for 2 years, or fine, or both.	Non-cognizable	Bailable	Any Magistrate.
224	Resistance or obstruction by a person to his lawful apprehension.	Imprisonment for 2 years, or fine, or both.	Cognizable	Bailable	Any Magistrate.
225	Resistance or obstruction to the lawful apprehension of any person, or rescuing him from lawful custody.	Imprisonment for 2 years, or fine, or both.	Cognizable	Bailable	Any Magistrate.
	If charged with an offence punishable with imprisonment for life or imprisonment for 10 years.	Imprisonment for 3 years and fine.	Cognizable	Non-bailable	Magistrate of the first class.
	If charged with a capital offence.	Imprisonment for 7 years and fine.	Cognizable	Non-bailable	Magistrate of the first class.
	If the person is sentenced to imprisonment for life, or imprisonment for 10 years, or upwards.	Imprisonment for 7 years and fine.	Cognizable	Non-bailable	Magistrate of the first class.
	If under sentence of death	Imprisonment for life, or imprisonment for 10 years and fine.	Cognizable	Non-bailable	Court of Session.
225A	Omission to apprehend, or sufferance of escape on part of public servant, in cases not otherwise provided for: (a) in case of intentional omission or sufferance.	Imprisonment for 3 years, or fine, or both.	Non-cognizable	Bailable	Magistrate of the first class.

contd

Section	Offence	Punishment	Cognizable or non-cognizable	Bailable or non-bailable	By what court triable
	(b) in case of negligent omission or sufferance.	Simple imprisonment for 2 years, or fine, or both.	Non-cognizable	Bailable	Any Magistrate.
225B	Resistance or obstruction to lawful apprehension, or escape or rescue in case not otherwise provided for.	Imprisonment for 6 months, or fine, or both.	Cognizable	Bailable	Any Magistrate.
227	Violation of condition of remission of punishment.	Punishment of original sentence, or if part of punishment has been undergone, the residue.	Cognizable	Non-bailable	The Court by which the original offence was triable.
228	Intentional insult or interruption to a public servant sitting in any stage of a judicial proceeding.	Simple imprisonment for 6 months, or fine of 1,000 rupees, or both.	Non-cognizable	Bailable	The court in which the offence is committed, subject to the provisions of Chapter XXVI.

STATE AMENDMENT

Andhra Pradesh:
Offence under Section 228 is cognizable.
[*Vide* A.P.G.O. Ms No. 732, dated 5th December, 1991].

Section	Offence	Punishment	Cognizable or non-cognizable	Bailable or non-bailable	By what court triable
[228A	Disclosure of identity of the victim of the certain offences, etc.	Imprisonment for 2 years and fine.	Cognizable	Bailable	Any Magistrate.
	Printing or publication of a proceeding without prior permission of court.	Imprisonment for 2 years and fine.	Cognizable	Bailable	Any Magistrate.

1. Ins. by Act 43 of 1983, sec. 5 (w.e.f. 25-12-1993).

Section	Offence	Punishment	Cognizable or non-cognizable	Bailable or non-bailable	By what court triable
229	Personation of a juror or assessor.	Imprisonment for 2 years, or fine; or both.	Cognizable	Bailable	Magistrate of the first class.

CHAPTER XII—OFFENCES RELATING TO COIN AND GOVERNMENT STAMPS

231	Counterfeiting, or performing any part of the process of counterfeiting coin.	Imprisonment for 7 years and fine.	Cognizable	Non-bailable	Magistrate of the first class.
232	Counterfeiting, or performing any part for the process of counterfeiting coin.	Imprisonment for life, or imprisonment for 10 years and fine.	Cognizable	Non-bailable	Court of Session.
233	Making, buying or selling instrument for the purpose of counterfeiting Indian coin.	Imprisonment for 3 years and fine.	Cognizable	Non-bailable	Magistrate of the first class.
234	Making, buying or selling instrument of the purpose of counterfeiting Indian coin.	Imprisonment for 7 years and fine.	Cognizable	Non-bailable	Court of Session.
235	Possession of instrument or material for the purpose of using the same for counterfeiting coin.	Imprisonment for 3 years and fine.	Cognizable	Non-bailable	Magistrate of the first class.
	If Indian coin.	Imprisonment for 10 years and fine.	Cognizable	Non-bailable	Court of Session.
236	Abetting, in India, the counterfeiting, out of India, of coin.	The punishment provided for abetting the counterfeiting of such coin within India.	Cognizable	Non-bailable	Court of Session.
237	Import or export of counterfeit coin, knowing the same to be counterfeit.	Imprisonment for 3 years and fine.	Cognizable	Non-bailable	Magistrate of the first class.
238	Import or export of counterfeit of Indian coin, knowing the same to be counterfeit.	Imprisonment for life, or imprisonment for 10 years and fine.	Cognizable	Non-bailable	Court of Session.

contd

Section	Offence	Punishment	Cognizable or non-cognizable	Bailable or non-bailable	By what court triable
239	Having any counterfeit coin known to be such when it came into possession, and delivering, etc., the same to any person.	Imprisonment for 5 years and fine.	Cognizable	Non-bailable	Magistrate of the first class.
240	Same with respect to Indian coin.	Imprisonment for 10 years and fine.	Cognizable	Non-bailable	Court of Session.
241	Knowingly delivering to another any counterfeit coin as genuine, which, when first possessed, the deliverer did not know to be counterfeit.	Imprisonment for 2 years, fine, or 10 times the value of the coin counterfeited, or both.	Cognizable	Non-bailable	Any Magistrate.
242	Possession of counterfeit coin by a person who knew it to be counterfeit when he became possessed thereof.	Imprisonment for 3 years and fine.	Cognizable	Non-bailable	Magistrate of the first class.
243	Possession of Indian coin by a person who knew it to be counterfeit when he became possessed thereof.	Imprisonment for 7 years and fine.	Cognizable	Non-bailable	Magistrate of the first class.
244	Person employed in a Mint causing coin to be of a different weight or composition from that fixed by law.	Imprisonment for 7 years and fine.	Cognizable	Non-bailable	Magistrate of the first class.
245	Unlawfully taking from a Mint any coining instrument.	Imprisonment for 7 years and fine.	Cognizable	Non-bailable	Magistrate of the first class.
246	Fraudulently diminishing the weight or altering the composition of Indian coin.	Imprisonment for 3 years and fine.	Cognizable	Non-bailable	Magistrate of the first class.
247	Fraudulently diminishing the weight or altering the composition of Indian coin.	Imprisonment for 7 years and fine.	Cognizable	Non-bailable	Magistrate of the first class.

contd

248	Altering appearance of any coin with intent that it shall pass as a coin of a different description.	Imprisonment for 3 years and fine.	Cognizable	Non-bailable	Magistrate of the first class.
249	Altering appearance of Indian coin with intent that it shall pass as a coin of a different description.	Imprisonment for 7 years and fine.	Cognizable	Non-bailable	Magistrate of the first class.
250	Delivery to another of coin possessed with the knowledge that it is altered.	Imprisonment for 5 years and fine.	Cognizable	Non-bailable	Magistrate of the first class.
251	Delivery of Indian coin possessed with the knowledge that it is altered.	Imprisonment for 10 years and fine.	Cognizable	Non-bailable	Court of Session.
252	Possession of altered coin by a person who knew it to be altered when he became possessed thereof.	Imprisonment for 3 years and fine.	Cognizable	Non-bailable	Magistrate of the first class.
253	Possession of Indian coin by a person who knew it to be altered when he became possessed thereof.	Imprisonment for 5 years and fine.	Cognizable	Non-bailable	Magistrate of the first class.
254	Delivery to another of coin as genuine which, when first possessed, the deliverer did not know to be altered.	Imprisonment for 2 years or fine, or 10 times the value of the coin.	Cognizable	Non-bailable	Any Magistrate.
255	Counterfeiting a Government stamp.	Imprisonment for life, or imprisonment for 10 years and fine.	Cognizable	Non-bailable	Court of Session.
256	Having possession of an instrument or material for the purpose of counterfeiting a Government stamp.	Imprisonment for 7 years and fine.	Cognizable	Non-bailable	Magistrate of the first class.
257	Making, buying or selling instrument for the purpose of counterfeiting a Government stamp.	Imprisonment for 7 years and fine.	Cognizable	Non-bailable	Magistrate of the first class.

Section	Offence	Punishment	Cognizable or non-cognizable	Bailable or non-bailable	By what court triable
258	Sale of counterfeit Government Stamp.	Imprisonment for 7 years and fine.	Cognizable	Non-bailable	Magistrate of the first class.
259	Having possession of a counterfeit Government stamp.	Imprisonment for 7 years and fine.	Cognizable	Bailable	Magistrate of the first class.
260	Using as genuine a Government stamp known to be counterfeit.	Imprisonment for 7 years, or fine, or both.	Cognizable	Bailable	Magistrate of the first class.
261	Effacing any writing from a substance bearing a Government stamp, or removing from a document a stamp used for it, with intent to cause a loss to Government.	Imprisonment for 3 years, or fine, or both.	Cognizable	Non-bailable	Magistrate of the first class.
262	Using a Government stamp known to have been before fine, used.	Imprisonment for 2 years, or fine, or both.	Cognizable	Non-bailable	Any Magistrate.
263	Erasure of mark denoting that stamps have been used.	Imprisonment for 2 years, or fine, or both.	Cognizable	Non-bailable	Magistrate of the first class.
263A	Fictitious stamps	Fine of 200 rupees	Cognizable	Non-bailable	Any Magistrate.

CHAPTER XIII—OFFENCES RELATING TO WEIGHTS AND MEASURES

Section	Offence	Punishment	Cognizable or non-cognizable	Bailable or non-bailable	By what court triable
264	Fraudulent use of false instrument for weighing.	Imprisonment for 1 year, or fine, or both.	Non-cognizable	Bailable	Any Magistrate.
265	Fraudulent use of false weight or measure.	Imprisonment for 1 year, or fine, or both.	Non-cognizable	Bailable	Any Magistrate.
266	Being in possession of false weight or measures for fraudulent use.	Imprisonment for 1 year, or fine, or both.	Non-cognizable	Bailable	Any Magistrate.

Section	Offence	Punishment	Cognizable or Non-cognizable	Bailable or Non-bailable	Court
267	Making or selling false weights or measures for fraudulent use.	Imprisonment for 1 year, or fine, or both.	Cognizable	Non-bailable	Any Magistrate.

CHAPTER XIV—OFFENCES AFFECTING THE PUBLIC HEALTH, SAFETY, CONVENIENCE, DECENCY, AND MORALS

Section	Offence	Punishment	Cognizable or Non-cognizable	Bailable or Non-bailable	Court
269	Negligently doing any act known to be likely to spread infection of any disease dangerous to life.	Imprisonment for 6 months or fine, or both.	Cognizable	Bailable	Any Magistrate.
270	Malignantly doing any act known to be likely to spread infection of any disease dangerous to life.	Imprisonment for 2 years, or fine or both	Cognizable	Bailable	Any Magistrate.
271	Knowingly disobeying any quarantine rule.	Imprisonment for 6 months, or fine, or both.	Non-cognizable	Bailable	Any Magistrate.
272	Adulterating food or drink intended for sale, so as to make the same noxious.	Imprisonment for 6 month, or fine of 1,000 rupees, or both.	Non-cognizable	Bailable	Any Magistrate.
273	Selling any food or drink as food and drink, knowing the same to be noxious.	Imprisonment for 6 month, or fine of 1,000 rupees, or both.	Non-cognizable	Bailable	Any Magistrate.
274	Adulterating any drug or medical preparation intended for sale so as to lesson its efficacy, or to change its operation, or to make it noxious.	Imprisonment for 6 month, or fine of 1,000 rupees, or both.	Non-cognizable	Bailable	Any Magistrate.
275	Offering for sale or issuing from a dispensary any drug or medical preparation known to have been adulterated.	Imprisonment for 6 month, or fine of 1,000 rupees, or both.	Non-cognizable	Bailable	Any Magistrate.

Section	Offence	Punishment	Cognizable or non-cognizable	Bailable or non-bailable	By what court triable
276	Knowingly selling or issuing from a dispensary any drug or medical preparation as a different drug or medical preparation.	Imprisonment for 6 month, or fine of 1,000 rupees, or both.	Non-cognizable	Bailable	Any Magistrate.

STATE AMENDMENTS (SECTIONS 272 TO 276)

Uttar Pradesh:

For the existing entries against sections 272, 273, 174, 175, and 176 in the First Schedule, the following shall be substituted—

Section	Offence	Punishment	Cognizable or non-cognizable	Bailable or non-bailable	By what court triable
272	Adulterating food or drink intended for sale, so as to make the same noxious.	Imprisonment for life, with or without fine.	Cognizable	Non-bailable	Court of Session.
273	Selling any food or drink as food and drink, knowing the same to be noxious.	Imprisonment for life, with or without fine.	Cognizable	Non-bailable	Court of Session.
274	Adulterating any drug or medical preparation intended for sale so as to lessen its efficacy, or to change its operation, or to make it noxious.	Imprisonment for 6 months, or fine of 1,000 rupees, or both.	Non-cognizable	Bailable	Any Magistrate.
275	Offering for sale or issuing from a dispensary any drug or medical preparation known to have been adulterated.	Imprisonment for 6 months, or fine of 1,000 rupees, or both.	Non-cognizable	Bailable	Any Magistrate.
276	Knowingly selling or issuing from a dispensary any drug or medical preparation as a different drug or medical preparation	Imprisonment for 6 months, or fine of 1,000 rupees, or both.	Non-cognizable	Bailable	Any Magistrate.

[*Vide* Uttar Pradesh Act 47 of 1975, sec. 4 (w.e.f. 15-9-1975)].

West Bengal:

For the existing entries against sections 272, 273, 174, 175, and 176 in the First Schedule, the following shall be substituted—

contd

272	Adulterating food or drink intended for sale, so as to make the same noxious.	Imprisonment for life, with or without fine.	Cognizable	Non-bailable	Court of Session.
273	Selling any food or drink as food and drink, knowing the same to be noxious.	Imprisonment for life, with or without fine.	Cognizable	Non-bailable	Court of Session.
274	Adulterating any drug or medical preparation intended for sale so as to lessen its efficacy, or to change its operation, or to make it noxious.	Imprisonment for life, with or without fine.	Cognizable	Non-bailable	Court of Session.
275	Offering for sale or issuing from a dispensary any drug or medical preparation known to have been adulterated.	Imprisonment for life, with or without fine	Cognizable	Non-bailable	Court of Session.
276	Knowingly selling or issuing from a dispensary any drug or medical preparation as a different drug or medical preparation	Imprisonment for life, with or without fine	Cognizable	Non-bailable	Court of Session.

[*Vide* West Bengal Act 34 of 1974, sec. 5 (w.e.f. 16-6-1974)].

277	Defiling the water of a public spring or reservoir.	Imprisonment for 3 months, of fine of 500 rupees, or both.	Cognizable	Bailable	Any Magistrate.
278	Making atmosphere noxious to health.	Fine of 500 rupees	Non-cognizable	Bailable	Any Magistrate.
279	Driving or riding on a public way so rashly or negligently as to endanger human life, etc.	Imprisonment for 6 months or fine of 1,000 rupees, or both.	Cognizable	Bailable	Any Magistrate.
280	Navigating any vessel so rashly or negligently as to endanger human life, etc.	Imprisonment for 6 months, or fine of 1,000 rupees, or both.	Cognizable	Bailable	Any Magistrate.

Section	Offence	Punishment	Cognizable or non-cognizable	Bailable or non-bailable	By what court triable
281	Exhibition of a false light, mark or buoy.	Imprisonment for 7 years, or fine, or both.	Cognizable	Bailable	Magistrate of the first class.
282	Conveying for hire any person by water, in a vessel in such a state or so loaded, as to endanger his life.	Imprisonment for 6 months, or fine of 1,000 rupees, or both.	Cognizable	Bailable	Any Magistrate.
283	Causing danger, obstruction or, injury in any public way or line of navigation.	Fine of 200 rupees	Cognizable	Bailable	Any Magistrate.
284	Dealing with any poisonous substance so as to endanger human life, etc.	Imprisonment for 6 months or fine of 1,000 rupees, or both.	Cognizable	Bailable	Any Magistrate.
285	Dealing with fire or any combustible matter so as to endanger human life, etc.	Imprisonment for 6 months or fine of 1,000 rupees, or both.	Cognizable	Bailable	Any Magistrate.
286	So dealing with any explosive substance.	Imprisonment for 6 months or fine of 1,000 rupees, or both.	Cognizable	Bailable	Any Magistrate.
287	So dealing with any machinery	Imprisonment for 6 months or fine of 1,000 rupees, or both.	Non-cognizable	Bailable	Any Magistrate.
288	A person omitting to guard against probable danger to human life by the fall of any building over which he has a right entitling him to pull it down or repair it.	Imprisonment for 6 months or fine of 1,000 rupees, or both.	Non-cognizable	Bailable	Any Magistrate.

180

289	A person omitting to take order with any animal in his possession, so as to guard against danger to human life, or of grievous hurt, from such animal.	Imprisonment for 6 months or fine of 1,000 rupees, or both.	Cognizable	Bailable	Any Magistrate.
290	Committing a public nuisance	Fine of 200 rupees	Non-cognizable	Bailable	Any Magistrate.
291	Continuance of nuisance after injunction to discontinue.	Simple imprisonment for 6 months, or fine, or both.	Cognizable	Bailable	Any Magistrate.
292	Sale, etc., of obscene books, etc.	On first conviction, with imprisonment for 2 years, and with fine of 2,000 rupees, and, in the event of second or subsequent conviction, with imprisonment for five years and with fine of 5,000 rupees.	Cognizable	Bailable	Any Magistrate.

STATE AMENDMENTS

Tamil Nadu:
In the first Schedule, in the entries relating to sections 292-A and 293, the following entries shall be substitutes, namely:

292A	Printing, etc. of grossly indecent of scurrilous matter or matter intended for blackmail.	Imprisonment of either description for 2 years, or fine, or both.	Non-cognizable	Bailable	Any Magistrate.

[*Vide* Tamil Nadu Act 30 of 1984].

293	Sale, etc., of obscene objects to young persons.	On first conviction, with imprisonment for 3 years, and with fine of 2,000	Cognizable	Bailable	Any Magistrate.

contd

Section	Offence	Punishment	Cognizable or non-cognizable	Bailable or non-bailable	By what court triable
		rupees, and in the event of second or subsequent conviction, with imprisonment for 7 years, and with fine of 5,000 rupees.			
294 *	Obscene songs	Imprisonment for 3 months, or fine, or both.	Cognizable	Bailable	Any Magistrate.
294A	Keeping a lottery office	Imprisonment for 6 months, or fine, or both.	Non-cognizable	Bailable	Any Magistrate.
	Publishing proposals relating to lotteries.	Fine of 1,000 rupees	Non-cognizable	Bailable	Any Magistrate.

CHAPTER XV—OFFENCES RELATING TO RELIGION

Section	Offence	Punishment	Cognizable or non-cognizable	Bailable or non-bailable	By what court triable
295	Destroying, damaging or defiling a place of worship or sacred object with intent to insult the region of any class of persons.	Imprisonment for 2 years, or fine, or both.	Cognizable	Non-bailable	Any Magistrate.
295A	Maliciously insulting the religion or the religious beliefs of any class.	Imprisonment for 2 years, or fine, or both.	Cognizable	Non-bailable	Magistrate of the first class.
296	Causing a disturbance to an assembly engaged in religious worship.	Imprisonment for 1 year, or fine, or both.	Cognizable	Bailable	Any Magistrate.
297	Trespassing in place of worship or sepulcher, disturbing funeral with intention to wound the feelings or to insult the religion of any person, or offering indignity to a human corpse.	Imprisonment for 1 year, or fine, or both.	Cognizable	Bailable	Any Magistrate.

Section	Offence	Punishment	Cognizable or non-cognizable	Bailable or non-bailable	By what court triable
298	Uttering any word or making any sound in the hearing or making any gesture, or placing any object in the sight of any person, with intention to wound his religious feeling.	Imprisonment for 1 year, or fine, or both.	Non-cognizable	Bailable	Any Magistrate.

CHAPTER XVI—OFFENCES AFFECTING THE HUMAN BODY

Section	Offence	Punishment	Cognizable or non-cognizable	Bailable or non-bailable	By what court triable
302	Murder	Death, or imprisonment for life, and fine.	Cognizable	Non-bailable	Court of Session.
303	Murder by a person under sentence of imprisonment for life.	Death	Cognizable	Non-bailable	Court of Session.
304	Culpable homicide not amounting to murder, if act by which the death is caused is done with intention of causing death, etc.	Imprisonment for life, or imprisonment for 10 years and fine.	Cognizable	Non-bailable	Court of Session.
	If act is done with knowledge that it is likely to cause death, but without any intention to cause death, etc.	Imprisonment for 10 years, or fine, or both.	Cognizable	Non-bailable	Court of Session.
304A	Causing death by rash or negligence act.	Imprisonment for 2 years or fine, or both.	Cognizable	Bailable	Magistrate of the first class.
1[304B	Dowry death	Imprisonment of not less than seven years but which may extend to imprisonment for life.	Cognizable	Non-bailable	Court of Session.

1. Ins. by Act 43 of 1986, sec. 11 (w.e.f. 19-11-1986).

Section	Offence	Punishment	Cognizable or non-cognizable	Bailable or non-bailable	By what court triable
305	Abetment of suicide committed by child, or insane or delirious person or an idiot, or a person intoxicated.	Death, or imprisonment for life, or	Cognizable	Non-bailable	Court of Session.

contd

Section	Offence	Punishment	Cognizable or non-cognizable	Bailable or non-bailable	By what court triable
		imprisonment for 10 years and fine.			
306	Abetting the commission of suicide	Imprisonment for 10 years and fine.	Cognizable	Non-bailable	Court of Session.
307	Attempt to murder	Imprisonment for 10 years and fine.	Cognizable	Non-bailable	Court of Session.
	If such act causes hurt to any person.	Imprisonment for life, or imprisonment for 10 years and fine.	Cognizable	Non-bailable	Court of Session.
	Attempt by life-convict to murder, if hurt is caused.	Death or imprisonment for 10 years and fine.	Cognizable	Non-bailable	Court of Session.
308	Attempt to commit culpable homicide.	Imprisonment for 3 years, or fine, or both.	Cognizable	Non-bailable	Court of Session.
	If such act causes hurt to any person.	Imprisonment for 7 years, or fine, or both.	Cognizable	Non-bailable	Court of Session.
309	Attempt to commit suicide.	Simple imprisonment for 1 year, or fine, or both.	Cognizable	Bailable	Any Magistrate.
311	Being a thug.	Imprisonment for life and fine.	Cognizable	Non-bailable	Court of Session.
312	Causing miscarriage.	Imprisonment for 3 years, fine, or both.	Non-cognizable	Bailable	Magistrate of the first class.
	If the woman be quick with child.	Imprisonment for 7 years and fine.	Non-cognizable	Bailable	Magistrate of the first class.

184

contd

313	Causing miscarriage without woman's consent.	Imprisonment for life, or imprisonment for 10 years and fine.	Cognizable	Non-bailable	Court of Session.
314	Death caused by an act done with intent to cause miscarriage.	Imprisonment for 10 years and fine.	Cognizable	Non-bailable	Court of Session.
	If act done without woman's consent.	Imprisonment for life, or as above.	Cognizable	Non-bailable	Court of Session.
315	Act done with intent to prevent a child being born alive, or to cause it to die after its birth.	Imprisonment for 10 years or fine, or both.	Cognizable	Non-bailable	Court of Session.
316	Causing death of a quick unborn child by an act amounting to culpable homicide.	Imprisonment for 10 years and fine.	Cognizable	Non-bailable	Court of Session.
317	Exposure of a child under 12 years of age by parent or person having care of it with intention of wholly abandoning it.	Imprisonment for 7 years, or fine, or both.	Cognizable	Bailable	Magistrate of the first class.
318	Concealment of birth by secret disposal of dead body.	Imprisonment for 2 years, or fine, or both.	Cognizable	Bailable	Magistrate of the first class.

CHAPTER XVI—OFFENCES AFFECTING THE HUMAN BODY

323	Voluntarily causing hurt.	Imprisonment for 1 year, or fine of 1,000 rupees, or both.	Non-cognizable	Bailable	Any Magistrate.
324	Voluntarily causing hurt by dangerous weapons or means.	Imprisonment for 3 years, or fine, or both.	Cognizable	Bailable	Any Magistrate.
325	Voluntarily causing grievous hurt.	Imprisonment for 7 years and fine.	Cognizable	Bailable	Any Magistrate.

Section	Offence	Punishment	Cognizable or non-cognizable	Bailable or non-bailable	By what court triable
326	Voluntarily causing grievous hurt by dangerous weapons or means.	Imprisonment for life, or imprisonment for 10 years and fine.	Cognizable	Non-bailable	Magistrate of the first class.
327	Voluntarily causing hurt to extort property or a valuable security, or to constrain to do anything which is illegal or which may facilitate the commission of an offence.	Imprisonment for 10 years and fine.	Cognizable	Non-bailable	Magistrate of the first class.
328	Administering stupefying drug with intent to cause hurt, etc.	Imprisonment for 10 years and fine.	Cognizable	Non-bailable	Court of Session.
329	Voluntarily causing grievous hurt to extort property or a valuable security, or to constrain to do anything which is illegal, or which may facilitate the commission of an offence.	Imprisonment for life, or imprisonment for 10 years and fine.	Cognizable	Non-bailable	Court of Session.
330	Voluntarily causing hurt to extort confession or information, or to compel restoration of property, etc.	Imprisonment for 7 years and fine.	Cognizable	Bailable	Magistrate of the first class.
331	Voluntarily causing grievous hurt to extort confession or information, or to compel restoration of property, etc.	Imprisonment for 10 years and fine.	Cognizable	Non-bailable	Court of Session.
332	Voluntarily causing hurt to deter public servant from his duty.	Imprisonment for 3 years, or fine, or both.	Cognizable	Bailable	Magistrate of the first class.
333	Voluntarily causing grievous hurt to deter public servant from his duty.	Imprisonment for 10 years and fine.	Cognizable	Non-bailable	Court of Session.
334	Voluntarily causing hurt on grave and sudden provocation, not intending to hurt any other than the person who gave the provocation.	Imprisonment for 1 month, or fine of 500 rupees, or both.	Non-cognizable	Bailable	Any Magistrate.

contd

335	Causing grievous hurt on grave and sudden provocation, not intending to hurt any other than the person who gave the provocation.	Imprisonment for 4 years, or fine of 2,000 rupees, or both.	Cognizable	Bailable	Magistrate of the first class.
336	Doing any act which endangers human life or the personal safety of others.	Imprisonment for 3 months, or fine of 250 rupees, or both.	Cognizable	Bailable	Any Magistrate.
337	Causing hurt by an act which endangers human life, etc.	Imprisonment for 6 months, or fine of 500 rupees, or both.	Cognizable	Bailable	Any Magistrate.
338	Causing grievous hurt by an act which endangers human life, etc.	Imprisonment for 2 years, or fine of 1,000 rupees, or both.	Cognizable	Bailable	Any Magistrate.
341	Wrongfully restraining any person	Simple imprisonment for 1 month, or fine of 500 rupees, or both.	Cognizable	Bailable	Any Magistrate.
342	Wrongfully confining any person	Imprisonment for 1 year, fine of 1,000 rupees, or both.	Cognizable	Bailable	Any Magistrate.
343	Wrongfully confining for 3 or more days.	Imprisonment for 2 years, or fine, or both.	Cognizable	Bailable	Any Magistrate.
344	Wrongfully confining for 10 or more days.	Imprisonment for 3 years and fine.	Cognizable	Bailable	Any Magistrate.

187

Section	Offence	Punishment	Cognizable or non-cognizable	Bailable or non-bailable	By what court triable
345	Keeping any person in wrongful confinement, knowing that a writ has been issued for his liberation.	Imprisonment for 2 years, in addition to imprisonment under any other section.	Cognizable	Bailable	Magistrate of the first class.
346	Wrongful confinement in secret.	Imprisonment for 2 years, in addition to imprisonment under any other section.	Cognizable	Bailable	Magistrate of the first class.
347	Wrongful confinement for the purpose of extorting property, or constraining to an illegal act, etc.	Imprisonment for 3 years and fine.	Cognizable	Bailable	Any Magistrate.
348	Wrongful confinement for the purpose of extorting confession or information, or of compelling restoration of property, etc.	Imprisonment for 3 years and fine.	Cognizable	Bailable	Any Magistrate.

CHAPTER XVI—OFFENCES AFFECTING THE HUMAN BODY

Section	Offence	Punishment	Cognizable or non-cognizable	Bailable or non-bailable	By what court triable
352	Assault or use of criminal force otherwise than on grave provocation.	Imprisonment for 3 months, fine of 500 rupees, or both.	Non-cognizable	Bailable	Any Magistrate.
353	Assault or use of criminal force to deter a public servant from discharge of his duty.	Imprisonment for 2 years, or fine, or both.	Cognizable	Bailable	Any Magistrate.
354	Assault or use of criminal force to a woman with intent to outrage her modesty.	Imprisonment for 2 years, or fine, or both.	Cognizable	Bailable	Any Magistrate.

Orissa:

Offence under Section 354 is Non-bailable.

[*Vide* Orissa Act of 1995, assented by the President on 10-3-1995].

355	Assault or criminal force with intent to dishonour a person, otherwise than on grave and sudden provocation.	Imprisonment for 2 years, or fine, or both.	Non-cognizable	Bailable	Any Magistrate.

STATE AMENDMENTS

Andhra Pradesh:

For the existing entries against sections 354 and 355, the following shall be substituted:

354	Assault or use of criminal force to a woman with intent to outrage her modesty.	Imprisonment for 7 years and fine.	Cognizable	Non-bailable	Court of Session.
355	Assault or criminal force with intent to dishonour a person, otherwise than on grave and sudden provocation.	Imprisonment for 2 years, or fine, or both.	Non-cognizable	Bailable	Any Magistrate.

[*Vide* Andhra Pradesh Act 3 of 1992, sec. 2 (w.e.f. 15-2-1992)].

356	Assault or criminal force in attempt to commit theft of property worn or carried by a person.	Imprisonment for 2 years, or fine, or both.	Cognizable	Bailable	Any Magistrate.
357	Assault or use of criminal force in attempt wrongfully to confine a person.	Imprisonment for 1 year, or fine of 1,000 rupees, or both.	Cognizable	Bailable	Any Magistrate.
358	Assault or use of criminal force on grave and sudden provocation.	Simple imprisonment for one month, or fine of 200 rupees, or both.	Non-cognizable	Bailable	Any Magistrate.
363	Kidnapping	Imprisonment for 7 years and fine.	Cognizable	Bailable	Magistrate of the first class.

contd

STATE AMENDMENT

Uttar Pradesh:

In the entries relating to section 363 in column 5, for the word "Bailable" the word "Non-bailable" shall be substituted.
[*Vide* Uttar Pradesh Act 1 of 1984, sec. 12 (w.e.f. 1-5-1984)]

Section	Offence	Punishment	Cognizable or non-cognizable	Bailable or non-bailable	By what court triable
363A	Kidnapping or obtaining the custody of a minor in order that such minor may be employed or used for purposes of begging.	Imprisonment for 10 years and fine.	Cognizable	Non-bailable	Magistrate of the first class.
	Maiming a minor in order that such minor may be employed or used for purposes of begging.	Imprisonment for life and fine.	Cognizable	Non-bailable	Court of Session.
364	Kidnapping or abducting in order to murder.	Imprisonment for life, or rigorous imprisonment for 10 years and fine.	Cognizable	Non-bailable	Court of Session.
[364A	Kidnapping for ransom, etc.	Death, or imprisonment for life, and fine.	Cognizable	Non-bailable	Court of Session.
365	Kidnapping or abducting with intent secretly and wrongfully to confine a person.	Imprisonment for 7 years and fine.	Cognizable	Non-bailable	Magistrate of the first class.
366	Kidnapping or abducting a woman to compel her marriage or to cause her defilement, etc.	Imprisonment for 10 years fine.	Cognizable	Non-bailable	Court of Session.
366A	Procuration of minor girl.	Imprisonment for 10 years fine.	Cognizable	Non-bailable	Court of Session.
366B	Importation of girl from foreign country.	Imprisonment for 10 years fine.	Cognizable	Non-bailable	Court of Session.

1. Ins. by Act 42 of 1993, Sec. 4 (w.e.f. 22-5-1993).

190

contd

Section	Offence	Punishment	Cognizable or Non-cognizable	Bailable or Non-bailable	Court
367	Kidnapping or abducting in order to subject a person to grievous hurt, slavery, etc.	Imprisonment for 10 years fine.	Cognizable	Non-bailable	Court of Session.
368	Concealing or keeping in confinement a kidnapped person.	Punishment for kidnapping or abduction.	Cognizable	Non-bailable	Court by which the kidnapping or abduction is triable.
369	Kidnapping or abducting a child with intent to take property from the person of such child.	Imprisonment for 7 years and fine.	Cognizable	Non-bailable	Magistrate of the first class.
370	Buying or disposing of any person as a slave.	Imprisonment for 7 years and fine.	Non-cognizable	Bailable	Magistrate of the first class.
371	Habitual dealing in slaves	Imprisonment for life, or imprisonment for 10 years and fine.	Cognizable	Non-bailable	Court of Session.
372	Selling or letting to hire a minor for purposes of prostitution, etc.	Imprisonment for 10 years and fine.	Cognizable	Non-bailable	Court of Session.
373	Buying or obtaining possession of a minor for the same purposes.	Imprisonment for 10 years and fine.	Cognizable	Non-bailable	Court of Session.
374	Unlawful compulsory labour.	Imprisonment for 1 year, or fine, or both.	Cognizable	Bailable	Any Magistrate.
[1][376	Rape	Imprisonment for life or imprisonment for ten years and fine.	Cognizable	Non-bailable	Court of Session.
	Intercourse by a man with his wife not being under twelve years of age.	Imprisonment for two years or fine or both.	Non-cognizable	Bailable	Court of Session.

Section	Offence	Punishment	Cognizable or non-cognizable	Bailable or non-bailable	By what court triable
376A	Intercourse by a man with his wife during separation.	Imprisonment for two years and fine.	Non-cognizable	Bailable	Court of Session.
376B	Intercourse by public servant with woman in his custody.	Imprisonment for five years and fine.	Cognizable (but no arrest shall be made without a warrant or without an order of a Magistrate).	Bailable	Court of Session.
376C	Intercourse by superintendent of jail, remand home, etc.	Imprisonment for five years and fine.	Cognizable (but no arrest shall be made without a warrant or without an order of a Magistrate).	Bailable	Court of Session.
376D	Intercourse by manager, etc., of a hospital with any woman in that hospital.	Imprisonment for five years and fine.	Cognizable (but no arrest shall be made without a warrant or without an order of a Magistrate).	Bailable	Court of Session.

1. Subs. by Act 43 of 1983, Sec. 5, for the entries relating to section 376 (w.e.f. 25-12-1986).

Section	Offence	Punishment	Cognizable or non-cognizable	Bailable or non-bailable	By what court triable
[1][377	Unnatural offences	Imprisonment for five years and fine.	Cognizable	Non-bailable	Any Magistrate.

1. Subs. by Act 30 of 2001, Sec. 3, and Second Schedule (w.e.f. 3-9-2001).

CHAPTER XVII—OFFENCES AGAINST PROPERTY

Section	Offence	Punishment	Cognizable or non-cognizable	Bailable or non-bailable	By what court triable
379	Theft	Imprisonment for 3 years, or fine, or both.	Cognizable	Non-bailable	Any Magistrate.
380	Theft in a building, tent or vessel.	Imprisonment for 7 years and fine.	Cognizable	Non-bailable	Any Magistrate.

contd

Section	Offence	Punishment			Court
381	Theft by clerk or servant of property in possession of master or employer.	Imprisonment for 7 years or fine.	Cognizable	Non-bailable	Any Magistrate.
382	Theft, after preparation having been made for causing death, or hurt, or restraint, or fear of death, or of hurt, or of restraint, in order to the committing of such theft, or to retiring after committing it, or to retaining property taken by it.	Rigorous imprisonment for 10 years and fine.	Cognizable	Non-bailable	Magistrate of the first class.
384	Extortion	Imprisonment for 3 years, or fine, or both.	Cognizable	Non-bailable	Any Magistrate.
385	Putting or attempting to put in fear of injury, in order to commit extortion.	Imprisonment for 2 years, or fine, or both.	Cognizable	Bailable	Any Magistrate.
386	Extortion by putting a person in fear of death or grievous hurt.	Imprisonment for 10 years and fine.	Cognizable	Non-bailable	Magistrate of the first class.
387	Putting or attempting to put a person in fear of death or grievous hurt in order to commit extortion.	Imprisonment for 7 years and fine.	Cognizable	Non-bailable	Magistrate of the first class.
388	Extortion by threat of accusation of an offence punishable with death, imprisonment for life, or imprisonment for 10 years.	Imprisonment for 10 years and fine.	Cognizable	Bailable	Magistrate of the first class.
	If the offence threatened be an unnatural offence.	Imprisonment for life.	Cognizable	Bailable	Magistrate of the first class.
389	Putting a person in fear of accusation of an offence punishable with death, imprisonment for life, or imprisonment for 10 years in order to commit extortion.	Imprisonment for 10 years and fine.	Cognizable	Bailable	Magistrate of the first class.
	If the offence be an unnatural offence.	Imprisonment for life.	Cognizable	Bailable	Magistrate of the first class.

Section	Offence	Punishment	Cognizable or non-cognizable	Bailable or non-bailable	By what court triable
392	Robbery	Rigorous imprisonment for 10 years and fine.	Cognizable	Non-bailable	Magistrate of the first class.
	If committed on the highway between sunset and sunrise.	Rigorous imprisonment for 14 years and fine.	Cognizable	Non-bailable	Magistrate of the first class.
393	Attempt to commit robbery.	Rigorous imprisonment for 7 years and fine.	Cognizable	Non-bailable	Magistrate of the first class.
394	Person voluntarily causing hurt in committing or attempting to commit robbery, or any other person jointly concerned in such robbery.	Imprisonment for life or Rigorous imprisonment for 10 years and fine.	Cognizable	Non-bailable	Magistrate of the first class.
395	Dacoity	Imprisonment for life or Rigorous imprisonment for 10 years and fine.	Cognizable	Non-bailable	Court of Session.
396	Murder in dacoity.	Death, imprisonment for life, or rigorous imprisonment for 10 years and fine.	Cognizable	Non-bailable	Court of Session.
397	Robbery or dacoity with attempt to cause death or grievous hurt.	Rigorous imprisonment for not less than 7 years.	Cognizable	Non-bailable	Court of Session.
398	Attempt to commit robbery or dacoity when armed with deadly weapon.	Rigorous imprisonment for not less than 7 years.	Cognizable	Non-bailable	Court of Session.

194

contd

399	Making preparation to commit dacoity.	Rigorous imprisonment for 10 years and fine.	Cognizable	Non-bailable	Court of Session.
400	Belonging to a gang of persons associated for the purpose of habitually committing dacoity.	Imprisonment for life, or rigorous imprisonment for 10 years and fine.	Cognizable	Non-bailable	Court of Session.
401	Belonging to a wandering gang of persons associated for the purpose of habitually committing thefts.	Rigorous imprisonment for 7 years and fine.	Cognizable	Non-bailable	Magistrate of the first class.
402	Being one of five or more persons assembled for the purpose of committing dacoity.	Rigorous imprisonment for 7 years and fine.	Cognizable	Non-bailable	Court of Session.
403	Dishonest misappropriation of moveable property, or converting it to one's own use.	Imprisonment for 2 years, or fine, or both.	Non-cognizable	Bailable	Any Magistrate.
404	Dishonest misappropriation of property, knowing that it was in possession of a deceased person at his death, and that it has not since been in the possession of any person legally entitled to it.	Imprisonment for 3 years and fine.	Non-cognizable	Bailable	Magistrate of the first class.
	If by clerk or person employed by deceased.	Imprisonment for 7 years and fine.	Non-cognizable	Bailable	Magistrate of the first class.
406	Criminal breach of trust.	Imprisonment for 3 years, or fine, or both.	Cognizable	Non-bailable	Magistrate of the first class.
407	Criminal breach of trust by a carrier, wharfinger, etc.	Imprisonment for 7 years and fine.	Cognizable	Non-bailable	Magistrate of the first class.
408	Criminal breach of trust by a clerk or servant.	Imprisonment for 7 years and fine.	Cognizable	Non-bailable	Magistrate of the first class.

Section	Offence	Punishment	Cognizable or non-cognizable	Bailable or non-bailable	By what court triable
409	Criminal breach of trust by public servant or by banker, merchant or agent, etc.	Imprisonment for life, or imprisonment for 10 years and fine.	Cognizable	Non-bailable	Magistrate of the first class.
411	Dishonestly receiving stolen property knowing it to be stolen.	Imprisonment for 3 years, or fine, or both.	Cognizable	Non-bailable	Any Magistrate.
412	Dishonestly receiving stolen property knowing that it was obtained by dacoity.	Imprisonment for life, or rigorous imprisonment for 10 years and fine.	Cognizable	Non-bailable	Court of Session.
413	Habitually dealing in stolen property.	Imprisonment for life, or imprisonment for 10 years and fine.	Cognizable	Non-bailable	Court of Session.
414	Assisting in concealment or disposal of stolen property, knowing it to be stolen.	Imprisonment for 3 years, or fine, or both.	Cognizable	Non-bailable	Any Magistrate.
417	Cheating	Imprisonment for 1 year, or fine, or both.	Non-cognizable	Bailable	Any Magistrate.
418	Cheating a person whose interest the offender was bound, either by law or by legal contract, to protect.	Imprisonment for 3 years, or fine, or both.	Non-cognizable	Bailable	Any Magistrate.
419	Cheating by personation.	Imprisonment for 3 years, or fine, or both.	Cognizable	Bailable	Any Magistrate.
420	Cheating and thereby dishonestly inducing delivery of property, or the making, alteration or destruction of a valuable security.	Imprisonment for 7 years and fine.	Cognizable	Non-bailable	Magistrate of the first class.

contd

421	Fraudulent removal or concealment of property, etc., to prevent distribution among creditors.	Imprisonment for 2 years, or fine, or both.	Non-cognizable	Bailable	Any Magistrate.
422	Fraudulently preventing from being made available for his creditors a debt or demand due to the offender.	Imprisonment for 2 years, or fine, or both.	Non-cognizable	Bailable	Any Magistrate.
423	Fraudulent execution of deed of transfer containing a false statement of consideration.	Imprisonment for 2 years, or fine, or both.	Non-cognizable	Bailable	Any Magistrate.
424	Fraudulent removal or concealment of property, of himself or any other person or assisting in the doing thereof, or dishonestly releasing any demand or claim to which he is entitled.	Imprisonment for 2 years, or fine, or both.	Non-cognizable	Bailable	Any Magistrate.
426	Mischief	Imprisonment for 3 months, or fine, or both.	Non-cognizable	Bailable	Any Magistrate.
427	Mischief, and thereby causing damage to the amount of 50 rupees or upwards.	Imprisonment for 2 years, or fine, or both.	Non-cognizable	Bailable	Any Magistrate.
428	Mischief of by killing, poisoning, maiming or rendering useless any animal of the value of 10 rupees or upwards.	Imprisonment for 2 years, or fine, or both.	Cognizable	Bailable	Any Magistrate.
429	Mischief by killing, poisoning, maiming or rendering useless any elephant, camel, horse, etc, whatever may be its value, or any other animal of the value of 50 rupees or upwards.	Imprisonment for 5 years, or fine, or both.	Cognizable	Bailable	Magistrate of the first class.
430	Mischief by causing diminution of supply of water for agricultural purposes, etc.	Imprisonment for 5 years, or fine, or both.	Cognizable	Bailable	Magistrate of the first class.

Section	Offence	Punishment	Cognizable or non-cognizable	Bailable or non-bailable	By what court triable
431	Mischief by injury to public road, bridge, navigable river, or navigable channel, and rendering it impassable or less safe for traveling or conveying property.	Imprisonment for 5 years, or fine, or both.	Cognizable	Bailable	Magistrate of the first class.
432	Mischief by causing inundation or obstruction to public drainage attended with damage.	Imprisonment for 5 years, or fine, or both.	Cognizable	Bailable	Magistrate of the first class.
433	Mischief by destroying or moving or rendering less useful a light-house or seamark, or by exhibiting false lights.	Imprisonment for 7 years, or fine, or both.	Cognizable	Bailable	Magistrate of the first class.
434	Mischief by destroying or moving, etc., a landmark fixed by public authority.	Imprisonment for 1 year, or fine, or both.	Non-cognizable	Bailable	Any Magistrate.
435	Mischief by fire or explosive substance with intent to cause damage to an amount of 100 rupees or upwards, or, in case of agricultural produce, 10 rupees or upwards.	Imprisonment for 7 years and fine.	Cognizable	Bailable	Magistrate of the first class.
436	Mischief by fire or explosive substance with intent to destroy a house, etc.	Imprisonment for life, or imprisonment for 10 years and fine.	Cognizable	Non-bailable	Court of Session.
437	Mischief with intent to destroy or make unsafe a decked vessel or a vessel of 20 tonnes burden.	Imprisonment for 10 years and fine.	Cognizable	Non-bailable	Court of Session.
438	The mischief described in the last section when committed by fire or any explosive substance.	Imprisonment for life, or imprisonment for 10 years, and fine.	Cognizable	Non-bailable	Court of Session.

198

contd

Section	Offence	Punishment			Court
439	Running vessel ashore with intent to commit theft, etc.	Imprisonment for 10 years and fine.	Cognizable	Non-bailable	Court of Session.
440	Mischief committed after preparation made for causing death, or hurt, etc.	Imprisonment for 5 years and fine.	Cognizable	Bailable	Magistrate of the first class.
447	Criminal trespass	Imprisonment for 3 months, or fine of 500 rupees, or both.	Cognizable	Bailable	Any Magistrate.
448	House-trespass	Imprisonment for one year, or fine of 1,000 rupees, or both.	Cognizable	Bailable	Any Magistrate.
449	House-trespass in order to the commission of an offence punishable with death.	Imprisonment for life, or rigorous imprisonment for 10 years and fine.	Cognizable	Non-bailable	Court of Session.
450	House-trespass in order to the commission of an offence punishable with imprisonment for life.	Imprisonment for 10 years and fine.	Cognizable	Non-bailable	Court of Session.
451	House-trespass in order to the commission of an offence punishable with imprisonment.	Imprisonment for 2 years and fine.	Cognizable	Bailable	Any Magistrate.
	If the offence is theft.	Imprisonment for 7 years and fine.	Cognizable	Non-bailable	Any Magistrate.
452	House-trespass, having made preparation for causing hurt, assault, etc.	Imprisonment for 7 years and fine.	Cognizable	Non-bailable	Any Magistrate.
453	Lurking house-trespass or house-breaking.	Imprisonment for 2 years and fine.	Cognizable	Non-bailable	Any Magistrate.

Section	Offence	Punishment	Cognizable or non-cognizable	Bailable or non-bailable	By what court triable
454	Lurking house-trespass or house-breaking in order to the commission of an offence punishable with imprisonment.	Imprisonment for 3 years and fine.	Cognizable	Non-bailable	Any Magistrate.
	If the offence be theft.	Imprisonment for 10 years and fine.	Cognizable	Non-bailable	Magistrate of the first class.
455	Lurking house-trespass or house-breaking after preparation made for causing hurt, assault, etc.	Imprisonment for 10 years and fine.	Cognizable	Non-bailable	Magistrate of the first class.
456	Lurking house-trespass or house-breaking by night.	Imprisonment for 3 years and fine.	Cognizable	Non-bailable	Any Magistrate.
457	Lurking house-trespass or house-breaking by night in order to the commission of an offence punishable with imprisonment.	Imprisonment for 5 years and fine.	Cognizable	Non-bailable	Magistrate of the first class.
	If the offence is theft.	Imprisonment for 14 years and fine.	Cognizable	Non-bailable	Magistrate of the first class.
458	Lurking house-trespass or house-breaking by night, after preparation made for causing hurt, etc.	Imprisonment for 14 years and fine.	Cognizable	Non-bailable	Magistrate of the first class.
459	Grievous hurt caused whilst committing lurking house-trespass or house breaking.	Imprisonment for life, or imprisonment for 10 years and fine.	Cognizable	Non-bailable	Court of Session.
460	Death or grievous hurt caused by one of several persons jointly concerned in housebreaking by night, etc.	Imprisonment for life, or imprisonment for 10 years and fine.	Cognizable	Non-bailable	Court of Session.

contd

461	Dishonestly breaking open or unfastening any closed receptacle containing or supposed to contain property.	Imprisonment for 2 years, or fine, or both.	Cognizable	Non-bailable	Any Magistrate.
462	Being entrusted with any closed receptacle containing or supposed to contain any property, and fraudulently opening the same.	Imprisonment for 3 years, or fine, or both.	Cognizable	Bailable	Any Magistrate.

CHAPTER XVIII—OFFENCES RELATING TO DOCUMENTS AND TO PROPERTY MARKS

465	Forgery	Imprisonment for 2 years, or fine, or both.	Non-cognizable	Bailable	Magistrate of the first class.
466	Forgery of a record of a Court of Justice or of a Registrar of Births, etc., kept by a public servant.	Imprisonment for 7 years and fine.	Non-cognizable	Non-bailable	Magistrate of the first class.
467	Forgery of a valuable security, will, or authority to make or transfer any valuable security, or to receive any money, etc.	Imprisonment for life, or imprisonment for 10 years and fine.	Non-cognizable	Non-bailable	Magistrate of the first class.
	When the valuable security is a promissory note of the Central Government.	Imprisonment for life, or imprisonment for 10 years and fine.	Cognizable	Non-bailable	Magistrate of the first class.
468	Forgery for the purpose of cheating.	Imprisonment for 7 years and fine.	Cognizable	Non-bailable	Magistrate of the first class.
469	Forgery for the purpose of harming the reputation of any person or knowing that it is likely to be used for that purpose.	Imprisonment for 3 years and fine.	Cognizable	Bailable	Magistrate of the first class.
471	Using as genuine a forged document which is known to be forged.	Punishment for forgery of such document.	Cognizable	Bailable	Magistrate of the first class.

Section	Offence	Punishment	Cognizable or non-cognizable	Bailable or non-bailable	By what court triable
	When the forged document is a promissory note of the Central Government.	Punishment for forgery of such document.	Cognizable	Bailable	Magistrate of the first class.
472	Making or counterfeiting a seal, plate, etc., with intent to commit a forgery punishable under Section 467 of the Indian Penal Code, or possessing with like intent any such seal, plate, etc., knowing the same to be counterfeit.	Imprisonment for life, or imprisonment for 7 years and fine.	Cognizable	Bailable	Magistrate of the first class.
473	Making or counterfeiting a seal, plate, etc., with intent to commit a forgery punishable otherwise than under Section 467 of the Indian Penal Code, or possessing with like intent any such seal, plate, etc., knowing the same to be counterfeit.	Imprisonment for 7 years and fine.	Cognizable	Bailable	Magistrate of the first class.
474	Having possession of a document, knowing it to be forged, with intent to use it as genuine; if the document is one of the description mentioned in Section 466 of the Indian Penal Code.	Imprisonment for 7 years and fine.	Cognizable	Bailable	Magistrate of the first class.
	If the document is one of the description mentioned in Section 467 of the Indian Penal Code.	Imprisonment for life, or imprisonment for 7 years and fine.	Non-cognizable	Bailable	Magistrate of the first class.
475	Counterfeiting a device or mark used for authenticating documents described in Section 467 of the Indian Penal Code, or possessing counterfeit marked material.	Imprisonment for life, or imprisonment for 7 years and fine.	Non-cognizable	Bailable	Magistrate of the first class.

contd

476	Counterfeiting a device or mark used for authenticating documents other than those described in Section 467 of the Indian Penal Code, or possessing counterfeit marked material.	Imprisonment for 7 years and fine.	Non-cognizable	Non-bailable	Magistrate of the first class.
477	Fraudulently destroying or defacing, or attempting to destroy or deface, or secreting a will, etc.	Imprisonment for life, or imprisonment for 7 years and fine.	Non-cognizable	Non-bailable	Magistrate of the first class.
477A	Falsification of accounts.	Imprisonment for 7 years, or fine, or both.	Non-cognizable	Bailable	Magistrate of the first class.
482	Using a false property mark with intent to deceive or injure any person.	Imprisonment for 1 year, or fine, or both.	Non-cognizable	Bailable	Any Magistrate.
483	Counterfeiting a property mark used by another, with intent to cause damage or injury.	Imprisonment for 2 years, or fine, or both.	Non-cognizable	Bailable	Any Magistrate.
484	Counterfeiting property mark used by a public servant, or any mark used by him to denote the manufacture, quality, etc., of any property.	Imprisonment for 3 years and fine.	Non-cognizable	Bailable	Magistrate of the first class.
485	Fraudulently making or having possession of any die, plate or other instrument for counterfeiting any public or private property mark.	Imprisonment for 3 years, or fine, or both.	Non-cognizable	Bailable	Magistrate of the first class.
486	Knowingly selling goods marked with a counterfeit property mark.	Imprisonment for 1 year, or fine, or both.	Non-cognizable	Bailable	Any Magistrate.

Section	Offence	Punishment	Cognizable or non-cognizable	Bailable or non-bailable	By what court triable
487	Fraudulently making a false mark upon any package or receptacle containing goods, with intent to cause it to be believed that it contains goods which it does not contain, etc.	Imprisonment for 3 years, or fine, or both.	Non-cognizable	Bailable	Any Magistrate.
488	Making use of any such false mark.	Imprisonment for 3 years, or fine, or both.	Non-cognizable	Bailable	Any Magistrate.
489	Removing, destroying or defacing property mark with intent to cause injury.	Imprisonment for 1 year, or fine, or both.	Non-cognizable	Bailable	Any Magistrate.
489A	Counterfeiting currency-notes or bank-notes.	Imprisonment for life or imprisonment for 10 years and fine.	Cognizable	Non-bailable	Court of Session.
489B	Using as genuine forged or counterfeit currency-notes or bank-notes.	Imprisonment for life, or imprisonment for 10 years and fine.	Cognizable	Non-bailable	Court of Session.
489C	Possession of forged or counterfeit currency-notes or bank-notes.	Imprisonment for 7 years, or fine, or both.	Cognizable	Bailable	Court of Session.
489D	Making or possessing machinery, instrument or material for forging or counterfeiting currency-notes or bank-notes.	Imprisonment for life, or imprisonment for 10 years and fine.	Cognizable	Non-bailable	Court of Session.
489E	Making or using documents resembling currency-notes or bank-notes.	Fine of 100 rupees	Non-cognizable	Bailable	Any Magistrate.
	On refusal to disclose the name and address of the printer.	Fine of 200 rupees.	Non-cognizable	Bailable	Any Magistrate.

204

CHAPTER XIX—CRIMINAL BREACH OF CONTRACTS OF SERVICE

491	Being bound to attend on or supply the wants of a person who is helpless from youth, unsoundness of mind or disease, and voluntarily omitting to do so.	Imprisonment for 3 months, or fine of 200 rupees or both.	Non-cognizable	Bailable	Any Magistrate.

CHAPTER XX—OFFENCES RELATING TO MARRIAGE.

493	A man by deceit causing a woman not lawfully married to him to believe that she is lawfully married to him and to cohabit with him in that belief.	Imprisonment for 10 years and fine.	Non-cognizable	Non-bailable	Magistrate of the first class.
494	Marrying again during the life-time of a husband or wife.	Imprisonment for 7 years and fine.	Non-cognizable	Bailable	Magistrate of the first class.
495	Same offence with concealment of the former marriage from the Person with whom subsequent marriage is contracted.	Imprisonment for 10 years and fine.	Non-cognizable	Bailable	Magistrate of the first class.
496	A person with fraudulent intention going through the ceremony of being married, knowing that he is not thereby lawfully married.	Imprisonment for 7 years and fine.	Non-cognizable	Bailable	Magistrate of the first class.

STATE AMENDMENTS

Andhra Pradesh:

Offences under Sections 494, 495, 496, shall be cognizable, non-bailable and triable by the Magistrate of the first class.
[Vide Andhra Pradesh Act 3 of 1992, Sec. 2 (w.e.f. 15-2-1992].

| 497 | Adultery | Imprisonment for 5 years, or fine, or both. | Non-cognizable | Bailable | Magistrate of the first class. |
| 498 | Enticing or taking away or detaining with a criminal intent a married woman. | Imprisonment for 2 years, or fine, or both. | Non-cognizable | Bailable | Magistrate of the first class. |

contd

Section	Offence	Punishment	Cognizable or non-cognizable	Bailable or non-bailable	By what court triable
	[1][CHAPTER XX-A—OF CRUELTY BY HUSBAND OR RELATIVES OF HUSBAND.				
498A	Subjecting a married woman to cruelty.	Imprisonment for three years and fine.	Cognizable if information relating to the commission of the offence is given to an officer-in-charge of a police station by the person aggrieved A6 by the offence or by any person related to her by blood, marriage or adoption or if there is no such relative, by any public servant belonging to such class or category as may be notified by the State Government in this behalf.	Non-bailable	Magistrate of the first class.

1. Ins. by Act 46 of 1983, Sec. 6 (w.e.f. 25-12-1983).

Section	Offence	Punishment	Cognizable or non-cognizable	Bailable or non-bailable	By what court triable
	CHAPTER XXI—DEFAMATION				
500	Defamation against the President or the Vice-President or the Governor of a State or Administrator of a Union territory or a Minister in respect of his conduct in the discharge of his public functions when instituted upon a complaint made by the Public Prosecutor.	Simple Imprisonment for 2 years, or fine, or both.	Non-cognizable	Bailable	Court of Session.

contd

	Offence	Punishment			Court
	Defamation in any other case.	Simple Imprisonment for 2 years, or fine, or both.	Non-cognizable	Bailable	Magistrate of the first class.
501	(a) Printing or engraving matter knowing it to be defamatory against the President of the Vice-President or the Governor of a State or Administrator of a Union territory or a Minister in respect of his conduct in the discharge of his public functions when instituted upon a complaint made by the Public Prosecutor.	Simple Imprisonment for 2 years, or fine, or both.	Non-cognizable	Bailable	Court of Session.
	(b) Printing or engraving matter knowing it to be defamatory, in any other case.	Simple Imprisonment for 2 years, or fine, or both.	Non-cognizable	Bailable	Magistrate of the first class.
502	(a) Sale of printed or engraved substance containing defamatory matter, knowing it to contain such matter against the President or the Vice-President or the Governor of a State or Administrator of a Union territory or a Minister in respect of his conduct in the discharge of his public functions when instituted upon a complaint made by the Public Prosecutor.	Simple Imprisonment for 2 years, or fine, or both.	Non-cognizable	Bailable	Court of Session.
	(b) Sale of printed or engraved substance containing defamatory matter, knowing it to contain such matter in any other case.	Simple Imprisonment for 2 years, or fine, or both.	Non-cognizable	Bailable	Magistrate of the first class.

CHAPTER XXII—CRIMINAL INTIMIDATION, INSULT, AND ANNOYANCE

Section	Offence	Punishment	Cognizable or non-cognizable	Bailable or non-bailable	By what court triable
504	Insult intended to provoke breach of the peace.	Imprisonment for 2 years, or fine, or both.	Non-cognizable	Bailable	Any Magistrate.
505	False statement. rumour, etc., circulated with intent to cause mutiny or offence against the public peace.	Imprisonment for 3 years, or fine, or both.	Non-cognizable	Non-bailable	Any Magistrate.
	False statement, rumour, etc., with intent to create enmity, hatred or ill-will between different classes.	Imprisonment for 3 years, or fine, or both.	Cognizable	Non-bailable	Any Magistrate.
	False statement, rumour, etc., made in place of worship etc., with intent to create enmity, hatred or ill-will.	Imprisonment for 5 years and fine.	Cognizable	Non-bailable	Any Magistrate.
506	Criminal intimidation	Imprisonment for 2 years, or fine, or both.	Non-cognizable	Bailable	Any Magistrate.
	If threat be to cause death or grievous hurt, etc.	Imprisonment for 7 years, or fine, or both.	Non-cognizable	Bailable	Magistrate of the first class.

STATE AMENDMENT

Andhra Pradesh:
Offences under Section 506 are non-bailable.
[*Vide* A.P.G.O. Ms. No. 732, dated 5th December, 1991.]

Uttar Pradesh:
Any offence punishable under Section 506, I.P.C., when committed in any district of Uttar Pradesh, shall be, notwithstanding anything contained in the Code of Criminal Procedure, 1973, cognizable and non-bailable. [*Vide* Notification. No. 777/VIII, dated 31st July, 1989, published in U.P. Gazette, Extra, Part-A, Section (Kha), dated 2nd August, 1989)].

Section	Offence	Punishment	Cognizable or non-cognizable	Bailable or non-bailable	By what Court triable
507	Criminal intimidation by anonymous communication or having taken precaution to conceal whence the threat comes.	Imprisonment for 2 years, in addition to the punishment under above section.	Non-cognizable	Bailable	Magistrate of the first class.

Andhra Pradesh:
Offence under Section 507 is cognizable.
[Vide A.P.G.O. Ms. No. 732, dated 5th December, 1991.]

STATE AMENDMENT

Section	Offence	Punishment	Cognizable or non-cognizable	Bailable or non-bailable	By what Court triable
508	Act caused by inducing a person to believe that he will be rendered an object of Divine displeasure.	Imprisonment for 1 year, or fine, or both.	Non-cognizable	Bailable	Any Magistrate.
509	Uttering any word or making any gesture intended to insult the modesty of a woman, etc.	Simple imprisonment for 1 year, or fine, or both.	Cognizable	Bailable	Any Magistrate.
510	Appearing in a public place, etc., in a state of intoxication, and causing annoyance to any person.	Simple imprisonment for 24 hours, or fine of 10 rupees, or both.	Non-cognizable	Bailable	Any Magistrate.

CHAPTER XXIII—ATTEMPTS TO COMMIT OFFENCES

Section	Offence	Punishment	Cognizable or non-cognizable	Bailable or non-bailable	By what Court triable
511	Attempting to commit offences punishable with imprisonment for life or imprisonment, and in such attempt doing any act towards the commission of the offence.	Imprisonment for life or imprisonment not exceeding half of the longest term provided for the offence, or fine, or both.	According as the offence is cognizable or non-cognizable.	According as the offence attempted by the offender is bailable or not.	The Court by which the offence attempted is triable.

II. CLASSIFICATION OF OFFENCES AGAINST OTHER LAWS

Offence	Cognizable or non-cognizable	Bailable or non-bailable	By what court triable
If punishable with death, imprisonment for life or imprisonment for more than 7 years.	Cognizable	Non-bailable	Court of Session.
If punishable with imprisonment for 3 years and upwards but not more than 7 years.	Cognizable	Non-bailable	Magistrate of the first class.
If punishable with imprisonment for less than 3 years or with fine only.	Non-cognizable	Bailable	Any Magistrate.

Cases

Glossary[1]

Abscond
To withdraw or absent oneself in a clandestine manner with an intent to run away in order to avoid a legal process.

Accused
A person against whom an allegation has been made that he or she has committed an offence, or who is charged with an offence.

Acquit
To set free, release or discharge as from an obligation, burden or accusation; to legally certify the innocence of one charged with a crime.

Advocate
One who renders legal assistance and pleads the cause of another before a court or a tribunal.

Affidavit
A written or printed declaration or statement of facts, made voluntarily, and confirmed by the oath or affirmation of the party making it, taken before a person having authority to administer such oath or affirmation.

Anticipatory bail
Bail granted by the High Court or the Court of Session where a person has reason to believe that he or she may be arrested on the accusation of having committed a non-bailable offence. When the anticipatory bail is granted, the accused is released immediately in the event of arrest.

Appeal
To resort to a superior court to review the decision of an inferior court or administrative agency. A complaint to a higher tribunal of an error or injustice committed by a lower tribunal, in which the error or injustice is sought to be corrected or reversed.

Appearance
A coming into court as party to a suit, either in person or by attorney, whether as plaintiff or defendant.

---

[1] Definitions are primarily taken from the *Black's Law Dictionary*, *Concise Law Dictionary*, and Section 2 of CrPC with modifications.

Arrest	To deprive a person of his or her liberty by a legal authority. An arrest is the beginning of imprisonment, where a person is first taken and restrained of his or her liberty by power or colour of lawful warrant.
Autrefois acquit	'Formerly acquitted.' The name of a plea in bar to a criminal action, stating that the defendant has been once already indicted and tried for the same alleged offence and has been acquitted.
Autrefois convict	'Formerly convicted.' A plea by a criminal in bar to an indictment that he or she has been formerly convicted of the same crime.
Bail	The security being taken to set free a person arrested or imprisoned, an assurance for his or her appearance in court on a certain day.
Bailable offence	An offence for which the prisoner may be admitted to bail. Bailable offences are generally considered less serious than non-bailable offences.
Charge sheet	Charge sheet is the form of sheet on which the officer-in-charge of a police station or lock-up enters the accusations or charges against persons brought there in custody, whether arrested with or without warrant.
Cognizable offence	A serious criminal offence, such as murder, rape, robbery, or sedition. A police officer can make an arrest for a cognizable offence without a warrant.
Cognizance	Judicial notice or knowledge; the judicial recognition or hearing of a cause.
Common law	Judge-made law as distinct from legislation and the rules of equity.
Complaint	Any allegation made orally or in writing to a magistrate, with an intention to take action under the CrPC, that some person, whether known or unknown, has committed an offence, but does not include a police report.
Compoundable offences	Offences that can be compounded under Section 320 of the Code of Criminal Procedure.
Conviction	The act of a legal tribunal adjudging a person guilty of an offence; finding of guilt.
Damages	A sum of money awarded to a person who suffered loss, detriment, or injury, whether to his or her person, property, or rights, through the unlawful act or omission or negligence of another.
Detention	Keeping in confinement or custody.
Detention, preventive	Confinement or detention in a prison under the preventive law, based on suspicion or reasonable probability that the person will commit an illegal act.

Detenu	A detainee; a person in detention.
Double jeopardy	A second prosecution after a first trial for the same offence, barred by Article 20(2) of the Constitution.
First Information Report (FIR)	First report of the alleged offence lodged with the police.
Fundamental rights	Those rights which have their source, and are explicitly or implicitly guaranteed, in the Constitution.
Habeas corpus	'You have the body.' A document in which a judicial authority directs the detaining authority to produce the detenu at a designated time and place.
Habitual offender	A person who repeatedly or persistently commits crimes.
High Court	The highest court of a state other than the Supreme Court of India.
Impeach	To challenge or call in question.
In camera	In chambers; in private; in the judge's private room; not in open court.
Incommunicado	A person accused of a crime who does not have the right of communicating with other than the ones in charge of his or her custody or the one investigating the crime.
Inquiry	An inquiry other than a trial, conducted under the CrPC by a Magistrate or court.
International Covenant on Civil and Political Rights (ICCPR)	An international treaty, entered into force in 1976, containing civil and political rights that were enumerated in the Universal Declaration of Human Rights, 1948. The Covenant is legally binding on those countries that have ratified it. India ratified ICCPR in 1979 with reservations.
Interrogation	In criminal law, the process of questions propounded by police to person arrested or suspected to seek solution of crime. Such person is entitled to be informed of his rights, including the right to have counsel present, and the consequences of his answers. If the police fails or neglects to give these warnings, the questions and answers are not admissible in evidence at the trial or hearing of the arrested person.
Investigation	Proceedings under the CrPC for the collection of evidence conducted by a police officer or by any person who is authorized by a Magistrate.
Joinder	A joining of parties as plaintiffs or defendants; a joining of causes of action or defence.

Judgement	The final adjudication of a court in a court case after due consideration of all of the evidence and arguments presented.
Jurisdiction	The power and authority of a court to hear and determine judicial proceedings.
Jurisdiction, subject matter	A term referring to a court's power to hear and determine cases of the general class or category to which the proceedings in question belong.
Jurisdiction, territorial	A term referring to the territory over which a government or court has jurisdiction, as the authority of any court is limited by the territorial boundaries thus fixed.
Juvenile	A young person under the age of 16 at the time of his or her appearance before the court, who should not be treated as an adult for purposes of criminal law.
Legal aid	Free legal services provided to those who cannot afford it.
Magistrate	A civil officer charged with the administration of the laws and having criminal jurisdiction of the first instance.
Mala fide	In bad faith. The opposite of bona fide.
Mental Retardation	A condition of arrested or incomplete development of mind of person which is specially characterized by sub-normality of intelligence. (Section 2(1)(h), Rehabilitation Council of India Act, 1992.)
National Human Rights Commission (NHRC)	A government body created by the Protection of Human Rights Act, 1993. Its functions include protecting human rights through inquiring, investigating and intervening in judicial proceedings and researching and making recommendations to government bodies.
Non-bailable offence	An offence for which bail cannot be claimed as a matter of right, but may be granted at the discretion of the court after considering the facts and circumstances of the case. Non-bailable offences are generally considered to be very serious offences.
Non-cognizable offence	A non-cognizable offence is an offence for which a police officer cannot make an arrest without a warrant, or investigate without an order from a magistrate. Such an offence is generally considered not as serious or immediately dangerous, such as contempt of court and neglect of public duty.
Petition	A formal application in writing made to a court for judicial action for something that lies in its jurisdiction.
Pleader	A person entitled to appear and plead for another in court, and includes an advocate, a *vakil*, and an attorney of a High Court.

Prima facie	On the face of it; at first sight; arising at first sight; based on the first impression.
Probation	The action or process of testing or putting to proof; a system of releasing on suspended sentence, during good behaviour, young persons and especially first offenders, and placing them under the supervision of a probation officer who acts as a friend and advisor.
Remand	An act of an appellate court when it sends a case back to a lower court and orders the conduct of limited new hearings or an entirely new trial, or to take some other further action.
Representation	A statement or account especially made to convey a particular view or impression of something with the intention of influencing action.
Search warrant	An order in writing signed by a Magistrate, commanding an officer to search for personal property and bring it before the Magistrate.
Seizure	Taking possession of property by an officer under legal process.
Self-incrimination	Acts of declarations either as testimony at trial or prior to trial by which one implicates himself or herself in crime.
Sentencing	The post-conviction stage of the criminal justice process imposing the sentence, a punishment.
Summons	A form of process issued by a court calling upon a person to appear before it to either give testimony or produce a thing; or to answer a particular charge.
Summons case	A case relating to an offence not punishable with death, imprisonment for life, or imprisonment for a term exceeding 2 years, the magistrate will issue a summons for the attendance of the accused.
Surety	One who has made himself or herself responsible for the performance or payment of a third person as a bondsman.
Torture	To inflict intense pain to body or mind for purposes of punishment, or to extract a confession or information, or for sadistic pleasure.
Trespass	An unlawful interference with one's person, property, or rights.
Trial	A judicial examination and determination of issues between parties to an action, either civil or criminal, before a court that has proper jurisdiction.
Undertrial	One who is in detention under official custody while waiting for his or her trial to begin.

Victim	A person who has suffered any loss or injury caused by reason of the act or omission for which the accused person has been charged and the expression 'victim' includes his or her guardian or legal heir. (Section 2(wa), Code of Criminal Procedure, 1973 introduced by the Code of Criminal Procedure (Amendment) Act, 2008.)
Warrant	An order issued by some authority, empowering an officer to make an arrest, seizure or search, or to execute a judicial sentence.
Warrant case	A case relating to an offence punishable with death, imprisonment for life, or imprisonment for a term exceeding two years. Magistrate may issue a warrant for the arrest of the accused.
Warrant of arrest	An order issued by some authority empowering a police officer to arrest the accused named in the warrant.
Witness	One who gives evidence in a case; a person sworn to speak the truth in a trial; one who is cognizant of something by direct experience.
Writ	A written command or a formal order issued by a court, directing or enjoining the person or persons to do or refrain from doing some act specified therein.

Select Bibliography

Bakshi, P.M. (2003), *Universal's the Constitution of India with Comments*, 5th edition, Universal Law Publishing Co., New Delhi.

Basu, D.D. (1973), *Criminal Procedure Code*, Prentice-Hall of India, New Delhi.

Basu, N.D. (2001), S.K. Bose (ed.), *Code of Criminal Procedure*, 9th edition, Ashoka Law House, New Delhi.

Black, Henry Campbell (1990), *Black's Law Dictionary*, 6th edition, West Group, St. Paul.

Goodman, Ryan (2002), 'Time to End Abuses,' *Seminar 512: States of Insecurity*, April, 20–6.

Jai, Janak Raj (2004), *Universal's Bail Law and Procedures*, 3rd edition, Universal Law, New Delhi.

Kelkar, R.V. (2001), K.N. Pillai (ed.), *Criminal Procedure*, 4th edition, Eastern Book Company, New Delhi.

Law Commission of India, Forty-First Report (1969), *The Code of Criminal Procedure, 1898*, volume I, Ministry of Law, Delhi.

Lijnzaad, Liesbeth (1995), *Reservations to UN-Human Rights Treaties: Ratify and Ruin?*, International Studies in Human Rights, Martinus Nijhoff.

Mahajan, V.D. (1991), *Constitutional Law of India*, 7th edition, Eastern Book Company, Lucknow.

Manohar, V.R. (2004), *Concise Law Dictionary*, 2nd edition, Wadhwa & Co., Nagpur.

Matthew, P.D. (2002), 'The Prevention of Terrorism Act, 2002 (POTA)', Indian Social Institute, New Delhi.

Matthew, P.D. (1996), 'Free Legal Services to the Poor', Indian Social Institute, no. 65/96, New Delhi.

National Human Rights Commission (2000), *NHRC Important Instructions/Guidelines*, New Delhi.

National Human Rights Commission (2002), *Annual Report 2001–2002*, NHRC, New Delhi.

SAHRDC (2001), 'Government Decides to Play Judge and Jury', *Prevention of Terrorism Ordinance 2001*, SAHRDC, Delhi.

SAHRDC (2000), *Preventive Detention and Individual Liberty*, SAHRDC, Delhi.

Sarkar, S.C. (2002), P.M. Bakshi (ed.), *Criminal Procedure*, 8th edition, Eastern Book Company, New Delhi.

Shukla, V.N. (2001), Mahendra P. Singh (ed.), *Constitution of India*, 10th edition, Eastern Book Company, Lucknow.

Singh, Subhash Chandra, 'Compensation and Restitution to the Victims of Crime: The Centuries Old Correctional Aim Modernised-Modernisation on the Basis of Public Responsibility Needed,' 1992, Cri LJ 100.

Talwar, Rajesh (1998), *How to Choose Your Lawyer*, Vision Books, New Delhi.

Thakker, C.K. (1994), *Criminal Procedure*, N.M. Tripathy Private Ltd, Bombay.

Universal's Criminal Manual (2004), Universal Law Publishing Co., New Delhi.

Index of Legal Provisions

Subject Index